RAISING THE TUDORS

RAISING THE TUDORS

Motherhood in Sixteenth-Century England

STEPHANIE KLINE

PEN & SWORD HISTORY

AN IMPRINT OF PEN & SWORD BOOKS LTD.
YORKSHIRE – PHILADELPHIA

First published in Great Britain in 2025 by
PEN AND SWORD HISTORY
An imprint of
Pen & Sword Books Ltd
Yorkshire – Philadelphia

ISBN 978 1 39903 937 6

A CIP catalogue record for this book is available from the British Library.

Typeset in Times New Roman 11.5/15 by
SJmagic DESIGN SERVICES, India.
Printed and bound in the UK by CPI Group (UK) Ltd.

The Publisher's authorised representative in the EU for product safety is Authorised Rep Compliance Ltd., Ground Floor, 71 Lower Baggot Street, Dublin D02 P593, Ireland.
www.arccompliance.com

For a complete list of Pen & Sword titles please contact:
PEN & SWORD BOOKS LIMITED
George House, Units 12 & 13, Beevor Street, Off Pontefract Road,
Barnsley, South Yorkshire, S71 1HN, England
E-mail: enquiries@pen-and-sword.co.uk
Website: www.pen-and-sword.co.uk

or

PEN AND SWORD BOOKS
1950 Lawrence Rd, Havertown, PA 19083, USA
E-mail: uspen-and-sword@casematepublishers.com
Website: www.penandswordbooks.com

MIX
Paper | Supporting responsible forestry
FSC® C013604

Contents

Acknowledgements

Writing books about British history while being an ocean away from one's subject matter is a challenge, yet one that has been made simpler thanks to the vast collections of online books and primary sources available. This simply must be my first thanks and acknowledgement, because without having had access to the incredibly valuable texts written during and around the sixteenth century, which are cited throughout this writing, thorough research on this subject matter would have been impossible. Sources such as British History Online and the University of Michigan Library's 'Early English Books Online' collections allowed me to access primary source materials from the Tudor period that would have otherwise been difficult or impossible to acquire. Similarly, Internet Archive, with its enormous collection of scanned books spanning centuries of publication, made digitised versions of texts available that I could not easily have accessed in person. I am indebted to these collections – and more, which are included in my notes and references – all of which have no doubt been tirelessly compiled for the sake of easier, more accessible research.

I must thank Sarah-Beth Watkins of Pen & Sword Books, to whom I first approached with this book proposal in the spring of 2023. After the wonderful experience I had with her and the whole Pen & Sword team during the writing and publication of my last book, *Edward VI: Henry VIII's Overshadowed Son*, I was thrilled that my idea for this project was accepted with such enthusiasm and that Sarah-Beth continued to be such a supporter throughout my writing. Thanks also go to Lucy May, Laura Hirst, Sarah Hodder, Teresa Hirst and the design, marketing, and editorial teams at Pen & Sword who all had a hand in bringing *Raising the Tudors* to life – taking it from a simple idea in my head to this beautiful, polished book that I am so incredibly proud of. I am lucky to have such talented, kind, and hard-working individuals helping me to see these projects through.

Whenever I sit down to research and write, I think back on the educators and examples who led me to where I am today. Never could I have dreamed that I would be writing books about the period of history I have been so passionate about (nearly to the point of obsession) since I was a young teenager. But as a young teenager, I spent time talking about the Tudor period with my high school history teachers, Mr Mark Alexander and Mr Jason Miller, both of whom, to this day, remain some of my favourite teachers, and who certainly lit the flame of my insatiable excitement for history. Not many 15-year-olds can get excited about Elizabeth I before eight o'clock in the morning, but I could – and it was thanks to them. My college composition professor at George Mason University, Dr Richard Nanian, was also a source of inspiration for me as he stood out to me as one of the most intelligent people I had ever met, and (if possible) his class made me love writing even more than I already had. In part, it was thanks to him that I felt qualified to apply to the University of Oxford for graduate school, which led me down the path of writing history books today. And my professors at Oxford, Dr Tracey Sowerby and Dr Steve Gunn were two immensely influential individuals who furthered my understanding of research methods, as well as my passion for the Tudor period. Conversations with them were thought-provoking, challenging, and exciting, and they made me want to be a thoughtful and thorough historian. I thank them both for the inspiration and guidance they provided.

To my *Tudor Enthusiast* community – I thank them for reading and supporting my writing since the advent of my blog and social media accounts in 2011. I know I don't post nearly as often as I used to, but when I do, they are there with their enthusiasm and conversation. I appreciate it so much. To my close friends who have supported my writing and encouraged me (even those who couldn't care less for history and I know won't read a word of this book), I am so appreciative of the check-ins, text messages, and reassurance as I have made my way through both this project and the last. To my parents, who were so incredibly proud of me for having fulfilled a lifelong dream with the publishing of *Edward VI* – look, I'm doing it again! I couldn't be more grateful for all that you've always done to encourage my passion for history and writing, and for the unwavering support you provide. To Jason, thank you for never feeling offended when I leave you to watch TV by yourself on the nights I'm writing, and for offering gentle and enthusiastic support on the days I need it. You encourage and celebrate with me every step of the way and I love you for it.

As I am a history lover, I often find myself asking 'What would this have looked like in the past?' when I'm doing perfectly normal, everyday things. I've done this for as long as I can remember and it's what has kept my curiosity and interest in the Tudor period alive. I contemplate what it must have been like for those living in that time period, but I have never questioned it quite so much as when I became a mother. Since having my son, Henry, in 2020, and then having my daughter, Mia, in 2022, I have found myself asking the question, 'What was motherhood like for sixteenth-century women?' It was a question that felt particularly relevant as I rocked Mia to sleep in the darkest hours of the night, while hanging onto my glowing iPhone – which helped me feel not only entertained, but also not nearly so alone as I might otherwise have. It was exactly this experience that made me think of the mothers nursing and rocking their own babies (*sans* iPhone) during the Tudor period – and I thought, certainly there would have been significant differences between my experience in motherhood and theirs. But also, I assumed, there would have been more similarities than I realised. And so, an idea was born, a book proposal was submitted, and the book you hold in your hands was written. None of it would have happened without those quiet, dark nights rocking my babies, where my mind was able to wander. Henry and Mia – for this reason and many more, this book is dedicated to you. Thank you for making me a mother, and for inspiring me to learn about the mothers of long ago. I love you more than you'll ever know.

Introduction

Tudor Womanhood

Tudor England was a man's world. When confronted with primary sources, descriptions and writings from the period, there can be little doubt or argument that women existed within a society that was ruled, governed, owned, and operated solely by their male counterparts. In it, they were largely expected to perform the roles that had been designated for them – again, by men. There were exceptions to this, of course, however few and far between they may have been. The Tudor period saw for itself two reigning queens, with one of them (the final monarch of the dynasty) regarded, even to this day, as one of England's most successful and impactful rulers. Certain women tested and stretched the bounds of decorum and responsibility that sought to control them, and carved their own way in a time when going against the grain was anything but easy and could even cost them their life. This book does not seek to discount the women who lived extraordinarily unusual lives, or who turned their noses up at the status quo and proved themselves powerful, influential, and even independent in their own right. Indeed, we know many of these women already as *these* are the women so often portrayed prominently in history books and on television screens. These women set themselves apart and dared to be different, whether choosing a life free of marriage (Elizabeth I), devoting their life's mission to religious reform and martyrdom (Anne Askew and Joan Bocher), or making any number of unconventional choices in between. But these are the women we have read and heard about many times before. Their stories have already been told.

We have only recently begun to scratch the surface of the typical Tudor woman's life, however. Historians like Elizabeth Norton should be credited with tackling this complicated and loaded subject in recent years, becoming one of the foremost experts on the lives of women during this period – from the poor and lowly to the most esteemed ranks of nobility and royalty. She has built upon decades of research by other notable historians, such as Alison Sim, Sara Read and James Daybell, among many others (several of whom are cited in this book). Through this research, the lives of ordinary sixteenth-century women have slowly but surely come to life, revealing to us more about how they lived, thought, spoke, and interacted with the world around them – in an entirely male-dominated culture. In addition to the strides already made by historians such as these, Nicholas Orme has recently uncovered the hidden stories of Tudor children – a subject untouched by most sixteenth-century historians. In it, he has offered a wealth of knowledge and insight into how adults viewed and interacted with children and how these children were brought up during the period. He, too, has expanded upon research by historians like David Cressy and Barbara Winchester, among others, all of whom have sought to make the Tudor family unit one that modern readers can more readily understand and, perhaps, relate to.

All of this research is invaluable and enters new and largely uncharted territory into the lives of sixteenth-century individuals who have been, until recently, mostly hidden from view. These are the people whose lives, triumphs, and challenges have been too often neglected in favour of the larger, louder personalities who broke the mould of conventional society during the Tudor period, and who have demanded to be remembered as such. But even in the midst of new sources uncovered, and new tales told about the ordinary women, children, and families of sixteenth-century England, a notable gap has been missed. The story of the typical Tudor mother – her entire adult journey from the advent of her fertility to the end of her childbearing years – has yet to have been fully revealed.

Motherhood in sixteenth-century England was often not a choice for women. There were those who never married, of course, whether or not by their own decision. Though exact statistics on the subject are difficult (if not impossible) to come by, it has been estimated that the percentage of unmarried women during the Elizabethan period (the latter half of the sixteenth century, from 1558–1603) might have hovered around sixteen per cent.[1] Those who avoided marriage were sometimes destined for the religious life, or otherwise that of spinsterhood. The latter occupation was one that presented a number of hardships for a woman, given that females during the period were generally set up to become not only a man's companion, but more importantly, his property. Without a husband, a woman had little-to-no power in her own right, and nor was she likely to have been educated to the degree to which she could earn a respectable wage and provide for herself. The independent, powerful, single woman was surely an anomaly in Tudor England – though some examples did exist. Most notably, however, positive examples of single women of the Tudor period were in fact widows – such as Katherine Fenkyll, who was fortunate enough to take over her deceased husband's successful business and then manage it with great success.[2] Ultimately, without being bound to a man for at least some portion of her life, the sixteenth-century woman had little hope of a comfortable livelihood or any kind of stability.

The only real 'viable alternative to marriage' in the late Medieval and first half of the Tudor period was the religious life.[3] Young women or girls who were sent to nunneries – often primarily for the benefit of a good education – found themselves to be a part of a 'socially prestigious community of unmarried women' and their only real honourable substitute to the social norm.[4] Even so, the parents of young women tended to have a strong preference for their daughters to marry rather than to join a nunnery, as evidenced by the dowry amounts proposed in either case.[5] Thomas West, Lord de la Warre, for example, declared he would reduce his daughter Mary's dowry from 500 to only 100 marks if she chose to enter the religious life rather than marry.[6] This showed a clear desire for his daughter to be wed and have children – an opinion held particularly highly by his fellow members of the aristocracy. In fact, as an already small proportion of the female population, nuns were made up of only a tiny percentage of daughters from noble families. In her work studying religious women in Norfolk and Suffolk between 1350 and 1540, historian Marilyn Oliva traced 542 nuns, only 7 of whom were members of the 'titled aristocracy', and 'fifteen per cent from the upper gentry'.[7] To put this into even closer perspective, the total number of nuns in Yorkshire at the time of the dissolution of the monasteries (between 1536 and 1541) was 230, as discovered by Claire Cross and

Noreen Vickers.[8] Comparing that number to the estimated population of 58,086 in the county of York, East Riding in the year 1570, this paints a striking (if admittedly imperfect) picture of the small number of nuns when compared to the rest of the female population.[9]

Without question, the vast majority of sixteenth-century women were encouraged to marry and procreate – and so most of them did. The typical Tudor woman would be shown little-to-no respect by society as a whole if she attempted to live as a single woman, particularly if she avoided the religious life as well. Of course, it could be argued that she was shown little respect – at least, on a personal level – whether she was married or not. In a time when women's '[d]owncast eyes' were meant to 'shield her thoughts from view', and her 'bridled tongue' should 'keep her silent', strong opinions and expectations on a woman's rightful place in society existed regardless of whether she was a wife.[10] However, unless she chose to play the role assigned to her simply by nature of her birth, she would likely be ostracised, avoided, and even feared – as her 'femaleness' was sure to be questioned, and society would have no choice but to view her as 'other'. But to argue that Tudor women were forced against their wills to be wives and mothers is anything but true. Indeed, it was the norm – expected and encouraged by parents across the country, and throughout the period. But to be a wife and mother was also viewed by most to be the most noble of callings – a gift and blessing by God (and the typical Tudor woman was nothing if not religious). This was a vocation that women could take pride in and devote themselves entirely to, and as the pages of this book will prove, the majority of them certainly did. Motherhood in the sixteenth century, as already stated, was not simply a choice. It was an identity, the very thing that proved a woman's femininity and female nature, as well as her worth and value in a society controlled by men.

Her physical body, mental capacity and emotional state were all characterised and controlled (in the eyes of male physicians) by her womb. The reproductive organs within her – still so fundamentally misunderstood, yet fascinatingly theorised upon since the time of the ancient Greeks – dominated nearly all medical understanding of both her physical and emotional health. Paramount importance was placed on menstruation and its regularity, the absence of which was thought to indicate poor health and even impending death, and was considered with the utmost seriousness. Medical texts of the time focused heavily on the physical differences that separated males and females; their very natures characterised in terms of the prevailing theory that had dominated medical thought for centuries – that of the four humours.[11] As ancient philosophers and physicians such as Aristotle, Hippocrates, and Galen had long ago asserted, women had always been – and continued to be, during the Tudor period – considered 'other' than their male counterparts. This 'otherness' centred upon a woman's reproductive anatomy and ability to birth children, as well as the frightening possibility that her uterus might be the cause of her own mental instability or, even more alarmingly, her physical demise.[12] The very nature of a woman's womb and its core functions of ovulating (as they understood it), menstruating, and carrying children is what gave that woman her female identity. It is also what made her, in Aristotle's words, a 'deformed male'.[13] In what was, inarguably, a very patriarchal society, this 'otherness' is what made a female able to be understood, categorised, and controlled by the men around her.[14]

For the average woman in sixteenth-century England, life changed drastically at the onset of her fertility. When she came of age to menstruate, she was no longer viewed as a child (no matter how young she might have been when this occurred). The onset of her fertility opened her up to a new stage of life, and as chapters one to three of this book will detail, everything about her health was understood – by men – through her humoural balance (or imbalance), her reproductive anatomy, and her ability to regularly menstruate. Once it had been established that she was able to menstruate and therefore was ready for marriage and children, her adult life could begin. Chapters four and five will explore the sixteenth-century concept of romantic love and marriage, how such unions were procured (oftentimes on behalf of young women, rather than through their own choosing), and the ultimate Christian duty of procreation by man and wife.

In chapters six through eight, the complex and extensive topic of Tudor pregnancy will be covered – a life event that the average Tudor woman endured roughly every other year throughout her marriage.[15] This was, without question, one of the most dangerous experiences of a woman's life during the period, and as primary sources such as Elizabeth Jocelin's *The Mothers Legacie* prove, expectant mothers often spent much of their pregnancy reflecting on the very real danger that lay ahead in childbirth, and the risk that they might not survive the ordeal at all. In addition to being dangerous (though less so than most modern readers likely assume), pregnancy was also one of the least understood conditions by medical professionals.[16] However, medical texts on the subject abounded – with theories surrounding the womb, the infant's development, and the process of birth often having been established centuries prior and parroted by authoritative men during the late medieval and Tudor periods. Invaluable texts from the period, such as *The Byrth of Mankynd,* originally written in German by Eucharius Rösslin and later translated by Richard Jonas, guide us through the understanding of the female body during pregnancy and through childbirth, as well as a vast number of complications that might have accompanied it. The fact that the author of this valuable pregnancy and childbirth guide was male is ironic (though unsurprising), given that the very nature of birth and the assistance provided by experienced midwives was largely 'women's work' – hardly involving men at all. Therefore, it is only fitting that these chapters (as well as the following) also heavily consult *The Midwives Book,* written by notable midwife Jane Sharp.[17]

Chapter nine will explore the process of childbirth – the rituals, beliefs and extensive practices surrounding this delicate, and often gruelling, work of bringing life into the world. This is followed by chapter ten exploring the infant's nursery, including the crucial choice of a Tudor mother to breastfeed or hire a wet nurse (a topic that was much more controversial during the period than modern readers might realise). Writing by Elizabeth Clinton, the Countess of Lincoln, sheds intimate light on a Tudor mother's own opinions and regrets regarding her decisions about feeding her babies, and her hopes for her daughter-in-law to choose differently. An exploration in the roles of wet nurses and nursemaids (including the aptly named job title of 'cradle rocker') gives insight into the inner workings of a Tudor nursery at the higher end of society, and the crucial roles these women played in raising babies of a certain status.

Chapters eleven to thirteen detail many aspects of childrearing in Tudor England, including parents' attitudes towards play, affection, discipline, and education. These chapters explore the extent to which mothers of varying social classes engaged with their children, from toddlerhood to adolescence and how society (and often, male authorities) dictated the way they parented. Women were, indeed, inundated with information on the rights and wrongs of childrearing – both from family members and friends, as well as published books like John Russell and Hugh Rhodes' *The Boke of Nurture*. An examination of different parenting styles viewed during the period – and how these were often correlated (whether rightly or wrongly) with varying social status – gives us a glimpse into the typical Tudor family home, and how children viewed, and were viewed by, their parents. This leads into chapter fourteen, and the surprisingly young age at which the sixteenth-century adolescent left home for higher education or work opportunities. Letters – such as those between Lady Katherine Paston and her college-aged son, William – grant us an intimate look at the bonds shared between mothers and their adolescent children. They show that very real and relatable concerns existed for mothers during this period, such as how their growing children were keeping up with their laundry, or if they were praying often enough.[18]

In the final chapter, an exploration of the ageing mother and her relationships with her adult children will take place. How did she assist in facilitating an appropriate marriage for her children – or fight against one that had been obtained without her consent, as in the case of Joan Thynne?[19] Following a marriage, how did she engage with her married children and their spouses, and what role, if any, did she play in the lives of her grandchildren? Crucially, how was she as a woman viewed by the rest of society, at an age when she was no longer menstruating and carrying within her the very thing that made her most valuable to a male-dominated world? Far from being protected and revered as she aged, the Tudor woman around the time of menopause and beyond often reverted back to an individual who was far less understood by her contemporaries – and was, in some drastic cases, feared and condemned.[20] Ultimately, the mother's final legacy will be discussed – through the combing-through of sixteenth-century wills and what they show us about bestowing personal items and clothing to children. Family portraits and their role in telling the story of a mother's life and her contributions to family lines is detailed, along with the more personal examples of nostalgic feelings for deceased mothers – even in the case of Henry VIII.

Until now, the all-encompassing story of Tudor motherhood – from menstruation to menopause – has not been told in one consolidated study. It is a remarkable journey, a thankless and overlooked job for the Tudor woman whose duty it was to procreate (often at a rate dictated by her husband) and to raise her children to be God-fearing, successful, and independent members of society. She was surrounded by men who did not understand her or her body, as well as authority figures who often sought to criticise and direct her at every turn. Her life was different from her neighbour's depending on her circumstances, and this is a theme and challenge that will run the length of this book. There is no generalisation to make about motherhood in sixteenth-century England, as so much about a mother's life depended on her social class, financial situation, and personal connections. Thus, it must be remembered that every phase of life covered in these chapters had a great deal of variability and no single book can feasibly account for all possibilities that a Tudor woman might have faced. If she was wealthy and married a successful husband with a house full of servants and staff, her life and motherhood journey would have looked far different from that of the poor, single mother whose lover might have abandoned her during her pregnancy. Likewise, the queen of England's pregnancies, births, and childrearing experiences were certainly worlds away from that of the shopkeeper's lowly wife, who had little help and few resources. At every opportunity, this book attempts to address these disparities and reinforce the reminder that, much like today, there is no single motherhood experience in Tudor England.

Similarly, there were a multitude of possible life circumstances outside of a woman's social class and financial status, which would have greatly impacted her motherhood experience. A huge number of Tudor women became stepmothers, for example – particularly when marrying older men who had been wed at least once before. Adoption – or perhaps 'wardship', as the closest equivalent in the sixteenth century – existed as well, and was another form of parenthood, or at least formal guardianship.[21] There were certainly cases of unplanned pregnancies – love affairs with unintended consequences – which sometimes resulted in tragedy for either the mother or baby (or both). There were women who were taken advantage of by their employers, left destitute with children they could not afford, or somehow otherwise provided for by family members and friends. Subjects and circumstances like these are indeed touched upon in this book, but they are not the focus. It is worth noting here that such women and stories should not be overlooked, ignored, or forgotten. But again, the extremely wide breadth of such an expansive topic as motherhood would require several books in order to tell the full story for every type of woman in sixteenth-century England. This book instead delves into the generally expected trajectory for women of the period, while acknowledging that it cannot possibly account for the experiences of every single one of them.

Regardless of who she was and what her circumstances were, the typical Tudor mother's story has been a largely silent one. Whether an impoverished farmer's wife or a great noblewoman who hailed from a historic, aristocratic family, hers is the story of a woman who followed the status quo. She married, birthed, and raised her children, and generally faded into obscurity, along with countless others. It was an obscurity that enfolded the vast majority of her time – to often only be remembered by her children (and if she was very lucky, her grandchildren). Until only relatively recently, her life remained a blurry mystery to modern readers of history, but we have now begun to peel back the layers of the complex role she played in her world, and all that her life entailed. Now, we peel back another layer – that of her fertility journey and motherhood – a portion of her life that spanned decades and constituted a large part, if not all, of her identity as an adult woman. No matter how obscure, how typical, or how hidden, hers *is* the story of the vast majority, the silent majority. It is now time to hear her motherhood story in full.

Chapter One

Sixteenth-Century Medical Theory: The Four Humours

While the sixteenth century understanding of males and females was inherently different – with women being undeniably less than their male counterparts in a number of physical, emotional, and intellectual ways – both sexes were considered similarly when it came to the prevailing medical theory of the time. There was one irrefutably popular philosophy regarding human health that dominated medical thought during the sixteenth century and, indeed, for several centuries prior, as well as a few still to come. This was known as the Humoural Theory, or perhaps more recognisably, the Theory of the Four Humours. With its origins dating back to the teachings of ancient Greek and Roman philosophers like Aristotle, Hippocrates and Galen, this theory asserted that the human body was comprised of four fundamental bodily humours: blood, phlegm, black bile and yellow bile. These were all believed to influence not only a person's physical health, but their mental health as well, and any possible ratio of the humours balanced against one another in an individual's body could have a multitude of effects on his or her health. Even more, they were thought to play a key role in determining one's personality and behaviour. In short, these four humours were given credit, as well as blame, for a great many aspects of a person's overall health, which renders the understanding of this theory critical in order to appreciate how Tudor physicians approached human health, and their understanding of the body as a whole. Through this examination, it will also shed light on how a female's body differed from a male's, as argued by the four humours theory.

The theory originated in a fifth-century treatise titled *The Nature of Man,* written by Hippocrates' student and son-in-law, Polybus.[1] It was then built upon by physician and surgeon, Galen, who incorporated the Hippocratic theory of humours into his own understanding of the human body. Several centuries following Galen's work, in late antiquity, the theory of the four temperaments were linked to the humours. An anonymous author writing around the same time asked the following question: 'How does it occur that amongst men, some are gracious, laugh and make jokes, others are sad, with a sombre air and doleful, others are quick-tempered, bitter and given to anger, others indolent, hesitant and pusillanimous? The cause is this, based on the elements', he then concluded in his treatise titled *On the Constitution of the Universe and of Man*. Thus, the full origin of the Humoural Theory, as the Tudors would come to know it, was reached.[2]

In it, the humours, also referred to as 'juices', which dominated the human body, were believed to correspond to a number of things – including organs, seasons, human age, temperatures and moisture levels within the body, and even planets. When all of the humours upheld their appropriate balance within one's body, optimal health was believed to have been achieved, and maintained for as long as that balance remained. However, an imbalance of the humours – called 'dyscrasia', or 'bad mixture' in ancient Greek – caused illness of the body and mind. Certain people were believed to have a 'natural disposition towards one type, illness or infection', due to the proportion of humours within their body.[3] Therefore, doctors needed to be able to recommend a wide and customisable range of explanations and remedies to combat humoural imbalances. These explanations often cited seasonal therapies that correlated to the time of year associated with the imbalanced humour, or offered some rationalisation regarding a specific sickness and its propensity to affect one of a certain age or stage of life.[4] The theory of the four humours – at times as wildly perplexing as it was ingeniously imaginative – remained the prevailing medical model for the human body up until the advent of germ theory in 1850.[5]

It is fitting to begin by examining the blood humour, as this was thought to correspond to the spring season and the advent of life, or childhood. Physiologically, this was because blood was considered to be hot and wet, produced by the liver and associated with a 'sanguine' temperament of joviality, liveliness, and enthusiasm.[6] The blood humour was believed to be ruled by the natural element of air and associated with the planet Jupiter. The anonymous author of *On the Constitution of the Universe and of Man* wrote that 'those who are composed of very pure blood are always friendly, joke and laugh; regarding their bodies, they are rose-tinted, slightly red and have pretty skin'.[7] In the sixteenth century, Thomas Elyot wrote that those dominated by the blood humour had large appetites for food, drink, and sex, and they tended to vividly dream, enjoy perfect digestion, and sweat profusely.[8]

Yellow bile, associated with adolescence and early adulthood, was of a hot and dry nature, and associated with the element of fire. Ruled by both the sun and Mars, and produced mainly in the gallbladder, it corresponded to a choleric disposition that was dominated by ambition, aggression, and short-temperedness. A dominance of yellow bile made one bitter and daring, and 'regarding their bodies, they are greenish and have yellow skin'.[9] In Elyot's interpretation, they were lean in body and often had dark, curly hair. They slept little, dreamt of their governing natural element of fire and were often constipated. For all the anger they naturally harboured, these choleric individuals were considered to be good, strong fighters.[10]

The third humour, black bile, was thought to be cold and dry, ruled by both the moon and Venus, and associated with a melancholic nature. The very word 'melancholy' derived from the Greek term for 'black bile' (*melaina kholé*). The governing organ that was believed to produce black bile was the spleen, and an excess of this humour in the body was known to cause increased depression, fear, and worry, though this relationship was questioned by Galen.[11] In general, they were seen to be sickly, with a weak pulse and slow, poor digestion, and to have a dark appearance with 'black eyes and black hair'.[12] According to Elyot, black bile was associated with the middle age of man – typically between ages 25 and 40.[13]

Finally, the fourth humour – phlegm – was associated with the soft and flabby, weak-pulsed and narrow-veined elderly life stage. This humour was considered to be cold and wet, ruled by the element of water, produced by the brain and lungs, and ruled by Saturn. Due to its cold and wet nature, it corresponded to the season of winter, and those suffering from an abundance of phlegm were thought to be listless, apathetic, dull in thought, and pale in appearance.[14] Our anonymous author wrote that phlegmatic individuals were 'despondent, forgetful; [and] regarding their bodies, they have white hair'.[15]

It was understood during the Tudor period that certain people were predisposed to an abundance of one of the four humours over the others.[16] It was thought that most people had one specific dominant humour within them, which influenced their overall health and personality.[17] At a high level, this was specific to sex, and could further vary depending on the individual within that sex. Women were thought to have, by nature, a colder and wetter bodily condition, being naturally more phlegmatic. Men, on the other hand, were seen as hotter and dryer, dominated by a choleric temperament. For women's health, this naturally cold, moist condition had a number of ramifications for her, including the belief that she tended to be over emotional and illogical when compared to her male counterpart. Physically, it was believed that she would not grow bald with age, as she did not have the heat within her to burn off her hair, as men did. Internally, her excess blood would be passed through menstruation (of which we will speak much more in the following chapters), while a man's natural heat was able to burn off that excess blood without the need for such menstruation. The understanding of how these humours reacted in different ways between the two sexes' bodies was vital to the understanding of how each should be treated in terms of diet and lifestyle.

This indicated their general temperament and overall health, although these things could also be impacted by external sources, known as the 'non-naturals', as they were referred to in medieval and early modern medical texts. According to physicians of the time, there were six dominant 'non-naturals' that had an effect on human health: diet, exercise, air, sleep, evacuation, and emotions.[18] Without question, the most important of these was a person's diet, as all four of the bodily humours were believed to be produced as part of the hepatic digestive process.[19] Sixteenth-century authors like Thomas Elyot, Andrew Boorde and John Partridge wrote extensively on the subject of diet and nutrition, advising the Tudor man and woman on the foods to avoid and indulge in based on the body's dominant humour(s). This was because food itself was thought to have its own humoural qualities, which could greatly affect an individual's health, mood, and overall wellbeing. As a general example, herbs were seen to harbour both a 'warm' quality – due to their leaves and affinity to air – as well as a 'dry' quality because they grew from within the earth. Therefore, adding herbs to dishes could be seen to balance out the 'cold' and 'wet' properties of commonly eaten foods, such as 'cucumbers, lettuce, spinach, pork, and veal'.[20]

Much of Elyot's *Castel of Helth,* published in 1541, is devoted to providing dietary advice with bodily organs and humourally-induced temperaments in mind. For example, he denotes foods such as garlic, onions and pepper as engendering choler (an increase in yellow bile), while pointing out that 'new cheese' and fish would increase phlegm. Meanwhile, 'salted flesh' and course brown bread would produce more black bile, thus increasing melancholy.[21] This is to say, of course, that individuals who were prone to the dispositions referenced by Elyot would be smart to stay away from the foods he listed, so as to reduce the dominance of that humour and the ill-effects associated with it. He also spent much time writing about certain foods' impact on various organs – fennel, saffron, cloves and rosewater being advised, among many other foods, for the good of the liver, and raisins, dates and almonds prescribed to improve lung function.[22] Much guidance on the proper foods to ingest and avoid – with consideration for one's temperament, dominant humour(s) and organ function – could be gleaned from Elyot's work.

Similarly, John Partridge's *Treasurie of Commodious Conceits,* published in 1573, provided copious instructions for a great number of recipes, both for general cookery (such as 'a sawce for a rosted Rabbet to King Henry the Eight'), as well as cures for maladies (like 'a receipt to restore strength in them that arr brought low with long sicknesse').[23] It was believed that, not only could food items themselves hold within them specific humoural properties, but various cooking and preparation methods could also play a role. Through seasoning with spices, dousing with sauces, and cooking through boiling (to moisten) or roasting (to dry), one could modify the hot, cold, wet or dry natures of the foods they prepared.[24] This book, in particular, is a wealth of information for the Tudor man or woman on many more topics, even those not related to diet, such as the specific instruction to 'breake [Rosemary] leves under thy bed, and thou shalt be delyvered of all evyll dreames'.[25]

Regarding the four humours and their particular association with temperature and moisture, Partridge assigned certain foods, herbs, and spices accordingly. Roses, for example, were cold and moist (aptly prescribed to be crushed and ingested in those who were thought to be naturally hot and dry). In addition, lilies were cold and dry (for wet, moist people), and rosemary was hot and dry (for those who were cold and wet). Sugar was known as a warming ingredient, as it heated and moistened the body, while salt was seen to dry it out (because of the thirst it created).[26] When ascribing these qualities to the foods he wrote about, Partridge noted, 'so sayeth Galyen' – thus reinforcing the ancient physician's prominence in this particular school of thought, and tying Tudor medical and dietary understanding to the Greeks who had written several centuries prior.[27]

Among the remaining five 'non-naturals' that impacted the sixteenth-century person's health, evacuation was arguably the next most important.[28] The purging, or releasing, of one excessive humour was thought to restore the body to its appropriate balance, with bloodletting being one of the most recognisable forms of evacuation. This method, of course, was meant to decrease the disproportionate amount of blood in one's body, typically via an incision in the ankle or wrist. Andrew Boorde, who wrote *A Compendious Regiment or a Dietary of Health*, published in 1542, instructed that 'yf blode do abounde, clense it with stufes, or by fleubothomye (phlebotomy)'.[29] However, he was also of the opinion that bloodletting was only particularly necessary for those who ate and drank to excess, while more temperate individuals did not require such a remedy. These people were better helped by 'bathes, exercise, walking, and riding moderately'.[30] Finally, it is important to note that bloodletting was not the only form of evacuation indicated by physicians and authors of the time. Just as important for the balancing of humours were the acts of vomiting, sweating, defecating and urinating. As an example, Boorde stressed in his chapter on individuals suffering from gout that they should not make the mistake of 'forgettyng them selfe to exonerate the blader and the bely whan need shall requyre'.[31]

This last note brings us to a brief examination of the remaining four 'non-naturals' and how they were believed to affect one's health. Boorde wrote more about some of these, including chapters in his *Dietary of*

Health that taught a man 'to buylde his howse in a pure and fresshe ayre, for to lengthen his lyfe' (chapter three), how he 'shulde exercise hym selfe for the helth of the soule and body' (chapter seven), and how he should 'order hym selfe in slepynge…' (chapter eight).[32] There was debate during this century regarding the types of exercise one should practise for optimal health, with the ancient Galen directing that it should be vigorous, while later physicians insisted that it was best to keep it moderate.[33] The quality of the air was also something to be considered, with Boorde cautioning his readers against exposing themselves to 'open ayer' when they were ill, and to 'fle from the contagious and infectious ayre' when disease was rampant.[34] This explains why so many citizens of crowded cities such as London viewed the air of the countryside to be healthier.

The ways in which a Tudor man or woman slept were also thought to influence their health – and in particular, their digestion. 'Moderate sleep', according to Boorde, would nourish the blood and heat the liver, which would make for perfect digestion. Conversely, 'immoderate sleep' would make the brain light and sluggish and increase a person's propensity for illness.[35] Finally, emotions were seen to impact health, primarily through their influence on a person's heart, which was responsible for heating the entire body. For example, an emotion such as anger might cause the body to overheat and dry out, which would (in the context of the four humours) result in an excess of yellow bile and a choleric temperament.[36]

Much more can (and has) been said on the topic of the Humoural Theory and its impact on the overall view of health and medicine in the sixteenth century, but this chapter is meant only to be an introduction to the subject. Our purpose in understanding the theory is to become familiar with the way Tudor physicians understood the human body, as well as how lifestyle and environmental factors could play a role in one's health. Most critically, it is important to see how males and females were viewed as intrinsically different, just based on this theory – without taking any other element of their physical bodies into consideration. Already, just by nature of her sex, the Tudor woman's health was approached differently than that of a man's, because her dominant body fluids were different than his were. As such, her physical and mental health were affected. As we will see in the following two chapters, however, the sixteenth century understanding of her body was only partly a result of a physician's knowledge of the Humoural Theory. It was combined with theories and assertions made about her anatomy – and more specifically, about how her reproductive organs differed from a man's. As we will see (and as the ancient Greeks had continued to point out), these organs played an even more intricate role in her life than by just giving her the ability to conceive and bear children. The Tudor woman's very anatomy had grave implications for her physical and mental health, and further separated her from the men who attempted to understand, write about, and medically treat her.

Chapter Two

Reproductive Anatomy of the Tudor Woman

Now, with a broad understanding of the dominating medical theory of the period, and a general familiarity with the factors that influenced a Tudor man or woman's overall health, it is time to explore the sixteenth-century human body – and more specifically, the female body. Just how was the anatomy of a woman understood at the time? And how did this understanding influence the overall view of a woman's role in fertility and conception by sixteenth-century physicians?

Just as the Tudor understanding of health and medicine originated with the ancient Greek way of thinking, so too did experts' understanding of gynaecology and the female reproductive system. It likely started with a sixth-century treatise entitled *Genecia,* written by Muscio, which is believed to have pulled heavily from the Greek physician Soranus of Ephesus' treatise, *Gynaikeia.* These ancient Greek works taught about both female reproductive anatomy, as well as positions of a foetus inside the womb, and included detailed birth figures that were referenced for centuries onwards. These would have astounded people in the sixteenth century, as they had likely never before been seen, up until the publication of Eucharius Rösslin's *Der schwangern Frauwen und Hebammen Rosengarten* in Germany in 1513, which translates to 'Pregnant wives and midwives rose garden'.[1] This information, which was highly acclaimed in Germany, was soon translated into French and Latin, and circulated to a much wider audience across Europe. A few decades later, in 1540, the English had their translation, with the publishing of Richard Jonas' *The Byrth of Mankynde.* He had translated it from the Latin version, titled *Rosengarten, De Parti Hominis*. This would later be translated yet again – and expanded upon – by Thomas Raynalde in 1545.[2] These English translations of Rösslin's original work would become an invaluable resource on female anatomy, pregnancy and childbirth during the Tudor period, and further inspire the writings of more books and pamphlets on the same subject.

But first, back to the Greeks. Unsurprisingly, the concept of female anatomy is tightly linked to the four humours discussed in the previous chapter. As already introduced, women were known to be of a wetter, colder condition than men and this lack of heat within their bodies led to a number of implications for her physical body. Perhaps the most shocking implication for her was the belief that a woman lacked the heat needed to force her genitalia out of her body, as a man's had. While his own bodily heat had forced his reproductive organs to the outside of his body, anatomically speaking, women were essentially viewed as deformed men.[3] This idea was backed by both Galen and Hippocrates, the latter of whom wrote, 'if the uteri fall completely outside the genitals, the ensemble hangs like a scrotum'.[4] In fact, it was thought that a woman's genitalia were actually identical to those of a man – 'the vagina taking the same form as a man's penis and two testicles nestling at the top of the vagina near the mouth of the womb'.[5] For this, as well as other reasons that will be discussed, the female body was commonly thought of and referred to as 'grotesque'.[6]

This brings us to the focal point of the female reproductive system, even as the Greeks viewed it: the uterus, or womb. There existed two schools of thought when it came to the uterus: (1) that it was simply a vessel into which a man's seed would fall, thus rendering the woman's part in conception entirely passive; and (2) that while certainly being a 'container organ', it was also 'a mobile living creature' capable of movement, and in particular 'toward sources of moisture'.[7] The latter argument was more widely accepted (at least, in part) during the sixteenth century, and this theory gave women's bodies a more active part to play in the role of reproduction, or 'generation' as it was termed by physicians of the period. With this view of the uterus in mind – being 'a female viscus, closely resembling an animal', in the words of the Greek physician Aretaeus of Cappadocia – the organ was not only capable of living and moving on its own, but it was also responsible for emitting its very own seed.[8] In fact, it was even termed 'leaky' by some – constantly releasing fluids into the body and adding to the female's 'natural grotesqueness'.[9] The uterus' 'seed' was considered 'thinner, colder, and feebler' than a man's, of course, but it was no less important for the act of generation, in this theory.[10] This theory, which will be expanded upon much more in chapter five, had its own negative implications for women, albeit rendering her a more active participant in the act of conception. More alarmingly for her, however, was the belief that her uterus was capable of freely roaming. This theory had potentially far graver, and more immediate, consequences for her health.

The ancient Greek philosopher, Plato, had his own descriptions of the womb, which he wrote in his fourth-century dialogue, *Timaeus*. In it, he described the uterus as being:

> … a living nature appetent of childbearing, when it is a long time fruitless beyond the due season, is distressed and sorely disturbed, and straying about in the body and cutting off the passages of the breath it impedes respiration and brings the sufferer into the extremest anguish and provokes all manner of diseases besides; until the passion and love of both unite them…[11]

With this, he introduced the controversial theory of the 'wandering womb', which built upon Hippocrates' earlier work in his publication, *Sicknesses of Women.* Here, he had coined the term 'hysteria' for this condition, which was based on the Greek word for uterus, *hystera*.[12] These ancient views painted a picture of a 'living thing inside another living thing' that was 'avid to conceive', and which, when denied a man's seed for too long, would wander around the woman's body in search of it.[13] This was believed to be due to the womb's inherent hot condition, though a woman was generally cold. In fact, the Greeks believed there was a good reason for this coldness in the rest of the woman – it was due to her body directing all of its heat to its internal 'oven'.[14] The hot womb's desire for moisture would cause it to rove around wildly, and this roving could then have serious health implications for the woman. For one, if the womb moved forward within the abdomen, or 'toward the hip', as

Hippocrates wrote, there was the risk that it might obstruct menstrual flow, which was critical to a woman's health. Similarly, he argued, 'if the orifice of the uteri withdraws, the menses do not come, and if they come, they are sparse and bad'.[15] Even worse, a journey upwards in the body might result in a collision with the diaphragm – which had the most disastrous effects for the woman, as this was believed to result in suffocation.[16] In short, the concept of a 'wandering womb' made for a perilous and anxiety-inducing image – a condition that was capable of wreaking havoc on a woman's health and creating, in Hippocrates' word, 'hysteria' within her.

But this argument was not met with acceptance by all Greek physicians. While Hippocrates, Plato and Aretaeus touted the theory of the womb's wild and roaming nature, Galen and Soranus did not believe in the 'wandering womb' concept at all, and even poked fun at the idea in later writings.[17] Even so, while this image of a ravenous, starved, and animalistic uterus was controversial even to the ancient Greeks, it managed to survive into and throughout the sixteenth century, and even lingered in some midwifery manuals of the eighteenth century.

For Tudor women of childbearing age, this idea would have understandably caused some unease. Not only was there a persistent belief that the restless womb could cause physical illness, but a publication at the very end of the Tudor period made it clear that such a condition could also result in negative psychological symptoms as well. The physician Edward Jorden's book *A briefe discourse of a disease called the Suffocation of the Mother*, published in 1603, detailed some very unsettling examples of the disease that he called *Passio Hysterico,* or 'suffocation of the mother' (in which the term 'mother' is a metaphor for 'uterus').[18] He writes about the 'passive condition of womankind' and describes her as a victim to her womb, building upon past arguments by the ancient Greeks. The symptoms of her 'wandering womb', he notes, are 'monstrous and terrible to beholde, and of such a varietie as they can hardly be comprehended…'.[19] Echoing the Greek theories from centuries earlier, Jorden describes the womb as being 'drawn upwards or sidewards above [its] natural seate … causing suffocation and difficultie of breathing'.[20] But he presses even further, insisting that the womb's movement is capable of causing 'perturbations of the mind', resulting in symptoms such as 'frenzies, convulsions, hickcockes [hiccups], laughing, singing, weeping, [and] crying'.'[21] These descriptions point to our more modern recognisable representations of the term 'hysteria'.

Ultimately, by offering these examples and explanations, Jorden was trying to dispel the accusations of witchcraft and supernatural possession in the case of an older woman named Elizabeth Jackson. She had been accused of bewitching 14-year-old Mary Glover in 1602, causing her to become very ill. Jorden was convinced that Glover simply suffered from a natural disease caused by her womb, which had both physical and mental consequences for her and had created symptoms similar to those caused by bewitching. This argument would have garnered the support of the ancient Greek Aretaeus, if not simply due to Mary Glover's young age. According to him, after all, a 'wandering womb' and the hysteria caused by it, was most likely to affect younger women, 'whose way of life and judgment are somewhat wandering, so that their womb is roving'. Older women like Elizabeth Jackson, he argued, would have been less prone to this condition, due to her 'more stable way of life, judgment', and, therefore, 'womb'.[22]

This wasn't enough to convince the judge at Jackson's trial, however. Jorden's testimony was unsuccessful, as it was difficult to change the commonly held Tudor perception that it was a melancholic disposition, not a hysterical one, that was most closely associated with the symptoms of bewitchment. The Tudors were nothing if not up to speed on the conditions caused by an imbalance of humours, after all. And in fact, the concept of 'hysteria' was an entirely new one in sixteenth-century England, despite having been written about centuries earlier. Jorden's *Suffocation of the Mother* was the first English book on the subject of hysteria, and the Merriam-Webster Dictionary points to the first English use of the word in 1603, due to this publication. Consequently, it should come as no surprise to us that the terms 'hysteria' and 'hysterical' are still used in modern day language to describe (typically women) 'feeling or showing extreme and unrestrained emotion'.[23] To some of the ancient Greeks' minds, as well as Edward Jorden's, these emotional outbursts just might be caused by a pesky, impatient 'wandering womb'.

Although the *Suffocation of the Mother* and the term 'hysteria' did not appear in English culture until the very end of the Tudor period, the concept of the 'wandering womb' – while still controversial – had persisted throughout the century. In fact, there was clearly enough anxiety about the womb's movement that certain remedies were written and spoken about. Recipes, tips and tricks were passed among women, meant to help keep the troublesome organ in its rightful place – or, if it had already wandered, to coax it back to where it belonged. According to physicians of the period, the womb was capable of travelling great distances – as far north as the throat, and as south as the knees.[24] In some cases, the womb could even prolapse out of the vagina, which was a real cause for concern.[25] One of the more common remedies practised during the sixteenth century had its roots in Aretaeus' ancient writings. He had long ago written that the womb 'flees from fetid things, and seeks after sweet', which introduced the concept of scent therapy.[26] A French surgeon named Ambroise Paré suggested that physicians should apply 'fetid and rank smells' to the nostrils if it had been suspected that a woman's womb had risen northwards in her body, thus to repel the uterus back downwards. He offered examples of such smells, like:

> … the snuff of a tallow candle when it is blown out, with the fume of a bird's feathers, especially partridges or woodcocks, of man's hair, or goat's hair, of old leather, of horse-hoofs, and such like things burned, whose noisome or offensive savour the womb avoiding, doth return unto its own place or seat again.[27]

Other sources provided alternative 'fetid' smells to try – such as 'a bath made of mugwort, flea-bane, juniper, camphire, and wormwood, boiled in water', which *A Rich Closet of Physical Secrets* proposed.[28] Applying recipes such as these to a woman's nose was meant to repel the womb and send it southward, back to its rightful place in the lower abdomen. Alternatively, if the womb had dropped low in the body, the herbal concoction would be administered via a vaginal pessary, in order to coax it upwards again. One example of a recipe meant for exactly this purpose was detailed in *The Secrets of the Reverend Maister Alexis of Piedmont,* translated to English from Italian and published in 1595.

It was titled 'To heale a woman that hath the Matrice [Matrix] out of her natural place'.

> Take a flint stone that hath beene always in the earth, and not taken the aire, and put it in some basket, covered in a greate faire: and when it is verie hotte, put it in a little tubbe or barrell, and wet it with vinegar cast upon it, and cause the woman to stande over it, to receive the smoake or perfume of it, and then let her goe to bed, for this must bee done at night.

This was, of course, to explain the use of a vaginal fumigation, but the author had yet another trick up his sleeve in order to coax that troublesome uterus back into place:

> Ye shall after this, take the juice of Rue, and make a little rounde ball of cotton, whereunto yee shall tie a thread: and then dippe the saied ball in the saied juice of Rue, and put it into the mouth of the Matrice, the which will incontinent take the ball, and drawe it in, and then it will returne into his natural place again.

Crucially, he also noted that 'you must binde and tie the ball sure and well, lest peradventure it should remain within'. This description was uncannily similar to the modern day tampon (without the dousing in rue). Combined with the action of inverting the woman's body in whichever direction the uterus needed to move – 'from night to night, three times' – it was said that she would be healed.[29]

Similarly, sweet smells could be administered in order to achieve a similar goal – that of attracting the uterus, rather than repelling it. Ambroise Paré recommended a pessary of 'sweet and aromatic fumigations', using cinnamon, aloe, labdanum, benzoin, thyme, pepper, cloves, lavender, calamint, mugwort, penny-royal, nutmeg, musk, and amber', as a means to attract the womb down when it had wandered upwards.[30] Referring specifically to the act of childbirth, but still regarding the drawing of a womb downwards, *The Byrth of Mankynde* stated that 'it shall also be very profitable for her to perfume the nether places with musk, amber, Gallia muscata which put on embers yield a goodly favor by the which the nether places open themselves and draw downward'.[31] Such a concept that a uterus could be drawn to or repelled by specific scents only built upon (albeit perhaps unintentionally) the argument for the womb being animal-like, given that it clearly had a sense of smell.[32] But this sort of vaginal fumigation had a humoural context too, as pessaries were considered to 'offer a purgative heat to release excess phlegmatic humours, returning the womb to its original place by humoural fumigation'.[33] As with all other medical topics at the time, scent therapy and its influence on the womb's position had its roots in the Four Humours Theory, although the 'non-naturals' were known to affect a 'wandering womb', as well.

Sleep, diet, exercise, air, emotions and evacuations all had their place in controlling the uterus' movement. Bloodletting, for example, was used to encourage the womb away from the liver, where it might be found seeking moisture.[34] Herbal baths were also recommended, along with lifestyle changes like adequate rest and sleep, as well as a moderate diet that supported proper humoural balance. The ancient Greeks had even suggested 'a series of physical manipulations and bindings of the abdomen to force the womb back in place'.[35] But perhaps the easiest remedy of all for a 'wandering womb' was simply sex. Hippocrates himself had written centuries earlier that 'a woman should marry young … engage in repeated intercourse with her husband and bear as many children as possible, so that the womb will always be moist and heavy and thus incapable of movement'.[36] Recall Aretaeus' assertion that a womb is more likely to wander in younger women who have just reached childbearing age, and we have the perfect recipe for 'the patriarchal ideal of a woman's life: early marriage and multiple pregnancies'.[37]

The anatomy of a sixteenth-century woman – particularly that of her reproductive organs – was a complex, loaded topic that further allowed for male control over her. Theories surrounding the structure of her genitalia, and particularly how they compared to a man's, as well as the nature of her animal-like womb and the havoc it might cause within her, created an anxiety both within her and *about* her, and set the stage for the path she was meant by society to follow. Moreover, these topics were shrouded by a fair amount of shame, hiddenness and secrecy. In the preface to the twelfth-century *Liber de sinthomatibus mulierum*, the author stated: 'and because only with shame and embarrassment do [women] confess the fragility of the condition of their diseases which occur around their more hidden parts … they do not dare reveal their distress to [male] physicians'.[38] References to women's 'secrets' and 'hidden places' increased in frequency during the thirteenth century, and gynaecological texts written in Europe during the fourteenth and fifteenth centuries continued with the phrases 'secret diseases', 'secret medicines', and 'secret places' – all indicating a vocabulary that was meant to conceal the taboo topics of female anatomy.[39] By the sixteenth century, when virtually all medical professionals, save midwives, were male, it is little wonder why these topics were fairly concealed to the work that had already been done centuries earlier. Women were not meant to question their own bodies or press for further answers regarding them. In fact, the very vocabulary placed upon their anatomy reminded women of their shame and embarrassment – and indeed, their own 'grotesqueness'. All of this forced such topics to hide behind virtually closed doors – only to be written about, prescribed upon, and judged by men.

So, while the nature of a Tudor woman's reproductive organs was largely left to centuries-old theories, one key concept had been well-established to encourage young women into early marriages and frequent childbearing. It had already been impressed upon young women that their wombs were prone to wandering – with one possible terrifying result being suffocation and an early death. Likewise, it was known that the simplest remedy for avoiding such a fate was to engage in frequent sexual intercourse (with one's husband, of course) and to become nearly perpetually pregnant with his children. With such teaching – and fear mongering – shouldn't every young sixteenth-century woman have desired matrimony and pregnancy as early as possible? To be sure, there were many other considerations at play regarding marriage and children, but perhaps it is worth questioning whether or not these ancient medical theories and fears played at least some role in a young Tudor woman's eagerness towards motherhood. The patriarchal society that had been perpetuating these theories about female bodies for centuries certainly seemed to know what it was doing.

Chapter Three

Flowers and Fertility

Girls living in the sixteenth century reached an important physiological milestone around the age of 12 to 14, on average. It should come as little surprise that this was typically the age range that she would experience menstruation for the first time ('menarche' being the medical term for the advent of menstruation). This biological transition from girlhood to womanhood was understood by the Tudors as being the onset of a female's fertile years, though many – particularly male physicians – shied away from speaking openly about it, given its hidden nature as a woman's 'secret malady'.[1] Still, men certainly knew what menstruation signified. We have evidence of this from a sixteenth-century man named Simon Forman, who expressed delight by writing in one of his personal notebooks that his wife had just had her first menstrual period at 17 years old, meaning that he could finally 'anticipate children by her'.[2]

The onset of a young woman's menstrual period tied back to the Humoural Theory, which we have already touched on. A woman's body was, again, seen as cold and wet, and unable to burn off any excess heat that she harboured inside of her – unlike the hot, dry nature of a man, who burnt it off through regular exercise and activity. Along this same line were the Hippocratic and Galenic theories that women had a 'more sedentary lifestyle' than men, and as such, 'her body was less efficient than a man's at utilising the blood that she produced'.[3] Women were, in fact, considered to have a higher blood volume than men (a false theory), which was even thought to manifest itself by creating a 'spongey' texture in their skin.[4] This excess blood was theorised by the ancient Greeks to be produced in a young woman from menarche onwards, and was absolutely critical to her health, as the root of all female health lay within her womb. Therefore, while menstruation was indeed termed a 'malady' throughout the centuries leading up to the Tudor period, it was nonetheless a necessary one. In a Hippocratic treatise titled *The Seed*, it was written, 'if the menses do not flow, women's bodies become prone to sickness'.[5] But more on that in a minute.

First, how did people in the Tudor period refer to a woman's menstrual period? The commonly-used modern term 'period' did not come into use until 1822, and 'menstruation' was not used in the English language until the 1680s, though *mensis* (the Latin word meaning 'month') was used by the ancient Greeks' in their writings.[6] Through the medieval period, common terms included 'the private malady', as well as 'the purgation'.[7] But for the Tudors, a woman's menstruation was most commonly referred to as her 'flowers', which conjures up images of springtime and rebirth. Indeed, this was exactly the point. The concept of 'flowers' to refer to menstruation was born out of a horticultural metaphor that was reinforced by the Bible. John 15:2 reads: 'every branch in me that beareth not fruit he taketh away: and every branch that beareth fruit, he purgeth it, that it may bring forth more fruit'.[8] The 'fruit' here was clear enough to the Tudors, in terms of menstruation – it signified the baby that was born from the womb. The womb, then, must be the flower that preceded the fruit – so to be purged monthly, in order to produce more. This connection between monthly menstruation and its role in conception was well understood at the time, and written about by seventeenth-century midwife, Jane Sharp. She even included a beautiful visual depiction of a pregnant woman's body as a flower, harbouring the 'fruit of her womb' (yet another biblical reference) in her 1671 publication, *The Midwives Book*.[9]

Other terms for menstruation during the sixteenth century included 'courses', 'monthlies', 'ordinaries', 'monthly sickness', and many more.[10] In short, there were a number of ways in which to refer to this time of the month, but the imagery surrounding 'flowers' was seen over and over again – notably in recipe books and domestic guides specifically directed towards women. And several such recipes existed during the period, aimed at adjusting menstruation in a number of ways. For example, one early modern Italian recipe instructed on 'how to restrain the natural course [*corso*] of a woman if her flowers [*fior*] were too abundant'. This involved applying an ointment over the pubis, and even referenced the bleeding's name once as *menstrua.*[11] Largely speaking, the reference to 'flowers' shed a positive light and image over the topic of menstruation – seeing it as an absolutely necessary physical function of the woman's uterus in order to maintain optimal health and, of course, fertility. At the same time, this positive imagery did not make the subject any less taboo or embarrassing.

In a medical sense, menstruation was the most common and 'normal' means of evacuation for females – one of the 'non-natural' methods associated with balancing her four humours.[12] It was caused by 'a chemical ferment … which reached critical mass once a month and broke forth from the uterus' – the absence of which was capable of causing anything from nosebleeds, as Hippocrates had warned, to the frightening 'suffocation of the matrix [uterus]'. This type of suffocation should not be confused with the suffocation described in the previous chapter, caused by a 'wandering womb'.[13] Instead, this instance of the term referred to a build-up of blood within the uterus that was, for some reason, unable to escape. The result of this was believed to be suffocation – and death – of the organ itself. Indeed, the majority of women's health problems were blamed on the uterus. One French physician named Lazare Rivière, writing in the mid-seventeenth century, stated that the womb was the source of 'six hundred miseries and innumerable calamities'.[14] Some of these calamities were believed to be caused by retained blood that did not purge from the female body as expected – as in, suffocation. As the ancient Greeks had taught, '[the menses'] absence, outside of pregnancy, was considered morbid, very worrisome, and often a forewarning of haemorrhages'.[15] Writing in 1652, Nicholas Fontanus summarised many of the problems that might follow retained menses:

> …[women] are immediately subject to the falling sickness, the palsy, the consumption, the whites, the mother, the melancholy, burning fevers, the dropsy, inward inflammations of all principal parts, the suppression of the urine, nauseating, vomiting, loathing of meat, yexing, and a continual pain in the head, arising from ill vapours communicated from the matrix to the brain.[16]

While the Greeks had written a number of their own remedies for absent menstruation in their time, the Tudors, too, had recipes and treatments for this serious condition. Amenorrhea, or the absence of a menstrual period, was by no means a rare occurrence for women in the sixteenth century, and it certainly did not always indicate a pregnancy. Poor diet, excessive physical exertion, as well as a number of undiagnosed and undiscovered medical conditions could have contributed to a young Tudor woman missing her monthly 'flowers'. But while this was relatively common, it was also considered very dangerous. Medieval writings on the subject, including the French translation of the *Aphorisms* (1362–1365) referenced several emmenagogues (formulas meant to induce menstruation), such as potions, fumigations, pessaries and suppositories.[17] Plant properties were very often recommended, even from the time of the ancient Greeks. Myrrh, basil, sisymbrium, spikenard, mugwort and chamomile were some examples of the numerous botanical suggestions made, and in 1655 Nicholas Culpeper's *The Complete Herbal* publication listed 80 different plant varieties that were believed to invoke menstruation.[18] Simon Forman's *Matrix and the paine therof,* published in 1596, listed another 140 plants for the same purpose, which he also referred to as 'flowares'.[19] Most of these remedies for amenorrhea were topical applications, or meant to be administered internally via the vagina. Some others were herbal drinks, including the crushed leaves or seeds from recommended plants, but far fewer were recommended to be eaten as food. A notable exception to this is a recipe detailed in *The Secrets of Alexis,* by Alessio Piemontese:

> Take a sweet Apple, and make him hollow within, make a pouder of Nutmegs, Mace, Synamon, of each halfe a dragme, Cloves halfe a scruple: put all this within the Apple with a little Suger, and rost it under hote ashes, and give of it onto the woman ever when the paine commeth onto hir.[20]

This pain, we can assume, referred to menstrual cramping, and the Italian author went on further to suggest a dosage of opium if the woman's discomfort should increase so much that 'hir life is in doubt'.[21] Another of the book's recipes was listed as a remedy 'to make a womans time to come', and detailed the following:

> Take two ounces of the juyce of Savyne, and puriffe it, mixing with it two dragmes of Synamon well made into pouder; sower grains of Saffron, two ounces of the water of Radish rootes distilled with a little sugar … this provoketh marveilously the flowers of a woman. Wherefore beware ye give it not unto a woman great with childe: For all that provoketh hir flowers, and maketh hir also to labour befor hir time.[22]

Indeed, it will come as little surprise that many of the ingredients meant to bring on menstruation also had abortifacient properties, and were often warned against if the woman knew herself to be pregnant. Culpeper's *The Complete Herbal* cautioned against this as well when speaking of certain plants – such as basil and the berries of bay trees, 'lest they procure abortion, or cause labour too soon'.[23] Thanks to modern day medical understanding, we know that if any ingredient is capable of bringing about menstruation, it is likely due to uterine contracting. This same contracting and constricting of the uterus would have had several effects, depending on the condition of the woman – to include the abortion of a foetus, the onset of labour contractions, and the expelling of a retained placenta following childbirth. We can see from many early modern recipes and texts that several of the same herbal ingredients were recommended in any of these cases, and so it fell to the woman (or her medical practitioner) to exercise caution and to understand exactly the specific outcome for which she was striving. As has already been mentioned, amenorrhea was not always due to pregnancy, though it certainly could be. Therefore, it is altogether possible that many young Tudor women simply did not realise that they were pregnant when they missed their monthly 'flowers'. In this case, a recipe meant to 'bring forth menstruation' might actually have caused an abortion – the woman being none the wiser. We will touch more on the methods used to recognise a pregnancy in later chapters, but for now it is worth briefly noting the multi-use nature of many of these popular menstruation-invoking recipes.[24]

While medically speaking, menstruation was considered to be vital to a woman's health, with far more published recipes directed at encouraging it rather than suppressing it, there was still nonetheless a secretive and taboo nature about the subject. Just as the vocabulary surrounding female reproductive anatomy in general had been given 'secret' and vague names throughout and since the medieval period, menstrual blood – and even the period of lochial flow following childbirth – continued to be referred to at times as a woman's 'issue'. Some religious authorities even debated whether or not a bleeding woman should be allowed to enter a church due to her inherent uncleanliness.[25] Due to this largely secretive nature of a woman's 'flowers', it should come as little surprise that we have very little evidence to suggest how Tudor women understood and dealt with this monthly occurrence. Such information was rarely documented or spoken about openly, though some detail does exist, particularly from the seventeenth century. Historians Liza Picard, Virginia Smith, and Patricia Crawford have written of women's usage of old rags, cloth and linen, repurposed to fit into a woman's skirts or to be pinned beneath her petticoat to collect and absorb menstrual flow, then to be washed and reused daily.[26] We can likely safely assume that sixteenth-century women used the same practices and materials, which remained common into the early twentieth century, with the emergence of disposable, single-use menstruation products.

Rags and fabrics used to absorb menstrual flow were often termed 'clouts', which generally referred to scraps of fabric that could be used for a variety of household purposes – such as dishrags, bandages, and even wiping material after using the toilet. Linen was perhaps the most chosen fabric for menstruation clouts, due to the belief that the material could efficiently draw out moisture from the body.[27] Alternatively, it seems equally likely that a number of women – particularly those of a lower status or with a limited supply of spare cloth – might just as well have used nothing at all to absorb their menstrual flow. In these cases, it would have simply seeped into the fabric of their shifts and underskirts, which would later have been washed. Indeed, it is extremely unlikely that any internal absorption measures would have been taken – such as through pessaries, or any form of the modern day tampon – as these would have been considered very dangerous to a woman's health.[28]

It is likely that much, if not all, of a young Tudor woman's knowledge on the subject of her 'flowers' came similarly as it does today – through friends, sisters, and perhaps most crucially, mothers. She would likely have known to expect her first menstrual flow somewhere between the ages of 9 and 18 (medieval and early modern writers on the subject found it difficult to pinpoint the exact age that menstruation should be considered 'normal').[29] She would have been taught to understand what this monthly bleeding meant – that it signified the arrival of her childbearing years and her ability to conceive, and thus, depending on her social standing and family situation, her readiness for marriage. It also would have been impressed upon her to pay some attention to its regularity, given the commonly held understanding that regular menstruation of around every thirty days, lasting for two-to-four days on average, was indicative of her overall health. Any deviation that she might notice in the characteristics, regularity, or (worst of all) absence of her 'flowers' would require the consultation of medical recipes to get her courses back on track. She would have been taught and guided in all manners of menstruation by the trusted women in her life, as they instilled in her the most important lessons of female health and prepared her for the obviously expected next chapter of her life: motherhood.

Chapter Four

A Time to Wed

Marriage in the Tudor period did not follow an exact formula or timeline. In fact, the circumstances, feelings, arrangements, and ages surrounding marriage were much more varied in sixteenth-century England than we are often led to believe. Not all teenaged young women were married off to middle-aged noblemen because their parents insisted on it, or because it was advantageous to the family. This certainly could – and did – happen, but younger marriages or provisional marriage agreements were more commonly seen among higher status individuals, such as members of the gentry, or even royalty. In fact, the average age for typical men and women to enter into marriage was the mid-to-late twenties, similar to today.[1] Around 1600, the average age for a first marriage for men and women was 28 and 25, respectively.[2]

But if menarche was expected to occur somewhere in a girl's early teenage years (in some cases earlier) then why such a gap in time between the beginning of her age of fertility and the age of marriage? In general, it was desirable that both a man and a woman – at least, of lower-to-middling classes – would have obtained many of the skills necessary to run a household and raise children before settling down and marrying. This meant that both girls and boys would be expected to carry out some sort of work experience while still quite young, which will be explored in much more depth later in this book. For now, the emphasis remains on young sixteenth-century men and women coming into and through adolescence, and paving the way to their finding a partner with whom to settle down. As has already been said, the vast majority of women and men did not meet their future husband or wife until they were well into their twenties, following what was usually a period of several years living and working outside of the familial home.

Another potentially surprising detail about the general attitude towards marriage in the Tudor period is that love (or at least fondness) was expected and desired across 'all social levels'.[3] In fact, it was the opinion of the Italian writer, Stefan Guazzo, at the time that 'the greatest joy and sweetest comfort that a man may have in this world is a loving, kind, and honest wife'.[4] Nevertheless, there were certain societal expectations for wives as well, beyond them simply being loving to their husbands and easy to love in return. Stefan himself was counselled to look for a woman who was 'demure', 'skilled in sewing, spinning, knitting', and who kept 'bashfully out of the way when strangers came to call'.[5] It should come as little surprise that a great deal of instruction and pressure was placed upon young women, considering the fragility of their reputations. Juan Luis Vives, who in 1529 published *A Very Fruitful and Pleasant Book Called the Instruction of a Christian Woman,* warned that 'if some slur has attached to a girl's reputation from men's opinion of her, it usually remains forever and is not erased except by clear proofs of her chastity and wisdom'.[6] She was expected, therefore, to be meek and pure, of course, as well as cognisant of how often and to whom she spoke – so as to strike the perfect balance of sounding educated, but not overly interested and flirtatious. In short, women of the time had many social rules to obey in order to attract a spouse and make a good match with their reputation firmly intact.[7]

Far from the oft-held belief that a 'normal' marriage arrangement in the Tudor period was that of a 15-year-old girl to a wealthy 60-year-old man (or some similar age gap), it seems that in most cases, such a union was viewed as unseemly. An Elizabethan writer stated on the subject, 'to match a young maid with an old man, it is miserable'.[8] *The Art of Love,* written in 1598, advised on this point:

> Chuse not a man either too yong, or over wearied with yeres: for no age can be more successful in loving, than when a man is in the state of firme strength and abilitie: which being already spent and gone in old men, makes them unapt or incapable of those sweet pastimes the case of love requires.[9]

Of course, not all young ladies were afforded an opinion on the subject – and neither were men, for that matter. In fact, it was never truly expected that the choice of one's spouse could be made entirely without the input of one's parents at all, regardless of social status. Across the board, to marry in secret or without the blessing and consent of fathers was deemed 'ungodly' – the gravity of which only increased in the higher, wealthier circles of society.[10] A pamphlet published in 1586 decreed 'that children are not to marry without the consent of their parents, in whose power and choice it lieth to provide wives and husbands for their sons and daughters'. And where the joining of lands, mingling of wealth, or rising of familial status was at stake, the seriousness of parental blessing on a potential marriage grew tenfold.

Indeed, among noble and royal families, marriage contracts brokered between parents on behalf of their children – particularly when they were very young – were more common. The case of Mary, Queen of Scots is an extreme example. At only a few months old, in the spring of 1543, betrothal plans were well underway to unite the kingdoms of Scotland and England in a marriage between her and the 5½-year-old Prince Edward, son of King Henry VIII.[11] These plans would never come to pass, but they were telling of the importance of merging political power, wealth and resources at the highest level of the period. Another slightly milder example is that of 12-year-old Lady Katherine Grey, who married 15-year-old Henry Herbert on 25 May 1553. This was another political arrangement made to assist the Duke of Northumberland in securing his new daughter-in-law, (Katherine's sister) Jane Grey's, succession to the English throne upon Edward VI's impending death.[12] Love, in these cases, was not even remotely within consideration by the families orchestrating the marriages. These were unions with a 'greater' purpose, and if the children were too young for the marriage bed (meaning that menarche had not yet occurred for the female), then it was a marriage on paper only – at least until menstruation began and the relationship could be consummated, thus making it official and legal.[13]

Such family pressures regarding marriage existed well beyond prepubescent children, however. Even an adult's choice of spouse was commonly regulated by mothers and fathers, with such parental involvement being not just tolerated, but expected. Vives reinforced this commonly-held notion in his *Instruction of a Christian Woman* by advising: 'it becometh not a maid to talk where her father and mother be in communication about her marriage, but to leave all that care and charge wholly unto them which love her'.[14] It was clearly understood that the arrangement of a child's prosperous marriage was one of a parent's primary responsibilities in life – but that didn't mean that such involvement was never challenged. Around 1523, for example, the 21-year-old Henry Percy was deeply in love with a soon-to-be very well-known lady named Anne Boleyn, despite having been technically betrothed to another (via his parents) since the age of 14. Once his parents, along with his employer, Cardinal Thomas Wolsey, discovered his planned betrothal to Anne, a swift stop was put to the love match and Henry was forced to marry the already agreed-upon Mary Talbot. In Anne's case, a similar arrangement had also already been discussed between her father, Thomas Boleyn, and the eighth Earl of Ormond – engaging her to the latter's son, James Butler. This agreement had been made with the intention to resolve a conflict between the Boleyns and the Butlers over claims to Ormond lands, and thus, neither Anne's nor James' happiness was of much concern. Despite Anne, Henry, James and Mary all having been in their twenties around this time, not a single one of them was afforded the luxury of choosing a partner whom they loved. Their betrothals – and many others like them – were meant to be familial alliances, treaty agreements, peace offerings and political transactions, but they weren't in the least about love.

Anne Boleyn, of course, would not in fact go on to marry James Butler at all. Instead, she would marry King Henry VIII, the man she truly wanted, in 1533. But even kings could not always have their pick of a partner, despite the proverbial mountains Henry had moved in order to rid himself of his first wife in order to acquire his second. He, too, would find himself forced into a political marriage just four years later in 1540, when his fourth wife, Anne of Cleves, arrived on English shores.[15] 'I like her not!' he passionately complained upon meeting her, though it mattered little. The political and religious alliance with the duchy of Cleves had been forged, and the king of England's hands were tied. That marriage, however, would be annulled just months later, in favour of another true love match (on the king's behalf, anyway) – this time with the decades-younger Katherine Howard.

Countless further examples could be explored here, regarding forced marriages among sixteenth-century nobility and royalty, but suffice to say, it happened often. Still, to return to the point that the general Tudor attitude towards marriage held love in high esteem, it can be argued that there was almost certainly the *hope* that many of these purely logistical marital arrangements might one day spawn feelings of affection and warmth. They might not be on par with the subjects of William Shakespeare's most romantic plays, but a general feeling of liking – and even one day, maybe loving – one's spouse was the goal of any sixteenth-century marriage, regardless of how the match had come to be. Henry Tudor and Elizabeth of York, who married in 1486 upon his ascension to the throne following the Battle of Bosworth, are a terrific example of this. Theirs was a marriage made strictly for political purposes – to unite the two long-warring noble houses of York and Lancaster, who had been engaged in a three-decades-long bloody conflict known as the Wars of the Roses. But their logistical and political union developed into one of real affection and love, so much so that when Elizabeth died from childbirth complications in 1503, the king was known to be devastated by her loss.[16]

In general, Tudor marriage was meant to result both in the 'personal happiness of the couples' as well as 'their future social status and economic security'.[17] Oftentimes, as in the case of Henry and Elizabeth, this worked out relatively well, and we can assume that this was likely the reality for a great many couples of the period across all social classes. Divorce rates throughout the sixteenth century remained quite low, probably due to the cost, legal inconvenience and stigma that came along with it. Therefore, marital conflict was often resolved quietly, or with the agreeable result that both parties would live separately while remaining legally married.[18] However, given the extremely high birth rates across the period, it stands to reason that many happy – or at least tolerable – marriages were indeed formed. If they couldn't be passionate love affairs, they might at minimum be emotionally satisfactory relationships that resulted in a great number of offspring.[19] And for a Tudor marriage, to produce children was – in most cases – almost entirely the point.

So, how might young men and women become acquainted and promised to wed in the first place? Aside from the obvious parental interference and matchmaking, as has already been discussed, there were a number of ways a sixteenth-century courtship might come to be. As briefly mentioned, young people might first be introduced to one another through their employment and service outside of the home. Social events, such as dances, were especially common up and down the social ranks of society, cultivating the perfect environment for the opposite sexes to mingle. While in wealthier circles, dancing was considered to be such a critical life skill that parents would pay for their children's dance instruction, the lower classes could content themselves to learn popular dances through watching their peers or learning from family members.[20] John Stow, a contemporary historian of the period, reflected on doing just that during his own youth in the 1540s when writing during the late Elizabethan period. He recalled 'the Maidens, one of them playing on a Timbrell, in sight of their Maisters and Dames, to daunce for garlandes hanged thwart the streetes…'. Crucially, he also pointed out that 'being now suppressed, worser practices within doors are to be feared'.[21] By this, he likely meant that the 'youths' he recalled in his writing were plagued by the pent-up sexual energy of adolescence and that dancing was at least a respectable and socially accepted form of releasing some of that vigour.

But let us not be fooled – young men and women of the sixteenth century were not so different from the young adults and teenagers of the modern day. It can be easy to assume, from the faraway lens with which we view the Tudor period, that the concept of premarital sexual relations was so morbidly anathema, that nobody was daring to do it. And while it is true that morality and abstinence had been preached about for centuries – and continued to be impressed upon young people throughout the sixteenth century – these people were, after all, only human. Homilies published in 1562 railed against 'whoredom, fornication, and uncleanness', proclaiming that the 'vice' of extra- or pre-marital fornication had 'grown unto such a height'. Similar to today (though perhaps with differing verbiage), the homilies complained that 'in a manner among many it is accounted no sin at all but rather a pastime, a dalliance and but a touch of youth, not rebuked but winked at, not punished but laughed at'.[22]

In short, though sexual intimacy among unmarried individuals was not to be condoned in society, it was also something to be understood – perhaps brushed under the rug or ignored – and seen to be the natural inclination for men and women of a certain age. The Tudors respected the Church's teachings, but they also had their sexual urges and they understood (as well as they could have) how their bodies worked. Therefore, it should be unsurprising that premarital sex certainly did occur across all social classes, and with varying degrees of chastisement. Depending on the circumstances, a pair of fraternising lovers might have been thrust into marriage by their parents, upon the discovery that they were already carnally involved. In other cases, public humiliation might have ensued, following the examination and punishment of a Church court or other town authority.[23] Somewhat surprisingly, however, babies born out of wedlock accounted for only four per cent of births across the country by the end of the Tudor period, which might have been owed to the Crown beginning to interfere in these 'sinful' relationships around 1576. Clearly, by the mid-sixteenth century, illegitimate children had become enough of a problem that the involvement of government was warranted – though in truth, no justices of the peace nor men of the cloth would ever truly curb what was known to be only basic sexual human nature.[24]

Even the ancient Greeks – who, as we know, were continuously cited throughout the Tudor period – had taught that exact sentiment regarding sex, by saying that it 'promoted good digestion and appetite, it made the body light and nimble, opened the pores and purged the phlegm. Minds became quicker when sex was properly partaken of; sadness, madness and melancholy were driven away'. However, it was also known to bring about a 'terrible weakness of both body and mind', according to the Greeks. It could sap strength, 'dragging a man down to the level of common beasts'.[25] And on that note, men were viewed quite differently from women when it came to sex. To return to the Humoural Theory for just a moment, it was well known that women were of a cold and wet disposition, which meant that their bodies craved the hotness of a man's seed. Due to this, women were considered to be far more prone to sin, having the wicked ability to lure otherwise strong and steadfast men into errant affairs. In fact, sex was seen as medically necessary for a woman's health, as her 'sexually ravenous body' needed to be satisfied – essential in order to avoid sickness caused by accumulated vapours from her womb (or worse, the dreaded organ's 'wandering', as discussed in the previous chapter).[26] Suffice to say, sex was a complicated and sensitive subject for young men and women of the period, and likely very much on their minds, whether they acted upon their urges or not. In any case, the subject of sexual intercourse and procurement of legitimately born children was the goal of any typical Tudor marriage – and if the average man or woman had reached their mid-to-late twenties and found themselves a partner (either through their own choosing or by way of parental involvement), this was precisely the immediate future that they were eyeing.

Marriage, however, was somewhat murky territory during the period, at least when it came to determining the legality of the union. The medieval period considered any union to be a valid marriage if the couple exchanged vows – regardless of whether or not such vows took place in a church. This continued throughout the sixteenth century, though in 1553, Archbishop Thomas Cranmer attempted to steer all valid wedding ceremonies into the holy confines of an actual church building. The law was never ratified, however, which meant that virtually any determined couple in love could become husband and wife, as long as they said something to the effect of 'I marry you'. This should not be confused with the phrase, 'I promise to marry you', as that would only have signified a betrothal, not an actual marriage. Of course, it helped if a witness was present to verify that vows had been exchanged, though this wasn't necessarily essential.[27] Consummation of the marriage afterwards, however, *really* sealed the deal, since this intimate act erased any real possibility of easily dissolving the union.[28] So, if a couple verbally committed themselves to one another, but one of them suddenly got cold feet before the consummation, was it truly a marriage at all? It seems the answer to this question depended upon who one asked, and how credible a couple's witness was – or indeed if there was anyone to corroborate the union's validity at all. Such grey area makes it difficult to pinpoint a reliable statistic on lawful marriages during the Tudor period, as it clearly depended on a multitude of factors – and a fair bit of subjectivity.

A sixteenth-century man could expect to receive a dowry from his new wife's father, particularly within aristocratic circles. Such dowries were seen as the daughter's sole inheritance from her family and it was her new groom's to do with as he saw fit.[29] In particularly wealthy families, a bride's dowry could have also included the income of familial estates, as well as lands that might be gifted from her family to her new husband. In essence, these were pure business transactions, negotiable between both parties, and likely to be far more generous if the bride was marrying 'up'. Upon the settling of such financial agreements, as well as the wedding ceremony itself (preferably taking place in a church and witnessed by the families of both individuals), the newlywed couple was ready to settle into their new marital home. This might have been a house or estate gifted from a family member, or paid for by the husband through purchasing or renting. This largely depended upon the husband's finances, of course, as well as the couple's social status. But no matter how it came to be, the newly minted husband and wife were now legally joined and ready to begin their next hotly anticipated duty: to produce children of their own. This may not have been such a simple task as one might think, however. The business of making children in the Tudor period, in fact, often involved explicit instructions, grim warnings and a fair number of eccentric theories about the human body and the process of conception. It was a lot more complicated than the simple act of hopping into the marriage bed.

Chapter Five

The Christian Duty

In this 'long and troublesome journey of matrimonye', wrote Edmund Tilney in 1568, 'the wise man maye not be contented onely with the Spouses virginitie, but by little and little must gently procure that he maye also steale away hir privat will, and appetite, so that of two bodies there may be made one onelye heart'.[1] These were some of Tilney's words of marital advice regarding sexual relations, published in a discourse titled *The Flower of Friendshippe.* They spoke of a popular attitude towards the importance of sex within a healthy Tudor marriage, citing romance and feelings of deep affection as reason enough for physical intimacy.

But according to Martin Luther, marriage and the procreation of children were godly works, and the Church itself conceded that sex within marriage – while being second-best to celibacy – 'represented a more biblically pure life for adults' in the sixteenth century.[2] It was essential, therefore, that a newly married man and woman should take to the marriage bed and see it as their Christian duty to procreate, given the Bible's decree for man and woman to 'be fruitful and multiply'.[3] In fact, childbearing was 'an obligation for married women', with the very nature of matrimony being explicitly linked to the procreation of children.[4] This was the essential expectation for married couples, not only because the Church commanded it of them but also because the promise of children signified the continuation of a familial, or even dynastic line. Estates, lands, wealth, titles and social status could only pass down so far as the family line extended, and so the Tudor man who found himself the only heir to his father's grand title and properties would be especially covetous of an heir for himself – and preferably a male at that. Otherwise, if he were to die childless, all that his family had earned throughout the generations prior to him would just as soon pass to a lateral relative, such as a cousin if one existed. Or worse, such titles would cease to exist and palatial family homes might fall into disrepair.

So essential was the topic of procreation within marriage that we see copious evidence of fertility symbols and imagery throughout the typical Tudor bedroom, as if to remind the married man and woman at every waking moment of exactly what they should be getting up to. Acorns were one such example that would often feature into the elaborate carvings of a grand Tudor bed. Representing new life, fertility and abundance (as the small acorn would one day grow into the mighty oak tree) it is the prominent focal point in the canopy of the ornate 1580s bed held today at Agecroft Hall in Richmond, Virginia.[5] The marriage bed of Henry VII and Elizabeth of York held plenty more examples of fertility images, including fruits like grapes and strawberries.[6] The Tudor bed is the greatest and most prominent example that we have of bedroom furnishings explicitly touting the significance of procreation within marriage, but such elaborately carved beds would have been cost-prohibitive for many in the sixteenth century. Other bedroom items with fertility images might have been much more subdued and humbler for those among the lower classes, perhaps including smaller pieces of artwork or wall hangings, often given as wedding gifts from family members.

The business of baby-making in the sixteenth century was so vital, in fact, that it appears a great number of couples took to the marriage bed *before* any official ceremony had been performed. A betrothal announcement was oftentimes thought to be legitimate enough, and 'considerable leeway could be afforded by many communities'. This appears to have been particularly true in Yorkshire, based on church records that indicate suspicious time intervals between marriage ceremonies and subsequent births.[7] Historians of the sixteenth and seventeenth century have concluded that many brides and grooms came to the altar already expecting a baby (perhaps one-third of Elizabethans) whether anyone else was aware of the circumstances or not.[8] No matter the timing – whether following a betrothal or an actual ceremony – there can be no doubt that children were important up and down the ranks of society. Exceptions were made, however, for betrothals and marriages that occurred when children were quite young, as was often the case among the aristocracy and royalty. As detailed in the previous chapter, Katherine Grey is one such example, but there were many others – such as Margaret Plumpton of Yorkshire, who married for the first time at age 5 and would not have consummated her union until her teenage years. Similarly, Agnes Barbron, who was the heiress to an impressive fortune and manor in Poulton, was arranged to be married at just 9 years old. But because she was a sickly child, her guardian allowed her to wait five years into her marriage (to his own son) before consummation.[9] Still, as early as could possibly be deemed respectable, consummation and babies – thus the securing of family ties in an arranged marriage – were vital. This was true from the humble merchant who hoped to pass along his home and business to his own child, all the way to the king of England, who needed to prove to his subjects that the throne and country were secure with an heir in line to inherit.

One needs only to look at the plight of King Henry VIII and his arduous task of acquiring a healthy male heir – marrying no fewer than three wives before Prince Edward was finally born in 1537. But six wives and nearly forty years of marriage altogether only produced a total of three legitimate children healthy enough to survive infancy. It is well known that he fathered at least one illegitimate child as well, but when it came to the king's marital relations, his and his queens' efforts returned relatively few rewards, despite several confirmed pregnancies between Catherine of Aragon and Anne Boleyn, many of which resulted in miscarriages or stillbirths. Each of these two wives produced daughters for the king – the future Queen Mary I and Queen Elizabeth I, respectively – but it was only Jane Seymour who gave him the son he most desired, the future King Edward VI.[10] So many years and so many wives later, King Henry must surely have questioned how the begetting of healthy children – and particularly sons – could be so difficult (and indeed he did question it). He was surely far from alone. As it turns out, the subject of conception was so hotly discussed throughout the sixteenth century that a staggering number of theories, instructions and recipes existed in order to help a couple along in their procreation process. There were even, supposedly, methods 'sure' to produce male children instead of female, if only the married couple knew just what to do.

First, as ever, we must consult the Theory of the Four Humours, as this was the basis by which the Tudors understood nearly everything to do with their bodies. It was helpful first for one to recognise their body's specific condition as it related to the humours, as this could very well determine their future success in the act of 'generation'. Colder people, for instance, were known to have little appetite for sexual intercourse – an interesting contradiction to the theories that women were naturally 'moist', yet also sexually ravenous and needy. Their hair – including that around their genitals – was sparse and slow-growing, and it should come as little surprise that they were most often associated with having more female children. Hotter people, on the other hand, were sexually voracious and more likely to beget boys. Even the individual's 'seed' (i.e. their reproductive bodily fluid, as the Tudors knew it to be) was affected by the body's condition. The dryer a person's bodily condition, the less seed they would produce during the act of sexual intercourse – but the seed that was emitted would be thick in substance. Wetter people, by contrast, had abundant but thin, watery seed.[11]

Of course, this 'seed' did not only refer to a man's semen; it was applicable to both males and females. Recall the writing of Aretaeus of Cappadocia, who while perpetuating the concept of the wandering womb, also theorised that the organ could produce its own 'thinner, colder, and feebler' seed to that of a man's.[12] The nature of this female seed, however, was not well understood. It was speculated by Tudor physicians that a woman might emit some watery substance that included an egg, thus, to meet with a man's seed during intercourse. It wasn't *too* far off the mark, though they also erroneously suspected that this egg was only emitted during female orgasm, which was a particularly troubling theory in cases of rape.[13] This theory frighteningly touted that, if a woman had successfully conceived a baby during the act of forced, unwanted sex, then it hadn't *really* been unwanted at all. Given that she would have had to experience orgasm in order to emit the seed capable of creating a child with her attacker's sperm, the offending man in question would have been virtually off the hook for having committed any violence against her. But if a woman was thought only to be capable of successful procreation if she enjoyed the act of sex and experienced orgasm, then her physical pleasure was actually something to be prioritised by a good, duty-bound Christian husband. This was emphasised in a fifteenth-century text called *The Book of Vices and Virtues,* which instructed a man in seducing his wife with the following words:

> … arouse a woman to intercourse [and] caress her breasts and touch [her] between the perineum and vulva and to strike her buttocks with the purpose that the woman desires … and when the woman begins to speak with a stammer, then they ought to copulate.[14]

Indeed, a married couple that prioritised both parties' sexual pleasure 'were able to feel that they were carrying out God's work'.[15] It might be a somewhat surprising notion for the period, that a female's pleasure was considered as important as a man's, but as a fascinating aside, it was indeed a sixteenth-century anatomist who 'discovered' the organ most responsible for female sexual pleasure – the clitoris – in 1559. Realdo Colombo, of Italy, wrote about it in his publication *De re anatomica,* following the dissection of a female corpse and describing the clitoris as being 'made with such art'.[16] But of course, it was not *all* about the woman. Pleasure was considered fundamental to a man's ability to procreate as well, and as is obvious and observable, the male 'seed' is indeed only released during orgasm. One fascinating – and perhaps superfluous – detail regarding a Tudor man's sexual pleasure has to do with the controversial subject of circumcision. There would have been no controversy during the sixteenth century, as foreskin heightened the pleasurable sensations of intercourse and was believed to speed along the conclusion of the act, thus rendering it arguably essential to generation, to the Tudor mind.[17] Thus, circumcision would have been a foreign and deeply unpopular concept.

But contemporary theories relating to successful conception were not all about orgasm or even the act of sexual intercourse itself. Interestingly, a lot of it went back to the topic of diet, as this controlled a great number of aspects to an individual's health. In fact, to return to a man's seed for just another moment, it was theorised that this seed arose 'within his body as a natural result of the digestive process' – and thus, mightn't that man's diet possibly influence the strength, vigour, and success of that resulting seed?[18] In fact, there was a lot to this. Strong sexual appetites, for one, were associated with certain foods, such as red meat and wine. The temperature of a woman's womb also influenced the diet that she should follow, in order to obtain the best chances of conception. In most cases, her womb was considered cold (to match the general cold, dry condition of the overall woman), and so she might be advised to eat a variety of warming foods, particularly warming spices, such as cinnamon, ginger, nutmeg and cloves.[19] This advice was another notable contradiction to the ancient Greeks' theory that the womb was a woman's internal 'oven', sapping all the heat from her body. But in addition to diet, the time of year for conception mattered, with colder seasons increasing the amount that a man might bundle up in warm clothes, therefore heating the sperm and requiring its output.[20] This particular theory seems to have been backed by Thomas Elyot, who wrote specifically on the subject.

In his *Castel of Helth,* Elyot described in great detail the precise foods that one should eat at the appropriate times of year, in order to attain the greatest success in sexual relations. He wrote, for example, that from 12 December until 9 March (certainly colder months, when a man might be tightly bundled), hot meats and drinks should be consumed in moderation. One should drink wine abundantly between these dates, with only little water, and 'the companie of a woman is not unwholesome to the bodie'. From 9 March until 25 April, he advised that sweet phlegm and blood would increase, so the individual should take in more juice, exercise the body diligently, 'then may ye use safely the companie of a woman'. Beyond the end of April, however, Elyot cautioned against carnal relations, pointing to choler increasing through 14 June, melancholy reigning between mid-June and 12 September, and thin humours abounding until 17 October. During this time, specifically, he warned that 'all fluxes and distillations be prohibited' and 'carnall occupations should then be eschewed'. Of the final two months of the year, Elyot didn't mention sex. He merely instructed the reader to use 'all bitter meates, sweet wines, fat meate, and much exercise'.[21]

Advice such as Elyot's informed the (typically male) reader about which seasons were encouraged for sexual intercourse – and a little bit about diet – but other contemporary sources were far more descriptive. Andrew Boorde, for example, in his *Dietary of Health*, specifically advised eating partridge, as it was 'soonest dygested', considered a 'restoratyve meate, and dothe comforte the brayne and the stomacke'. Most importantly, he insisted that it could 'augment carnall lust'.[22] Vegetables that grew into phallic shapes were also thought to be good for reproductive health, as it was a popular theory during the period that texture and appearance of foods were key indicators about their influence on the body.[23] Towards the end of the sixteenth century, Alessio Piemontese also wrote in great detail a recipe that he named 'For to make a woman beare children, although it bee not always assured, yet it is the best remedie that can be found'. In it, he directed:

> … let her eat of the flesh of a hare, and the man also as much as is possible, that is to saie, leaving all other kind of fleshe, then take the kinde of that Mercurike that hath curled or wrinkled leaves, Mugwort or Motherwort, Valerian, and make thereof long or round morsels … with grease, spices, cheese, and egges, and let hir eate nothing else in the morning with bread, three times a weeke continuallie, and let her drinke good wine.

He also advised the woman's husband to concoct a powder by taking 'the small scraping of Cypres, a dram and a halfe of Nasturtium, long pepper, nutmegs, fine wood of Aloe', and most interestingly, 'the kidney or stones of a hedgehog dried and not burned'. These ingredients together, the author wrote, would produce a powder that both husband and wife should take three times with malmsey wine. Then, the husband was instructed to 'remaine eight daies without the companie of her'.[24]

There was plenty of other advice provided for a newlywedded couple who hoped for children, however. While diet and time of year for sexual relations certainly played their roles in the process of procreation, so too did perfuming one's body with 'Frankinsence, Bay leaves, nutmegs, Begewine, and a little muske', according to Piemontese.[25] Even more intriguingly, he offered this final advice:

> … having companied with her let her slepe, and carie upon her left arme an eagle stone, not of the common sort, but of those

> that be as hard as steele, and let her also keep everie day upon the raines of her backe a new laid egge, beaten with five or six drops of strong black vinegar, and remove it everie day.[26]

This set of explicit instructions was thought to give a sixteenth-century couple fairly good odds of conceiving a child, though it 'bee not always assured', as the recipe's disclaimer stated. But if one had not read Piemontese's writing – or they were living prior to its publication in 1595, there were a number of other factors they could consider instead.

The timing of intercourse was certainly something to note. As if Tudor couples were not already limited by the number of holy days and seasons on which they were expected to remain abstinent (Fridays, Sundays and fasting days, to name a few), the actual timing within a woman's cycle was also vitally important.[27] An empty, 'clean' womb was thought to be ideal for conceiving – this being in the days directly following menstruation, when it had been adequately purged and prepared to receive a man's seed.[28] Having relations during menstruation was ill-advised, according to experts such as Thomas Elyot, who noted that doing so might produce 'small, unhealthy children'.[29] It was also believed to cause unsightly birthmarks or red hair in infants.[30] The time of day for sexual relations was also important, and it was thought that the middle of the night was best, as it was far enough removed from dinnertime so as not to feel weighed down and sluggish, and rested enough by a couple of hours' sleep.[31] Another vital consideration was sex position, as it was well known that if engaging in sexual intercourse while standing up, the man's seed would simply drain out and conception could not occur.[32] This same fate was also suggested if a woman stood up too quickly, hurried down a flight of stairs, or jumped up and down after the act was complete.[33] Any and all of these things might have affected a couple's chances in the marital bed, but beyond the mere possible success of conceiving a baby, was it possible that they could influence the gender of that baby as well? As it turns out, the Tudors certainly believed that they could.

It was widely accepted at the time that the right side of the body was associated with maleness, while the left correlated to femaleness. Therefore, a woman lying on her right side – both during sex, if possible, and certainly afterwards – was thought to encourage her fertilised egg's implantation on the right side of her uterus, being likely to result in a male child.[34] In the same vein, tying a ribbon around a man's left testicle during intercourse was also meant to prevent female sperm from being ejaculated. The theory behind this notion touted that blood supply to the right testicle was stronger, coming directly from the heart. The left, on the other hand, was believed to receive a weaker supply of blood, and thus more likely to produce female babies.[35] Piemontese had something to say on the subject as well, with a recipe 'to make a woman that is wont to have daughters, to beare sonnes also'. His instructions were as follows:

> … to make a woman that beareth always daughters, to beare also sonnes, it is a thing verie easie, and hath good successe, and hath bin diverse times proved. Wherefore, if you will that your wife shall have male children, eat an herbe called in English Mercurie … which hath only two seedes, like unto the genitories of a man, and make her also eat of it before you companie with her, and eat both of you the right stones of some beastes, and of the scraping of an elephants tooth.[36]

How simple it was for a sixteenth-century man or woman to acquire the scrapings of an elephant's tooth is difficult to know, but the author seemed rather confident that this guidance would prove successful and result in the birth of at least one son. Perhaps this was due to a warming property of the mercury herb, as it was also well known that a warmer womb was more likely to grow a male child, given that he would be of a hotter nature than a female. Heating foods would therefore always have been encouraged, so as to promote a more welcoming environment for such specifically male seed to take root and flourish.

Of course, despite the countless instructions on lifestyle and sexual rituals for the purpose of succeeding in the married couple's Christian duty, it was at the end of the day – and certainly to the typical Tudor man and woman's mind – in the hands of God. The most frequently used method to achieve conception, therefore (besides sexual intercourse itself), was probably through prayer, as this was a deeply entrenched ritual in the everyday sixteenth-century individual's life. Prayers for male children, specifically, were routinely said, especially among aristocratic and royal families, who depended on sons for their family names and dynasties' survival.

But no matter how often a couple might pray, or avoid sexual relations while standing, or ingest the scrapings of an elephant's tooth, there were – as there are today – many couples who had trouble conceiving. This is evident enough by the writings of Piemontese, who advised on the issue of barrenness through several recipes in *The Secrets of Alexis.* Rather unsurprisingly, this issue of barrenness was most often placed on the woman as her own failing, as opposed to a matter of infertility in her husband. This is evident by the wording of published recipes aiming to resolve the problem, with none of them mentioning the male partner as the subject of focus. Piemontese wrote one such method meant to determine whether or not conception was even possible for a particular woman, instructing the following:

> Take of the ruen of a hare, and having fraied and consumed it in hot water, give it the woman to drinke in the morning at her breakfast: then let her stand in hot bathe, and if there come a greefe or paine in her bellie, she may conceive: if not, she shall never conceive.[37]

Intriguing as this advice was, it spoke of a common enough issue that the author felt the need to write of it multiple times. Even he could not invoke miracles, however, as he clearly stated that 'it is a hard thing for a barrain woman to beare children, and a great gift and grace of God to obtaine it, because the causes of sterilitie and barrainnesse be diverse and without number'.[38] Any mention of the possibility of male infertility is nowhere to be found in his writing. He, too, advised seeking help from God by invoking prayer, and he was certainly not alone in not knowing what the cause of such infertility in a woman might be.

Philip Barrough, who wrote *The Method of Physicke* in 1590, wrote the following on the subject: 'They which be married, and cannot use the act of generation, because of the sluggish impotencie and weakness of their members: coming of a cold distempute wherewith they be vexed, or of some other cause...'. He didn't seem to know the source of such 'sluggish impotencie', but here he did, in fact, seem to acknowledge the fact that both partners' 'members' were worth taking into consideration when attempts at conception were unsuccessful. The coldness he referenced could be remedied by a man who 'exercise[d] the nether partes, and [used] meates that doe heate and engender good humours, as is the flesh of hennes, capons, partrich, feasauntes … and specially sparrows, cockes stones and such like'.[39] He further emphasised 'windy meates' – as it was thought that a man's 'yard' was 'inflated by the wind' when aroused.[40] Such 'windy meates' were described as 'chickens, beans, scalions, leekes, the roote and seede of persneppes, pine nuts, rape roots', and 'the egges of partriches', which 'doe stirre up carnal lust'.[41] Finally, Barrough advised – following the warming, windy diet – to 'let the patient sleepe in a soft bedde, and let him reade things that doe stirre up lust, or let him heare them read. Let his privie members be continually chafed and rubbed with oyles, ointments and other heating medicines'.[42] It is somewhat refreshing to see that Barrough pointed towards remedies to help a *man* who was having trouble procreating, rather than focusing solely on his wife's barrenness. However, the issue appeared to be centred solely on the usefulness of a man's reproductive organs. Medical advice was only offered in the cases of erectile dysfunction. Otherwise, if a man could attain and maintain an erection, then penetrate and ejaculate during sexual intercourse, then he was considered perfectly fertile. If conception was still unsuccessful, then the issue clearly lay with the woman.[43]

It is worth mentioning that while this was still almost certainly not the typical attitude towards infertility among married couples, the Tudor man did have a very serious mental investment in his own fertility. To be an infertile male would have questioned his inner morality as a Christian – and perhaps worse, it would have threatened his masculinity. It was much easier and beneficial to a man, therefore, to lay the burden of infertility upon his female partner. We see this very clearly in the case of Henry VIII, who in 1519 became the father to an illegitimate son born of his mistress, Bessie Blount. This birth came after nearly ten years and six pregnancies in his queen, Catherine of Aragon, who had produced only one healthy daughter and one son who had lived for just fifty-two days. This lack of healthy male issue, of course, had created a dynastic crisis in Henry's mind, but the successful pregnancy and birth of a son by his mistress – albeit an illegitimate one, unfit to inherit the throne of England – placed the blame of the situation squarely on Queen Catherine's shoulders. To Henry's mind, it was not *he* who was incapable of begetting healthy boys, it was his wife. Far from the 'emasculated' king who suffered from 'impotency' of his own members, he realised that he had simply been trying to procreate with an incapable woman, and he would take the next several years rectifying the situation and remarrying, in the hopes of more reproductive success.[44]

However, this was not entirely due to his own selfishness (though far be it from this book to try to redeem any of King Henry VIII's marital behaviours). In fact, the idea that an infertile couple was ill-matched, or even that their union was null and void due to that fact, was a common enough belief that would be echoed a century later by the well-known midwife and writer, Jane Sharp. She would go on to warn that marriage was for procreation, 'and if a person had married knowing themselves to be infertile, because of some deformity for example, then the marriage was void'. Even if there was no intentional deception in the matter, an infertile couple could, in some cases, be a sign of God's displeasure with the union.[45] In the case of his marriage to Catherine of Aragon, this was precisely Henry VIII's theory, and the ultimate reason for its demise.

John Partridge, in his *Treasurie of Commodious Conceits,* had yet another recipe for a woman to try: to 'take of those little sea fishes, called in Latine *Polipi* or *Polipodes,* and roast them upon the embers without oile, and let the woman eate of them, and it shall profite and help very much, having in the meane time the companie of a man'.[46] He also offered guidance on ingredients to 'strengthen the seed' – advising that a man should 'take Succorie, Endive, Plantin, Violet flowers & the leaves, Clarie, Sorrel, of each half a handful, with a peece of Mutton, make a good broth, and to eat it evening and morning…'.[47]

But if a man and woman were lucky enough – whether by following popular dietary and medical advice or by simply doing their Christian duty while invoking God's good favour – they might find that a baby was indeed on its way. And after so much preparation, with only a meagre (at best) understanding of her own body, the Tudor woman stepped into what is generally believed to have been the most perilous and formidable period of her entire life.

Chapter Six

To Be with Child

It is probably no surprise that determining pregnancy in the sixteenth century was not nearly so easy as it is today. There were no instant digital tests available for purchase, capable of measuring detectable levels of elevated hormones in a woman's urine. The French surgeon, Jacques Guillimeau, noted how frequently, therefore, mistakes could be made in the diagnosis of pregnancy, when he wrote *Child-birth or, The happy deliverie of women* in 1612:

> For there is nothing more ridiculous, then to assure a woman that shee is with childe; and afterward, that her natural sicknesse, or store of water should come from her: and in stead of a childe, some windie matter should breake from her, and so her belly fall, and grow flat againe, which hath hapned unto many men....[1]

Indeed, reliable pregnancy tests would not begin to be made available for roughly another four centuries, which left some degree of mystery to an early pregnancy in the Tudor period.[2] But even then, urine could, in fact, still play a role and tell a great deal about an individual's health. There was some weight placed on the characteristics of urine in general, as being a fair indicator of a wide range of medical conditions. John Partridge devoted two brief chapters at the end of his *Treasurie of Commodious Conceits*, detailing many features of urine and what they might signify, and pregnancy was indeed mentioned. He asserted that a woman's urine 'that is cleare and shining in the urinal as silver, if she cast oft, and if shee have no talent to meat, it betokeneth she is with child'.[3] Any modern day woman who has experienced pregnancy might attest that frequent urination and an early aversion to certain foods (such as meat) might indeed indicate a pregnancy, though 'clear', 'shining', and 'silver' urine might be up for some debate as a reliable signifier.

One of our best resources about the period's understanding of conception is Jane Sharp, a seventeenth-century midwife who wrote *The Midwives Book: or the Whole Art of Midwifery* in 1671. Though this is, of course, a woman and resource of the Stuart, rather than Tudor, dynasty, it is no less useful to our understanding about the early modern popular theory of the subject. She wrote extensively and in detail, for example, about the process of conception and how a woman might learn that she was with child. First, she described the nature of conception in vivid detail, writing:

> True conception is then, when the seed of both sexes is good, and duly prepared and cast into the womb as into fruitful ground, and is there so fitly and equally mingled ... that a perfect Child is by degrees framed; for first small threads as it were of the solid and substantial parts are formed out, and the womans blood flowes to them, to make the bowels and to supply all parts of the infant with food and nourishment.[4]

Jane Sharp alleged that conception was 'performed in less than seven hours after the seed is mingled', and early symptoms of a pregnancy would swiftly follow.[5] Firstly, she asserted that 'when the seed is cast into the womb, [the woman would] feel the womb shut close, and a shivering or trembling [would] run through every part of her body'. The reason for this, she explained, was 'by reason of the heat that draws inward to keep the conception, and so leaves the outward parts cold and chill'. Next, she described the pleasure that a woman would feel as 'the mans seed comes not forth again, for the womb closely embraceth it, and will shut as fast as possibly may be'. Thirdly, Sharp noted that 'the womb sinks down to cherish the seed, and so the belly grows flatter than it was before'. Then, she warned that a woman might feel a pain 'that goes about her belly, chiefly about her Navel and lower belly', and then the *real* early pregnancy symptoms would begin.[6]

According to Sharp, the woman's stomach would next become 'very weak, she hath no desire to eat her meat, but is troubled with sowr belchings'. After that, menstruation might cease 'at some unseasonable time that she lookt not for'. Next, the cravings would ensue – and some of these cravings, according to her, were rather interesting. She noted that women often 'hath a preternatural desire to something not fit to eat nor drink, as some women with child have longed to bite off a piece of their Husbands Buttocks'. Sharp then went on to describe other, more recognisable, early pregnancy symptoms, such as changes to the breasts, constipation, and general fatigue.[7]

As Jane Sharp did not write this midwifery manual until late into the following century, much of this knowledge of early symptoms in young Tudor women would have been passed down by mothers, sisters and other close female companions who had previously experienced pregnancy for themselves. It is certainly likely that any Tudor wife would have known of some of these physical signs to look for, as might their husbands. Jacques Guillimeau had one rather intimate suggestion for a man to be on the lookout for, which involved going to bed with her yet again. He wrote, 'If he finde an extraordinarie contentment in the companie of his Wife; and if he feele at the same time a kind of sucking or drawing at the end of his yard; if he returne from the field of nature, not over-moyst, these are signes that a woman may have conceived'. He claimed that this particular practice had assured numerous men that they had impregnated their wives, 'as soone as they have had their company'.[8] Women, too, could look for the 'symptom' of 'receiv[ing] the extraordinarie delight in the comfort of her Husband', which might indicate that she had conceived.[9] Turning to a more conventional approach to recognising early pregnancy, there was one symptom in particular that was a bit more of a mystery to a Tudor woman. The absence of a woman's menstrual period could very well have indicated a pregnancy in the sixteenth century – but it just as easily did not. As noted by Guillimeau, some women even experienced menstruation throughout their pregnancy, which was even more reason not to trust the symptom alone.[10] As discussed in chapter three, the 'flowers' of a woman's monthly cycle were affected by any number of things, such as poor diet or intense physical exertion. This would have been particularly true for women among lower classes, who might have been labouring in fields or tending a busy household or business.

But mysterious illnesses that might have included the symptom of amenorrhea would also have fooled more than a few women of the period up and down the ranks of society, with one example being Queen Mary I. In 1554, with the absence of her menstruation, she believed herself to be with child – even going so far as to formally begin her 'lying in' (a topic which will be discussed later) – but no baby was ever born. Her false condition, as described by Venetian ambassador, Giovanni Michieli, had reportedly been present 'from her youth', as her menstrual cycle had never been reliable. As such, she had long suffered the 'retention of menstrual fluids' and the 'strangulation of her womb'.[11] To add insult to injury, she later believed herself to be pregnant again in 1557, but waited to inform her husband until what she believed to be her sixth month of gestation. By then, her belly had likely swelled to some convincing degree, but alas, the cause of this was probably a growing uterine or ovarian tumour, which would ultimately cause her death in November 1558.[12]

If the absence of menstruation was not a guaranteed indicator of pregnancy, the onset of the 'flowers' at their expected time was a sure sign that conception had not occurred. Sixteenth-century men and women were educated enough on the topic of menstruation to know that regular monthly bleeding was indicative of an empty womb, as evidenced by a diary entry of Sir Archibald Johnston. Though he lived during the seventeenth century, it can be inferred that such knowledge was relevant decades earlier among men, as well. He wrote in his personal diary regarding his wife, Helen's condition: 'This night my wife told me something of hir auen flouers coming on hir now at the turne of the moneth, which shew that she was not with child'.[13] Amenorrhea might indeed have been some women's first hopeful sign of conception, but she likely would not have rested easily in the knowledge that she was truly 'with child' until several other symptoms proved themselves. There was one particularly vital sign that would verify conception once and for all, however, and for that, a woman had to wait several weeks.

The 'quickening', or the first foetal movements felt inside the womb by the mother, was the only real indicator of a guaranteed pregnancy during this period.[14] The timing of these fluttering sensations inside a woman's belly might have been anywhere from fifteen to twenty-five weeks of gestation, as an estimate, and so a Tudor woman might have been quite far along in her pregnancy before she ever realised she was actually carrying. Lady Anne Clifford was one such example, as she did not inform her husband or her sisters that she was pregnant until she felt she was 'quick with child' in 1619.[15] Other symptoms were often too easily misdiagnosed or overlooked. Plenty of other medical conditions could produce a slightly swollen belly, nausea and food aversions, or (as noted) the cessation of menstruation. So, the quickening was considered to be relatively foolproof evidence of pregnancy, which meant that when the stakes were higher, some women might have chosen not to tell their husbands about their suspicions at all until they could be absolutely certain that they had felt the child move. Queen Catherine of Aragon was another example of this, as she had suffered one stillbirth prior to becoming pregnant again in the spring of 1510, and wished to keep the news private until she reached the third month of gestation. This was, according to the Spanish ambassador at the time, in order to quell King Henry's 'annoyance'.[16]

Once the assurance of a pregnancy had been confirmed, a woman could predict with varying degrees of accuracy when she might expect her baby to be born. Women of the period did, in fact, judge forty weeks – or roughly nine months – to be the estimated length of a healthy gestation, as evidenced by a man named Hugh Cholmley, who made the comment soon after the close of the Tudor period in 1624, 'My wife would not be persuaded but she went full forty weeks'.[17] It was also recognised that a baby born around seven months could survive, though interestingly, not at eight, according to *The Byrth of Mankynde*.[18] Likely, it would have been previously pregnant women who would educate a newly pregnant wife on the length of her condition. And due to the quickening being the first sure sign, an estimated due date probably wouldn't have been discussed with much certainty until those first movements were felt. Once they were, the woman would have been advised that she had roughly six or so months to go, and larger announcements to the community might have been made about the impending arrival.

It did not take long before the expecting mother and those surrounding her would begin to wonder whether she was carrying a son or a daughter.

Like the various conception methods already discussed, designed to increase the odds of conceiving a boy, there were believed to be signs, symptoms and tests during pregnancy that could foretell the baby's sex, although these were up for some debate. The French royal physician, Dr Guillimeau, for one, insisted that 'it is very hard to know at the first whether the woman be with child or no … so by great reason must it needs be far more difficult to discern and distinguish the difference of the sex, and to determine whether it will be a boy or a wench'.[19] In fact, many during the period held the controversial belief that the sex of the child wasn't even determined until a few months after conception, and that this date was different for males versus females. This was all to do with the timing that the infant's soul was believed to have entered the foetus, and one school of thought asserted that this happened at forty-six days gestation for a boy and ninety days for a girl. This was a matter of much debate, however, with other experts insisting that a baby's ensoulment occurred at the same time (forty-six days), regardless of gender.[20] Ensoulment was also thought to correspond with the 'quickening' of the child, however – though how many babies were felt inside the womb at only forty-six days gestation is impossible to know.

Nevertheless, this ensoulment period for the foetus was vitally important to the Tudors, as before this occurred the child was not considered to be human at all. Ensoulment was the moment that God 'implant[ed] its rational side', and thus, also signified the time at which the idea of an abortion became morally problematic.[21] Since the thirteenth century, abortion following the foetus' ensoulment was illegal, but the period beforehand was murky territory that both 'allow[ed] for life in the womb from conception' while it also refrained from fully condemning the termination of the pregnancy.[22] Actions taken to 'disrupt' the pregnancy at this early stage (before being fully touched by the hand of God) 'did not register as foetal murder' to the Tudors.[23] In fact, throughout the early modern period, the term used in medical manuals to describe a foetus' destruction in early pregnancy, 'intentional or not', was simply 'miscarriage'.[24] The concept of actively killing an unborn child was not described as such until at least a few months of gestation had passed, with both the ensoulment and the quickening guaranteeing the true human form of the baby within.

Unsurprisingly, male babies were thought to give their mothers far less trouble in the womb than females. Jane Sharp wrote that a woman who carried a boy was 'more cheerful and in better health, her pains are not so often, nor so great'. But aside from feeling better, she looked different as well, with a lighter walk and a higher, rounder bump than if she were carrying a girl.[25] Female babies were known to make their mothers sicklier during the first few months of pregnancy, as well as to cause excess weight gain and more general fatigue. But physical symptoms alone weren't the only thing that Tudor woman used in order to gauge the gender of her unborn baby. The sixteenth-century physician and translator of *The Byrth of Mankynde,* Thomas Raynalde, took things a step further with a specific test the pregnant woman might try. He advised squeezing a drop of milk from her breast during pregnancy onto a shiny surface, and noting whether or not the milk began to flow freely. If it did, the child was a girl, but if the milk was slower to flow and more solid, it was sure to be a boy.[26] According to Raynalde, this milk that 'commeth chiefly by a privie natural instinction … [drew] unto itselfe greater abundaunce of bloud, converting and altering the same by the propertie of the place, into convenient mylke'.[27] In his understanding, the breastmilk that began its production during pregnancy was simply converted blood, inexplicably transformed by the body to prepare to nourish its infant. And as if this wasn't miraculous enough, its flow during pregnancy could also predict the baby's sex.

But whether or not a woman subscribed to the theories surrounding gender prediction through physical signs alone, she paid particular attention to how sick her pregnancy made her feel. Specifically, she often considered this to correlate directly to the baby's condition within her. A relatively sickly first few months was thought to be indicative of a healthy, thriving child, while a well-feeling pregnant woman might worry after her baby's health. Frances Hatton was concerned about exactly this when she said during her pregnancy, 'I am very well and never was as fat in my life, makes me fear yt my child does not thrive I doe so much'.[28] Indeed, it appears to have been much more the usual experience of women to have felt ill during those first few months, and therefore to have been relatively sure of their baby's healthy growth. One of many examples is Alethea Talbot, born in 1585 and pregnant six times by her husband,

Thomas Howard. She was described by her mother as having a difficult time in pregnancy, when she stated, 'I besech our Lord send hir much comfort of hir children for she breeds them very painfully'.[29]

The idea of a woman possibly conceiving and carrying multiple children was certainly known to the Tudors, though it was thought to be relatively uncommon. Such pregnancies were written about by both Nicholas Culpeper and Jane Sharp – and both mentioned the legendary tale of the thirteenth-century countess, Margaret of Henneberg, who allegedly bore 364 living children from a single pregnancy.[30] But regardless of how many babies a sixteenth-century woman was actually suspected to be capable of bearing, there existed two separate theories about how multiples came to be. The first assumed that the seed must divide in the womb, creating more than one baby. In this theory, it would be expected that the babies would be identical, regardless of the number. But a second theory allowed for the possibility that an already pregnant woman might engage in intercourse, only to have her womb reopen and create the possibility of a second joining of seeds.[31] This idea spurred on the belief that non-identical (fraternal) twins could actually be fathered by different men, though this theory had its origins in ancient Greek and Roman writings. Much later, in a 1646 book titled *Pseudodoxia Epidemica,* Sir Thomas Browne would cite the writers Pliny and Hippocrates in describing this phenomenon:

> '... after reception of its proper Tenant, may yet receive a strange and spurious inmate [...] as also in those superconceptions where one child was like the father, the other like the adulterer, the one favoured the servant, the other resembled the master.[32]

There would have been no difference in determining the conception of multiples versus a singleton pregnancy in the sixteenth century, though some might have begun to suspect that a woman carried more than one baby if her bump developed unexpectedly early, or if her abdomen grew to be larger than was thought 'typical'.

While physically, the pregnant Tudor woman would likely have been feeling nauseated, excessively hungry (while possibly shying away from foods she had previous loved), and feeling the general discomforts that most women experience in those first few months, she would also have had a mental challenge to face. The journey of pregnancy was by no means an easy one in the early modern period, though it has, admittedly, been villainised more than it rightfully deserves. Popular modern day depictions of Tudor pregnancies and births paint a rather dreary picture of near-certain death, as if it was almost nothing short of a miracle to survive the entire ordeal. But the truth is that the maternal mortality rate of the Tudor period has been estimated to have been around one per cent.[33] For context, today's maternal mortality rate in the United Kingdom hovers around one hundredth of a per cent (0.01%), or roughly ten maternal deaths per every one hundred thousand babies born.[34]

And while the estimated rate in the Tudor period is certainly bleaker than modern day numbers (as well it should be), its risk seems magnified in part due to how many times a woman in the sixteenth century would have likely faced childbirth. Differing from today's averages of one-to-four pregnancies in a woman's lifetime, the Tudor woman was more likely to experience an average of six or seven, and (in more extreme circumstances) upwards of twenty pregnancies. It has been estimated that the average sixteenth-century woman was pregnant roughly every other year once she was married, which amplifies the supposed risks of childbearing. However, the actual statistics regarding Tudor maternal mortality do not quite fit the narrative perpetuated by historical fiction that the experience of childbearing and birthing would so often end in death. In fact, according to social historian, Roger Schofield, this risk was really no different than that of dying of some infectious disease of the period. He went on to write, 'in the distant past women will have known of others who died giving birth to a child; but they may also have considered it such a rare event that there was little risk that the tragedy would befall them'.[35]

Still, women would have been understandably apprehensive at the thought of something horrible happening during birth, and there is plenty of evidence that this could plague their minds during the course of pregnancy. One such example of this anxiety is the case of Elizabeth Jocelin, who wrote a letter that was later published as a book, titled *The Mother's Legacie to her unborn Childe,* prior to the birth of her child in

1622. In it, she aimed to teach her unborn baby everything that he or she might need to know in life in case she did not survive the ordeal of birth. While her tone throughout the text remained joyful and excited at the prospect of being a mother, it acknowledged the perils of pregnancy and birth, and directed whoever might need to raise the child in her absence to follow her specific wishes. More than anything, it instructed her son or daughter to be a dutiful Christian and to avoid sin at all costs, noting:

> I know in fewer words there might much more have beene said against this sinne, but I know not who will say so much to thee when I am gone. Therefore I desire thou maist bee taught these my instructions when thou art young, that this foule sinne may be weeded out before it take deepe root in thy heart.[36]

The majority of the letter comprised Jocelin's heartfelt advice on the subject of virtue and a steadfast relationship with God in her son or daughter. She even took care to reassure the following: 'If thou beest a daughter, thou maist perhaps thinke I have lost my labour; but reade on, and thou shalt see my love and care of thee and thy salvation is as great, as if thou wert a sonne, and my feare greater'.[37] She also acknowledged how strange it might seem to some for her to write such a letter, but she explained herself by saying, 'I write not to the world, but to mine own childe, who it may be, will more profit by a few weake instructions comming from a dead mother (who cannot every day praise or reprove it as it deserves) than by farre better from much more learned'. Heartbreakingly, she opened the main body of the letter with the words, 'Therefore, deare childe, reade here my love, and if God take mee from thee, bee obedient to these instructions, as thou oughtest to bee unto mee…'.[38] Even more heartbreakingly, Elizabeth Jocelin died nine days following the birth of her daughter, Theodora, making the tone, meaning, and significance of this text all the more striking.

This is only one example of what was probably a fairly common occurrence in the early modern period, where expectant mothers wished to leave behind some words of advice for their children, in the case that they did not survive to raise them. Equally, it was not at all uncommon for a woman to write her will as she approached the end of her pregnancy, no matter how unlikely the prospect of death might have felt to her. She would also often written prayers upon which to meditate during labour, and so to plead with the Lord to spare her life in what was known to be a particularly precarious time for any woman.[39] But while pregnancy and birth in the Tudor period were understandably and recognisably hazardous experiences in a woman's life, it was not all doom, gloom and foreboding for an expectant mother of the sixteenth century. In fact, it was quite the opposite in most cases, with a great deal of rejoicing, nurturing and preparing for birth and the mothering years ahead. Indeed, the typical Tudor wife took great pride in the knowledge that she was with child, soon to transition into the respected status of matron – that which was arguably the most coveted and noble role for a married woman of any social class.

Chapter Seven

The Expectant Tudor Mother

One indicator to the pride and joy felt by expectant mothers of the Tudor period – as well as that of their husbands – is the influx of pregnancy portraiture that became popular during the Elizabethan period. A very recognisable example of this is the 1562 portrait of the visibly pregnant Catherine Carey, Lady Knollys, who was painted beside her lap dog by Steven van der Meulen.[1] In it, she is finely attired in a fur-lined coat, a modest bonnet, and an Elizabethan collar, while holding a pomander at her waist and a pair of gloves in her left hand, signifying her enviable social status. But what is on full display for the viewer to see here is her open coat, which reveals a protruding pregnancy bump clothed in a silver gown – a colour often worn in these portraits to represent the woman's chastity.[2] What cannot be missed is the hint of a smile on Catherine's face as she stares directly at the viewer – pleasure mixed, perhaps, with a 'need for recognition of what [she] has achieved'.[3] She is one of several women of the period to pose with a pointed, smiling expression as she shares her pregnancy through portraiture. Another example is an expensively and lavishly dressed unknown woman – again in silver, bedecked with several strands of pearls to signify her purity. Painted in 1595 by Marcus Gheeraerts, this woman's smile is even more apparent than Catherine's, as she glows in her obviously late stage of pregnancy.[4] Further examples (several painted by Gheeraerts) exist throughout the late Elizabethan period and into the Stuart dynasty, such as the extravagantly dressed unknown pregnant woman in crimson, painted in 1620, and a smilingly pregnant Lady Anne Fanshawe, painted in 1630.[5] These portraits conveyed an important message about the 'earthly imperative of procreation and the chaste state of an icon, similar to the Virgin Queen'. They were perhaps, first and foremost, meant to be visual reminders of the Tudor wife's primary duty.[6]

These paintings may have become so popular towards the end of the Tudor period, not because Elizabethan women were prouder of their pregnant state than the generations before them had been, but perhaps instead largely because of the Protestant Reformation. In the Catholic view, which had dominated English thought during the first half of the century, virginity was seen as the paramount and preferred state for a woman. An outward showing of pregnancy, therefore, was somewhat complicated – a happy occasion, to be sure, but also proof of a woman's sexuality and impurity. This was relatively problematic, and might explain why portraits of individual pregnant women did not truly flourish in England until the Protestant Church (and specifically Martin Luther) decreed that pregnancy was indeed a holy state for a woman.[7] Perhaps this was why the family portrait was also popular through the entirety of the Tudor period; it still proved a woman's fertility, as she was painted alongside several children and her husband but it was not so overtly 'sexual' by showing a pregnancy bump.

Paintings such as these, aside from giving us a glimpse into the Tudor woman's pride, happiness, and expectation in her pregnant state, also give us some idea of the way she clothed herself during this time of her life. The extra ties and fabric – particularly in Catherine Carey's portrait – indicate how a pregnant woman's dress would have had to be modified to accommodate her growing midsection. Additional stomachers (the triangular panel that filled the front opening of a gown or bodice) were used to allow for the same gowns to be used both pre- and throughout pregnancy.[8] In addition, 'self-grow' waistcoats, kirtles and gowns could be worn throughout pregnancy and let out as needed to accommodate for the woman's growing size. And of course, she could also simply unlace her gowns as needed, as was probably done more often among women who had fewer resources and options for modified clothing.[9] However, the Tudor period was a restrictive time for women's clothes, with stiff boning comprising a vast number of corsets, especially among those of higher rank. Corsets in general were worn among all social classes during this period and those who favoured the more constricting bone-reinforced corsets were often criticised for placing their own vanity before the health of their unborn child. But as is evident in many pregnancy portraits, it appears that it was possible to position a lady's corset to fall just above her bump, which often gave the illusion of a much lower-than-natural swollen belly. Women would surely have taken some care to ensure that their vanity, and the preferred style of the period, did not come at the cost of their unborn baby's healthy growth and they may very well have only worn these tight, stiff corsets for public occasions.[10]

Aside from the way she dressed and presented herself during pregnancy, how else would a sixteenth-century woman have cared for herself, and what would her lifestyle have been during this time? As one might imagine, this answer would have varied greatly depending on her social class. The higher born expectant Tudor lady would have been much more able, for example, to rest and refrain from any strenuous activity during these crucial nine months than would her lower-class counterpart. Those who fell within the lower ranks of society would almost certainly have been expected to continue working, whether that meant supporting their husband's businesses, working the fields, or tending to busy households with, potentially many additional children to look after. Expectant mothers in wealthier circles would have had households to attend to as well, but would undoubtedly have had extra help in the form of ladies' maids, servants, governesses, and cooks. So, the lifestyles of pregnant Tudor women would have looked quite a bit different from one another based on these factors, but an over-arching look at sixteenth-century antenatal care practices and professional medical advice can give at least some clues into the general attitudes towards pregnant women of the time period.

There was no concept of a 'normal' or 'abnormal' pregnancy in the sixteenth century, and no differing standards of antenatal care designed to distinguish between any abnormalities. The guidance regarding the management of a pregnant woman's health was relatively standardised, and seemingly solely focused on the avoidance of spontaneous abortion (or miscarriage).[11] Failed pregnancies were common during the period with an estimated one in two conceptions sadly ending in miscarriage.[12] Thus, instructions on proper prenatal care were strict and exact. Diet was of primary importance, as food choices were known to play a vital role in the balancing of humours and a person's overall health. But nearly just as important (depending on rank) was the limiting of strenuous exercise and activity, the avoidance of sexual intercourse, and the mental wellbeing of the expectant mother. Finally, there was instruction even for the husband once his wife was known to be with child; far from being encouraged to take a passive or dismissive role once his procreative duty was over. In fact, William Gouge, writing in the early seventeenth century, instructed that 'husbands also in this case must be very tender over their wives, and helpful to them in all things needfull'.[13] The dutiful husband, in this case, would dote upon his expectant wife, as well as help in preparing for the baby's arrival later in pregnancy.

To first look at a pregnant woman's prescribed diet, it is clear from source material from the period that medical professionals recognised that certain foods were more likely than others to make a pregnant woman feel ill – or perhaps make her unable to digest them at all. Meat seems to have been particular noteworthy, as in the case of the many writers who discussed a woman's sudden aversion to meat and how this symptom could be used to tentatively diagnose a pregnancy. This was clearly a relatively common aversion, as evidenced by a letter written to Anne, Countess of Leven by her mother, who worried after her condition during pregnancy. 'I am very sory you are still so much troubled wt the collick', the letter states. 'I fear you eat too much fruit or heavy meats both wich are very ill for you … You never told me if you use to vomet yr meat. I intret you strive against it for it [will] destroy yr stomach and give you perpetuell paines'.[14] Though this particular letter was written in the seventeenth century, the aversion to meat during pregnancy was documented frequently enough throughout the sixteenth-century medical and dietary texts, that we can infer similar advice was given by mothers to their pregnant daughters.

In general, women of the period were also advised to avoid especially salty or spicy foods, as well as any baked meats – anything that could disrupt their digestion and therefore jeopardise their baby's nourishment. Guillimeau, in his *Happie deliverie of women,* cited the ancient warnings of Aristotle and Pliny, that 'if a woman with child eate much salt meate, her child will be borne without nayles; which shewes, that he will not be long lived'.[15] He offered a number of specific examples regarding her ideal diet, noting that her 'bread must be of good Wheate, well kneaded, light, and also well baked'. The meats that she should choose from were 'Henne, Chicken, Capon, yong Pigeons, Turtle, Pheasants, Larks, Partridge, Veale, & Mutton', and he advised on specific herbs like 'Lettuse, Endive, Borage, Buglosse, and Sorrell', but specifically instructed to avoid all raw salads.[16] Regarding the quantities that she should consume, he wrote the following:

> The quantitie must be sufficient both for her selfe, and for her child, and therefore they are to be dispenced withal from fasting at any time: for sometime too much abstinence makes the child weake and sickly, and causeth him often to be borne before his time, seeking after nourishment, which he cannot find within his Mothers body.[17]

Such leniency regarding fasting days is echoed in a seventeenth-century example of one Anne D'Ewes, who 'took some small sustenance' during a 1634 fast day while pregnant. It is clear from contemporary examples that expectant mothers were allowed – and possibly encouraged – to eat on traditional and religious fast days, for the sake of their own wellbeing and for the health of the child.[18] The amount of food that the pregnant woman consumed, however, was generally left up to her own discretion. According to contemporary midwifery treatises, she could usually 'rely upon her appetite to regulate the proper amount of food to nourish her and her foetus'. This appetite was recognised to change and adapt throughout the course of gestation, with midwives advising, 'when the child is bigger, let her diet be more, for it is better for women with child to eat too much than too little, lest the Child should want nourishment'.[19] Another notable detail about diet is the recognition of odd cravings, including those that were not actually food at all. Guillimeau notes a woman's desire to 'eate Coles, Chalke, Ashes, Waxe'... and to drink 'Veriuice, and Vinegar'. However, he advised that 'they must refraine and over-maister themselves' in order to avoid eating such things.[20]

A 'temperate' diet was deemed best – one that would provide 'adequate nourishment for the mother and foetus while minimising digestive difficulties and avoiding foods that might bring on dangerous health situations such as constipation, vomiting, terms, and fluxes'.[21] Such temperance extended itself to a woman's drink of choice, as alcoholic beverages were never off-limits, though expectant mothers were instructed to avoid 'strong alcohol' and to instead ensure that it was 'well temper'd with water'.[22] Guillimeau echoed this sentiment by recommending mature Claret wine, 'and not too strong'. He indicated that wine 'hath power to comfort and strengthen the stomacke, and all the other parts serving for nourishment and generation'. He offered alternatives, however, such as Hydromell or barley water 'well boyled'.[23]

In addition to diet, Guillimeau referenced the other four 'non-naturals' in *The happy deliverie of women,* to include 'aire', 'exercise and rest', 'sleeping and waking', 'fulnesse and emptinesse', and the 'passions of the minde'. Of the air, he indicated that the expectant mother 'must dwell and live in a good and well-tempered aire, which is neither too hote, nor too cold, or waterish: not subject to any foggie mists, or winds, and especially the South-wind'. According to Hippocrates, he noted, such south winds could blow 'upon every light occasion' and cause miscarriages. The north wind, however, was also said to be problematic, causing 'thin rheumes, distillations, & troublesome Coughs in great-bellyed women'. These symptoms were also known to cause miscarriage or pre-term labour. Ill smells were to be avoided at all costs, as the air that a woman might breathe into her lungs was thought to have the potential for devastating impacts on her unborn child. Once again, the ancient advice of Aristotle was invoked, with Guillimeau writing, 'the smell of a Candle put forth, may cause a woman to abort'.[24]

In terms of exercise and rest, the general guidance towards pregnant women was to avoid over-exerting themselves – though again, this depended upon how much physical work a woman of a particular social class was required to do in order to survive. Those in more privileged positions would have been better able to put their feet up and to have relaxed throughout the day, perhaps while being doted upon by servants and staff. Lower-class women, on the other hand, would likely have had little choice in their activity levels. Most of them would have been expected to carry on as usual with their daily labours, simply because it was necessary for their lifestyle and the wellbeing and livelihood of their families. But even if a woman had the ability to rest and avoid over-exertion, not all Tudor women did so to the extent that their family members deemed appropriate. A young woman named Cicelea was one such example, who at five months pregnant was apparently sewing too much for her mother-in-law, Elizabeth Hatton's liking. Elizabeth wrote, 'I would by noe means have her work [sew] now because it is not good for her'.[25] Indeed, according to Guillimeau, exercise must be taken only in moderation (though one might wonder what he would have said about sewing). He wrote that 'violent motion loosneth the Cotiledons or vessels of the Matrice whereby the child receives his nourishment'.[26] This was of particular concern regarding travel via horseback or in 'waggins or coaches' and it was considered especially dangerous in the first three months, 'for as upon a small occasion we see the fruits and flowers of trees do fall'.[27] This warning was enough to scare a great many women away from the supposed risk of travelling. such as in the case of the early seventeenth-century woman Elizabeth Isham, who lamented that she could not visit her father because of 'my present condition, my burthen, disabling mee for travel'.[28]

Apparently, however, it became common enough that women took this advice to rest and avoid excessive exercise to an extreme, particularly if they had reason to fear for the health of their baby. In the case of Lady Anne Clifford, an illness at four months gestation during her second pregnancy caused her to take to her bedchamber and remain there, refusing to cross the threshold until her child was born.[29] Another example of this was Lady Frances Hatton, who was 'content to be a prisoner to hir condition; and is perswaded to begin hir lying in three quarters of a year before hand…'.[30] Such extreme action, however, was not exactly 'moderate' in the eyes of many medical professionals of the period – though this was a matter of some debate. It was not healthy, argued the physician John Locke, who wrote on the subject several decades later in a letter to Henry Fletcher regarding his wife, Margaret:

> If she be with child let her not do as is usually with women of [her] condition, mew herself up in her chamber for fear of miscarrying, much lesse confine herself to her bed. This makes ye body and spirite weak which is one great cause of miscarriage.[31]

Again, though this letter was written in the late seventeenth century, the phrase 'as is usually with women of [her] condition' implies that it was well and frequently documented that women had been doing this for some time. We can assume, therefore, that such practices of taking oneself to bed for fear of miscarrying, and therefore choosing to do as little physical activity as possible, was certainly common throughout the Tudor period as well. Guillimeau had stressed this advice enough in his writing, instructing women to 'walke gently' and to take special caution in their movements particularly in the first three months of pregnancy. 'Too much labour', he warned, was 'hurtfull and dangerous for her; as also to fret, chide, or laugh immoderately'. Interestingly, he advised further on the amount of activity she could enjoy as her pregnancy progressed: 'the fourth, fifth, and sixth moneth she may use more libertie, the seventh and eight she must keepe herselfe stille and quiet, but when she is in her ninth moneth, then may she use more stirring, and exercise'.[32] Perhaps John Locke had taken the advice of Guillimeau when he later warned Henry Fletcher about his wife's inactive lifestyle, as *The happy deliverie of women* decreed 'that women with child should not be sedentary, nor live too nicely, but that since God hath blessed them to beare children, they should dayly visit the Temples of the Gods for their exercise'.[33] Fascinatingly, he also cited ancient Plato's assertion that, far from endangering their unborn babies and causing a difficult labour, 'in the Countrey … where women accustome themselves to labour, they are brought abed more easily, and with lesse paine. In briefe, where women exercise themselves, they are sooner delivered'.[34] As with most pieces of advice regarding antenatal care, it seemed there was a happy medium to find here. While differing schools of thought preached about the subject of exercise and rest for a sixteenth-century pregnant woman, it appears that some degree of moderation was key.

In a similar vein, however, was the guidance to avoid a terrible fright in pregnancy. 'Great noyse and sounds' such as thunder, artillery and even loud bells were to be avoided at all costs – as the ancient Galen had written in his own book *de Theriaca* of pregnant women who had died from such fearsome noises, or lost their babies to them. This was – as with many similar warnings – of especial concern early on in pregnancy, as Guillimeau noted 'a woman may easily loose her burthen the first moneth, because her child (though he be but little) is not yet firmely fastned and tyed to the wombe, so likewise being great or big through his weight, he may fall downe and come forth'.[35] Regarding a pregnant woman's sleeping habits, 'her sleepe must be in the night' and 'she must avoid sleeping after dinner'. Morning naps were acceptable, though Guillimeau warned against 'turning (as some great Ladies do) the day into night, and the night into day'. It was clearly unhealthy, to the Tudor mind, to sleep the day away, even when with child.[36] Sexual intercourse was another matter that warranted some advice, though this one seemed to have been somewhat controversial, dating all the way back to the ancient Greeks. According to Guillimeau, Aristotle had been of the opinion that a woman with child should avoid the company of her husband, while Hippocrates disagreed, noting that intercourse was perfectly acceptable further along in pregnancy: 'toward the time of their lying in, thereby to shake the child, and make him come the more readily forth'. The reason for this ease in coming forth was, apparently, at least partly due to the baby being 'enwrapped and compassed with slime' following intercourse.[37]

Finally, the things surrounding a pregnant woman in the Tudor period – particularly anything that she might gaze upon – was of the utmost importance to both her health and her baby's condition. It was believed that she was far more than simply a vessel by which to carry the child to term. Indeed, her own mind was a powerful thing, capable of transporting images both good and bad to the baby, with very real consequences. Jane Sharp wrote on the subject in the following century, describing the power of the expectant mother's imagination:

> Imagination can do much, as a woman that looked on a black-more brought forth a child like to a blackmore; and one that I knew, that seeing a boy with two thumbs on one hand, brought forth such another; but ordinarily the spirits and humours are disturbed by the passions of the mind, and so the forming faculty is hindered and overcome with too great plenty of humours that flow to the matrix.[38]

It was generally advised, therefore, that women with child should remain in the happiest, most peaceful state of mind possible. She should avoid looking at anything ugly or upsetting, which might fester within her unsettled mind and create unsightly birthmarks in her child, as well as abnormalities in hair or skin tone, as noted by Jane Sharp. Thomas

Lupton, who published *A Thousand Notable Things* in 1589, even noted abnormalities in babies' lips – such as cloven or 'hare lips' (a cleft palate) due to the mother's 'sudden seeing of a hare, or for the desire or longing to eat of the same'.[39] Instead of risking any such conditions in their unborn children, Tudor women were encouraged to look at beautiful things, such as angelic and saintly images as frequently as possible – at least, prior to the Reformation.[40] Beyond the woman's sight, however, was the power of her mind and motivations. As Sharp wrote, if 'some women with child will desire to steal things from others', her child, too, might grow to be a thief.[41] Virtually anything that she viewed, thought, or did during pregnancy was believed to influence the very nature of her unborn baby's physical and mental condition and therefore, how she conducted herself during these critical forty weeks was paramount. Reflecting on God and her own faithful life and charitable works, as well as gazing only upon beautiful (preferably religious) artwork, and conversing pleasantly and calmly throughout pregnancy was recommended by virtually all medical authorities of the period. This particular belief regarding a woman's deep influence on her unborn child would live on for several generations beyond the sixteenth century.

As most women would have had a fairly good idea of how far along they were in pregnancy – due to the swelling of their bellies and the timing of their baby's quickening – the majority of them would have had the chance to adequately prepare for the impending birth. For the average Tudor housewife who awaited the birth of her child and approached the end of her gestation, there would have been a number of things she might have done to arrange for the big day. Not only might she have been busily writing her will – just in case the worst should happen – she would have also been gathering essential supplies, such as linens and handmade baby clothes. She might also have been hiring or arranging for midwives and female attendants to care for her and the baby during birth, and depending on her social class, she would have been preparing for her own lying-in period – there to await the baby's arrival from the comfort of her bedchamber. But as we have learned already about all aspects of pregnancy in the sixteenth century, such birth plans and preparations were widely varied and depended greatly on the woman's status, means, and the support she had surrounding her as she approached this momentous time in her life.

Chapter Eight

Preparing for Delivery

Any modern day mother might recognise the joy and anticipation that comes with gathering the first items of clothing or soft bedding and blankets as they prepare for the birth of their baby. Tudor women, too, would have experienced a similar thrill and eagerness as they readied their baby's layette and ensured that everything was meticulously sewn, cleaned, and organised. However, there was another side to these preparations that must be acknowledged, though it was as equally macabre as it was essential. Indeed, in the sixteenth century, a woman had to be ready to prove that she had truly prepared for the baby's arrival – in case she gave birth unexpectedly to a stillborn child, and was later accused of having murdered it. By gathering the essential items, such as newborn clothes, blankets and other essential linen that the baby would need, she was proving that she was taking adequate steps to welcome a living, healthy child.[1] Of course, it is unspeakably unfortunate that such drastic accusations might have been made against a mother, but it was not at all uncommon during the Tudor period, due to many unforeseen and unfortunate circumstances that could accompany births.

An aristocratic or royal lady of the Tudor period would have had quite an elaborate preparation as she reached the end of her pregnancy. In addition to gathering linen and clothing items (or sewing them herself), she would also have procured furniture items for the bedchambers where her baby would be tended. In most cases, these rooms would not have been the mother's, but rather those of the child's nurse. Such furniture would have included, at the very least, a cradle for the baby, complete with a cushioned wool mattress.[2] Depending on her condition and how she was feeling in her final months, the expectant mother might have begun her 'lying-in' period, also known as her 'confinement', a few weeks or even months before delivering. The timing of this would have largely depended upon how well she felt, how frequently she might have been experiencing early labouring pains, and how her physicians or midwives advised her.

Husbands were expected to assist in preparing for this confinement period in most cases and if they didn't it was cause for some concern and criticism. One such example of negligence on the husband's part is from 1590, when Elizabeth Molys' daughter was preparing for her upcoming birth and her 'intollerabley badd husband' was refusing to make appropriate plans for her lying-in and delivery. Elizabeth wrote the following to her son-in-law's mother, beseeching her 'to allowe and provide for her that ys mete for a woman in her case, and that she maye be accompanied with suche honest matrons as maye be for her saffetie for yt ys evident that he [the husband] hathe no car[e] for the preservacon of her lyffe'.[3] A few decades later, another instance would warrant Thomas Peyton writing to Henry Oxinden, regarding his opinion that his 18-year-old pregnant daughter was not being properly looked after by her husband. In the letter, he described his son-in-law as caring about her upcoming lying-in merely as much as 'cowes calving'.[4] Indeed, it was a good Tudor husband's duty to take an active role in the arranging of his wife's confinement as well as in the notifications to her attendants and midwives whenever the crucial time came. *The Batchelars Banquet,* published anonymously in 1603, speaks cynically about the hardships that middle-class men might endure in marriage, citing exactly this expectation of them. A woman's entry into her confinement marked the beginning of her husband's need 'to play both husband and housewife' according to this text – arranging and financially providing for her entourage of female companions, while seeing to (or hiring out) the necessary work to be done around the house in her absence.[5]

Queen Elizabeth of York settled into her confinement on All Saints Day, 1 November 1489, following an elaborate religious ritual meant to prepare the way for her to begin this sacred, private period of time. She first attended Mass in her private chapel, which was sung by the Bishop of Exeter, Richard Fox. There, the devoutly Catholic queen received confession before being given holy communion, as two earls held towels beneath her chin to catch any crumbs of the consecrated wafer. Following communion, she processed to her 'great chamber', flanked by noble men and women who accompanied her and prayed for her safe delivery. As she entered the most public of her rooms along with her retinue of well-wishers, her lord chamberlain beseeched everyone present to pray for the queen and her unborn baby. Finally, she disappeared into her inner chamber, not to be seen by the outside world again until her baby was born.[6]

Queen Elizabeth's confinement would have been quite similar to other queens of the period, with an ornately and peacefully decorated bedchamber that was designed specifically with childbirth in mind. Fertility imagery, saintly relics and angelic artwork would have donned the room (at least up until the Reformation) – centred, naturally, by a magnificent, canopied bed, luxuriously swathed with the softest of linens. The lord chamberlain would have been the last to leave the room, drawing a curtain and leaving the queen with the promise that he would instruct the prayers of all the country's nobility to cover her as she awaited the birth of her child. And once he was gone, she would only have been attended by her trusted female companions.[7] At this time, only lady servants and midwives would have been allowed to attend the queen, though over the course of the Tudor period, this would change, allowing for male physicians to replace female midwives in some cases. This was, in fact, the case during the labour and delivery by Henry VIII's ill-fated third wife, Queen Jane Seymour.[8]

The reason for the attendance of a male physician in this instance was, presumably, that the king of England considered the professionalism and medical expertise of a physician to exceed that of a humble midwife. But such thinking couldn't have been further from the truth, at least, in the case of sixteenth-century childbirth. In fact, it has been theorised that Jane Seymour's lack of a midwife during the difficult birth of her son, Prince Edward, may have contributed to her own demise soon after, which was due to postnatal complications.[9] Interestingly, it has also been supposed that the slow replacement of midwives in favour of male physicians (and consequently, a more medicalised approach to birth) contributed to the overall maternal mortality rate jumping from around one per cent during the Tudor period to roughly four per cent in the Victorian era.[10] There was just no substitute for the hands-on training and familiarity with a woman's body – not to mention a midwife's sole professional focus on childbirth. Even the most well intentioned and educated of physicians likely lacked a great deal of knowledge and first-hand expertise that midwives had, and pregnant mothers and their babies would suffer for it in the coming centuries.

But queens would likely have been afforded little choice in the matter regarding their medical care in childbirth – depending on her husband, of course. For Henry VIII, who had fought long and hard for decades prior, going through two previous wives and still without a living male heir by 1537, he called the shots when Jane entered her confinement in mid-September, there to bide her time until her labour pains began on 9 October. A woman of lower status, ironically, would have been afforded a more traditional birth, likely influenced by her mother and other female relatives and friends. If she was of some rank, she might have had her own household with ladies attending her daily, and these attendants would almost certainly have remained with her during her lying-in period. Those of lesser status might only have had close female family members or dear friends, though in truth, most lower-class women of the period would hardly have been afforded a confinement period at all, due to the need for them to continue working right up until the birth. But regardless of the scale of company and attendants a woman might have received during these weeks (or months, in some cases), the largest parallel that spanned all social classes regarding this tradition was that the birthing chamber was meant to be an exclusively *female* space. These attending females were termed 'gossips' – deriving from the phrase 'god-sib' – or 'sister in the Lord'.[11]

The universality of this exclusively female concept is seen in the Middle English romance story *Bevis of Hampton*, which was popular throughout the Tudor period. In it, Bevis' pregnant wife Josian, who goes into labour while travelling with him through the forest, sends him away so that she may deliver in private – away from the eyes of a man.

> Sir Bevis gan her service bed, for to helpe her at her needed.
> She thanked him and said nay, for Gods love go hence away.
> Go and play you with Terry, and let me worke & our Lady.
> Shall never womans privitie, to man be shewed for me…

> After that Bevis was gone her fro, she was delivered of children two.[12]

Of course, Josian was not lucky enough to have the services of a midwife in the forest, but in most cases during the sixteenth century, a midwife would have dominated the scene and acted as the central figure during a woman's labour. For some, such a midwife might have been the very one to attend their mother at their own birth decades earlier. She would likely have trained for years – perhaps several decades – and apprenticed under an experienced midwife for some period of time before taking on her own 'practice' and attending women herself. Depending on the pregnancy, the attending midwife might have been acquainted with the expectant mother throughout her entire gestation, perhaps already being aware of any complications, illnesses, or concerns that she might have had. It is unlikely, however, that she would have remained with the labouring woman for the entirety of her confinement, as this period was known to last anywhere from a few days to a few months' time. In most cases, a midwife was simply sent for as 'the tyme drawes nye at hand' – as her true purpose was to supervise and assist in the delivery and birth, rather than the full pregnancy itself and all of its preparations.[13]

The vast majority of women who were able to enjoy a confinement period would have done so in their primary residence, as there was no such thing as a hospital during this period. Exceptions to birthing at home would have been in the case of an outbreak of illness in a city or cramped quarters and only if the family had the luxury of a secondary home or relative's residence removed from the contagion or risk of disease. We see instances of these relocations, particularly out of London and into the countryside, throughout the Tudor period. London was known to be a more dangerous place to give birth (as well as simply to live) due to the far increased risk of disease in the city. It has been estimated that the maternal mortality rate ran significantly higher in London than elsewhere in England by the end of the Tudor period, with 23.5 deaths per one thousand births in Aldgate parish during the 1590s.[14] Aside from the fear of disease and contagion, however, many more of these relocations were for women who served at court, but were expected to retire to a country estate in order to give birth and recover, before returning again to service.

In the case of a queen, however – as in our examples of Elizabeth of York and Jane Seymour – their homes were, of course, at the royal court. They may have chosen their favoured palace in which to birth their children, or the location may have been dictated by the king and his choice of residence at the time. In the case of Elizabeth of York, she was at least given the opportunity to select her preferred room for the occasion. In the preparations leading up to her confinement, her ladies would have been sent to work to ready the bedchamber – 'covering the ceiling, walls and even the windows with rich hangings to create a dark, stuffy space in the early summer heat'.[15] This was, in essence, in order to create a 'womb-like' environment for the queen and her unborn baby.[16] Most windows in the room would have been tightly closed against the potentially toxic outdoor air, though in this case one window was left merely curtained, able to be opened to 'have light when it pleaseth her'.[17]

Regardless of the season or natural temperature of the room, the bedchamber's hearth would likely have been lit, and in the queen's case, candles would have illuminated the room. In the homes of poorer women who likely could not have afforded the luxury of candles, this would not have been the case. Fabric would have covered nearly every surface of the room, thus muting the sounds within and providing a quiet, dark, and warm (perhaps uncomfortably so) space for the queen to relax. As has been mentioned, the imagery that would have decorated the walls would have been only pleasant art – uncomplicated and unlikely to unsettle her mind.[18] As she was giving birth early in the Tudor period, religious art and saintly relics would have been abundant, though this would surely change by the time of Jane Seymour's confinement in 1537, when the Protestant Reformation would do away with such things. Most of these items, being so commonly used in childbirth, would have been destroyed by this time, with the notion of such rituals and religious talismans being highly discouraged and even prohibited. Pre-delivery superstition did not entirely end with the Reformation, however, as evidenced by the writings of Reginald Scot from 1584. He noted that pregnant women in one town would 'run to church, and tie their girdles or shoe latchets about a bell, and strike upon the same thrice, thinking that the sound therof hastened their good delivery'.[19]

Of course, no matter how many rituals, relics, and 'superstitious acts' were effectively done away with by the Protestant Reformation, the importance placed on prayer never wavered, no matter the dominant religion in England. A woman nearing her time was expected to place the appropriate weight upon her spiritual life as she approached this most precarious transition in her life. Religious men of the Tudor and Stuart periods wrote extensively on this subject, with John Oliver being one such example in his publication, *A present for teeming women*. In it he wrote that women in their confinement would 'make no other preparation for lying in than what is common, if they only get linen and other necessaries for the child, a nurse, a midwife, entertainment for the women that are called to their labour, a warm convenient chamber...'. He rebuked this, pointing out that many women coming out of childbirth would 'need no other linen shortly but a winding sheet, and have no other chamber but a grave'.[20]

For Queen Elizabeth in her time, however, she was able to take things a step further by arranging for a very specific and cherished relic – the girdle of the Virgin Mary, held by Westminster Abbey – to be sent to her prior to each of her births. She paid a monk six shillings and eight pence to bring the sacred girdle to her, as it was so necessary in order to protect her during childbirth.[21] It would be placed upon her belly during her labour, so as to invoke the Virgin's assistance, minimise her birthing pains, and – God willing – bring both herself and her babe safely through the ordeal.[22] This particular form of labour preparation was common throughout the early decades of the sixteenth century, even among women who could not arrange for the Virgin's own girdle to be sent to them. Many parish churches held similar items, even multiple girdles believed to have been worn by the Virgin, or chains that were said to have been used in St Peter's imprisonment (used for the same purpose as a girdle).[23] But in the cases where such holy relics were not accessible, birth girdles were fashioned by female attendants who would use written down prayers on scrolls of paper to create belts. These would be wrapped around the woman's belly or thigh to intercede for her safe delivery.[24] Girdles such as these might have been made by the expectant mother's ladies during the weeks of her confinement as a way to pass the time, and to keep the thoughts and energies in the room focused on praying for the upcoming birth.

While certain queens and the highest-ranking ladies in England might have been attended in birth by a male physician, as decreed by the king, the majority of women would have had the opportunity to select a midwife for the occasion. How this was done would have depended on the family's connections and resources, as well as their proximity to the midwife, as she would likely be called to attend the labouring woman as soon as her pains began. The name 'midwife' is a literal Old English translation of the phrase 'with woman', and she would indeed be expected to answer the call as soon as she was needed, then to remain 'with the woman' until delivery was complete. One of the instructions that Jane Sharp gave in her writing was that midwives would also be expected to keep the labouring woman's spirits high throughout the process. The same advice was true for her entourage of gossips.[25]

Midwifery as a career was largely unregulated, though some midwives were licensed through local parishes – likely due to the need for them to occasionally perform emergency baptisms for babies who were near death at the time of their delivery.[26] The translator of *The Byrth of Mankynd,* Thomas Raynalde, described midwives as 'right expert, diligent, wise, circumspect, and tender about such business' though it was also noted that there were 'many more [who were] full indiscreet, unreasonable, churlish, and far to seek in such things'.[27] Guillimeau wrote that a midwife must be 'wise, discreet, and witty, able to make use sometime of faire and flattering speeches … to busie and beguile the poore apprehensive women'.[28] Theirs was one of the most highly sought-after occupations of any Tudor woman.[29] For most, the knowledge that an educated and experienced midwife would attend them in their hours of need would surely have been cause for some comfort, especially given that the final weeks of pregnancy were likely a time of some stress and fear for them.

Though the risk of death in or immediately following childbirth was relatively low during the Tudor period, it is probable that most women knew of – or had at least heard of – someone having died during the process. The risks in giving birth, however small, were nevertheless at the centre of the typical woman's mind as she approached her time. Furthermore, despite complications being relatively uncommon, it was nevertheless acknowledged that if a complication did arise and the birth went awry, death was 'almost certain' to follow.[30] This did little good for a woman's mental health as she neared the end of her pregnancy, and the anxiety appears to have been unaffected by the number of successful births a woman might have already previously endured. Every pregnancy and delivery carried its own risks, with the fear of death never being far from the birthing chamber.[31] As we have already seen, wills, letters, and even poetry was often written in these final weeks and months, serving as preparation by the mother in case the worst should happen. One further example of this comes from Anne Bradstreet, who fled England as a puritan migrant in 1630, and penned the poem 'Before the Birth of One of Her Children'. In it, she wrote specifically to her husband Simon, 'How soon, my Dear, death may my steps attend, /How soon't may be thy lot to lose thy friend'. Additionally, she encouraged him to remarry in case she died in childbirth, yet to also ensure that he keep his focus on their living children (particularly in the case of an unkind stepmother):

> And when thy loss shall be repaid with gains,
> Look to my little babes, my dear remains.
> And if thou love thy self, or loved'st me,
> These O protect from step-dame's injury.[32]

For the lady enjoying a confinement surrounded by her gossips and attendants, the final weeks of pregnancy would have most likely consisted of a great deal of praying and meditation, reading (or being read to), sewing, conversing, and biding her time as she waited for the first indications that her labour was beginning. Depending on her preferences, she may or may not have seen her husband in person at all leading up to the birth, though it is well documented that she generally wished for him to be within close proximity. Elizabeth of York enjoyed her husband, King Henry VII's company from time to time throughout her tedious days of confinement.[33] And lower down the social ranks, Sabine Johnson, who in 1546 was preparing to give birth at Glapthorn, requested that her husband John swiftly return home from business in time for her labour. She wrote, 'What a great comfort it shall be to me to have you here at that time'.[34] Loving husbands generally wished for this too, as they were often just as anxious for the impending arrival as were their wives.

When those first labour pains did arrive, the advice given to Tudor women was sensible and recognisable even to our modern times. Jane Sharp wrote in the following century that the labouring woman should immediately walk to the birthing chamber (if she was not already there for her confinement, of course). There, she was advised to 'lye down, keep her self warm, rest her self and then stir again, till she feels the waters coming down and the womb to open'. Sharp advised against too much lying around – encouraging the labouring woman to remain as active as possible, though noting that brief periods of rest would strengthen both herself and the child.[35] It would have been at this point that a midwife would be called to the house under normal circumstances, and she would arrive carrying a bag filled with supplies – tools, herbs, oils, and clouts.

The first thing she was likely to do upon arriving would be to pray for the safe delivery of mother and child, as no one in the period was more acutely aware of the possible dangers of childbirth than she. Finally, she would locate the labouring woman, perhaps having brought along her own attendants. She would meet her patient's gossips in the birthing chamber and begin to call out instructions as she appraised the situation and how far the labour might have already progressed. In the case of a particularly long labour and an especially exhausted labouring woman, the midwife's first action might have been to rejuvenate her with some 'chickens broth of the yolk of a potched egg, with a little bread' along with some wine or water.[36] But then, the real work would begin. With any luck, the expectant Tudor woman was in strong, capable hands as she gathered all of her strength and prepared herself to do her most noble and holy duty.

Chapter Nine

The Tudor Birthing Chamber

Contemporaries believed that a woman could often tell that labour was approaching once 'certaine dolours and paines begyn to growe about the guttes, the navyll, and in the raynes of the backe, and lykewyse about the thighes and the other places beyng neare to the privie partes'.[1] The sixteenth-century woman would have been no stranger to the notion of pain in childbirth – it was an accepted fact that the process would be painful, as indeed it was meant to be. As the Bible and scripture played a role of the utmost importance in most Tudor families' lives, Adam and Eve's plight in the Garden of Eden in the Book of Genesis would have been as recognisable a story to them as any other. God's curse upon Eve and all women following her, with the words 'I will greatly multiply thy sorrow and thy conception; in sorrow thou shalt bring forth children', (3:16) was reason enough for most women of the period to accept their fate in enduring a painful childbirth.[2] This humble acceptance wasn't necessarily true for all women, though, with one slightly later example being from a seventeenth-century minister reporting on a Warwickshire woman:

> … being in travail and sorely afflicted with pain, they could not rule her, but sent for my Lady Puckering to try what she could do; when she came she exhorted her to patience, and told her that this misery was brought upon her sex by her grandmother, Eve, by eating an apple. 'Was it?' says she, 'I wish the apple had choked her', whereupon my lady was constrained to turn herself about, and go out of the room and laugh.[3]

Little was generally done to aid in the relief of labour pains and what recipes and remedies did exist were (unsurprisingly) fairly ineffective throughout most of the period. The majority of such remedies that were published and shared were focused more on speeding up the process rather than alleviating discomfort. This was largely because long labours were known to be more dangerous, often resulting in complications either for the mother or baby (or both). Thus, contemporary writers put forth suggestions to help the birth along as quickly as possible, and to reduce the chances of something going seriously wrong.[4] Among those most prone to long, hard, and exceptionally painful labours were believed to be particularly young women under the age of 12 or 15, according to Raynalde ('whiche chaunseth sometime, though not very often').[5] Others who were more at risk included those of 'weake and of feble complexion, or of nature very colde, or to younge, or very aged, or exceadyng grosse and fatte, or contrarywyse too spare and leane'. Being too fearful about childbirth could also produce a more 'paynefull, cruell and dolorous' labour according to contemporary experts.[6] Unsurprisingly, it was also believed that the birth of a son would be less painful than that of a female – as the son would have also caused her less trouble throughout pregnancy.

In any case, once the midwife was at the side of the labouring woman, she was expected first to question the woman about the nature of her pains. According to Guillimeau, she should ask:

> what manner they bee, where they begin, and where they end: and whether they bee little or great, and frequent: whether they begin at the backe, running downe all along the belly, without staying at the Navell: and chiefly if they run along the groine, and end in the bottom of the belly inwardly.[7]

Such questions and their answers could help the midwife predict exactly how difficult the labour was expected to be. Manuals on the subject gave guidance as to the location and severity of pains and what they might mean for the duration of the woman's labour. For example, *The Byrth of Mankynd* noted pains in the 'forepart of the bottome of the belly' (as well as frequent stirring of the child, along with a strong and mighty nature in the woman) to signify 'good spede and lucke in the labour'. Conversely, if she were to feel pain 'only in the backe and above the navel, and not under' it was a bad sign for a hard labour.[8] Any information the midwife could glean from the labouring mother would be helpful as she anointed her hands with 'fresh butter, hogs grease, or some other ointment' such as the oil of almonds or white lilies.[9] Then, she would 'thrust up her hand' to check 'the inner and outer orifice of the womb' for dilation and to get some sense for exactly how the situation was progressing.[10]

Perhaps the most crucial thing that a midwife was feeling for in this scenario was whether or not the birth was 'natural' or 'unnatural' – in the words of Raynalde. A natural birth was one in which not only the baby was born in 'due season' (around the estimated due date of nine months' gestation), but also in 'due fashion' – meaning head-first. The proper position of the child was described to be 'first the head commeth forwarde, then foloweth the necke & shoulders, the armes with the hands lying close to the body towarde the feete, the face and forepart of the chylde, being towards the face and forepart of the mother'.[11] With this knowledge, the original writer noted that throughout pregnancy, the baby had likely been positioned opposite (head up, feet down), but would have moved into this 'natural' position as delivery approached. The 'unnatural' birth, therefore, was one where the baby had not moved into this expected head-first position, and instead 'both the legges proceade first, or one alone, with both the hands up, or both downe, other els the one up and the other downe'.[12] An experienced midwife would have been able to feel the position of the child, and would have well known the possible dangers and complications that could arrive from the 'unnatural' (or in modern terms, 'breach') position.

A feet-first labour was recognised to be more painful and difficult – as well as longer and riskier to both the mother's and baby's survival – so it was often imperative that the midwife should use her well-oiled hands to manoeuvre the baby into the correct position, if needed. With 'all her diligence and payne' it was deemed possible in some cases for the baby to be turned.[13] If it could not, a healthy delivery was still possible, though considered 'jeopardous' and requiring diligent and skilful care by the midwife.[14] Raynalde listed several positions in which a baby could present for birth and he included thirteen illustrations of a singleton child in utero (with an additional four depicting possible positions for twins). No matter what the midwife felt when first physically examining her labouring patient, she would hopefully have known exactly how to prepare and plan for the delivery, being aware of the most effective manoeuvres, birthing positions, tools, and remedies to use for any situation.

She would also likely have brought along with her a variety of herbs, salves, and tinctures – meant to help the labour along and either speed up the process or offer some marginal pain relief. Midwives were often known to tend their own physic gardens, growing 'lilies and roses, cyclamen or sowbread, columbine or aquilegia' – all believed to assist in childbirth.[15] Later, during the Elizabethan period, laudanum would be added to this otherwise natural list of ingredients used to dull the ache of labour.[16] Betony and sage were also used in drinks for the woman to sip throughout labour, with the hopes that the herbs might speed things along.[17] In general, midwives would not have gotten their recipes from medical texts of the time. They would have learned through hands-on care and the passing down of information from other midwives and female relatives – not from male-written informative publications. Still, plenty of midwifery direction was written – such as Raynalde's instruction for her to comfort the labouring woman with 'sweete wordes' and to stroke her belly 'above the Navell, for that helpeth to depresse the byrth downewarde'.[18]

It was well documented that labouring women could give birth – and were supported – in a number of positions, not limited to their beds. Women could lie down and push from their backs if they chose, but they were equally encouraged to stand while being supported either by furniture or female attendants, to sit in a chair, or to use a new invention called the 'birthing stool'. This stool, with a large horseshoe shaped cut-out in the seat to allow for the baby to fall through (and into the waiting hands of the midwife, preferably) grew in popularity throughout the seventeenth century. It was probably less common during the sixteenth, though instances of its use were mentioned and promoted.[19] Beds, when they were used, were encouraged to be 'of a reasonable bigness, strong and firm', and of a height and position so that the midwife could easily move about all sides as she worked.[20] White linen sheets would be strewn over the bed, with plenty of extra cloth and clouts to assist in cleaning up the eventual mess. The labouring woman, while likely in pain and relying on the direction of her midwife, would spend as much time as possible walking and moving around the bedchamber. She would take breaks as needed – perhaps sipping a tincture or a bit of broth to regain her strength, while being advised on different positions or movements to try. Intermittently, the midwife might have continued to check for dilation and the positioning of the baby's head, as it would have been greatly hoped for that the child would have been in the 'natural' head-first position.

In some cases, as Raynalde described, it was necessary for an experienced midwife to manually break the woman's water. If it had not already broken naturally through the course of labour and the midwife had reached a point where she decreed the process to be taking dangerously too long without much progress, then she might have:

> … with her nayles easely and genteelly to breake and rent it, or yf that maye not conveniently be done, then rayle up between [her] fingers a peece of it, and cut it of with a payre of sheeres, or sharpe knyfe, but so that [she] hurt not the byrth with the cut.[21]

It was known that the breaking of a labouring woman's waters precipitated the birth of her baby, so however this might have come to be, it was imperative that the process did not take too long, lest it should endanger the mother's or baby's life. According to Raynalde, the breaking of the waters should 'immediately' bring forth the baby's birth – but in cases where it was delayed, the midwife could apply some lubrication (such as the oil of white lilies, or even a beaten egg) in order to create a 'slypperye and slydyng' condition.[22]

In a 'natural' birth, it was expected that the midwife should only need to offer a supporting hand and some gentle words once the baby began descending and the labouring woman was pushing. Perhaps she might only be needed to help guide the baby's way and to catch it gently in clean linen once it was born. But in 'unnatural' circumstances, her hands would face a more challenging task – that of turning and rotating the tiny body until it was properly facing downwards into the 'natural' position. Of course, if at any point during delivery the baby become stuck, the midwife would be expected to expertly adjust and loosen it – to do her utmost to avoid the tragedy that too often befell the birthing chamber after a difficult and complicated delivery. All the while, her assistants and the mother's chosen female family members and attendants would be dutifully wiping her brow, encouraging her with their words, and gripping her hands, while doing anything and everything they could to assist the midwife. Most critically of all, they would have been praying.

Caesarean sections, or the surgical birth of a baby via incision in the mother's abdomen, would never have been performed on a living Tudor mother – at least prior to the 1580s. Texts from the middle ages gave specific instructions on performing this lifesaving (for the baby) surgery once its mother had already died – with particular guidance to keep the woman's mouth open throughout the procedure, so as to possibly infuse the child with any final remnants of breath she had inside her. Otherwise, such surgery was known to be performed in order to baptise a baby who had been in the process of birth when its mother had passed. In these cases, it would have been likely that the child had already died, too.[23] Until the publishing of Francois Rouset's *L'hysterotomotokie ou enfantement cesarien* (*The Hysterotomotokie or Caesarian Birth*) in 1581, no surgeon in England would have considered such an operation possible while maintaining the life of the woman.

But this Parisian physician (the personal physician to the Duke of Savoy) referenced no fewer than ten successful caesarean sections performed on French women (six of which he had assisted with himself) and argued in his writing that this intervention could be seen not only as a last resort to save the baby of an already deceased mother, but in fact one that had been already been proven multiple times to save both lives.[24] His work was scoffed at and disbelieved by physicians and surgeons around Europe, who had only ever heard of performing such a surgery if the labouring woman had already died during childbirth. But his work on the subject was nevertheless groundbreaking regarding caesarean sections (the name of which he himself coined, referencing the supposed birth of Julius Caesar).[25] Giving descriptions of how this procedure could be performed with a suturing needle, it not only introduced the theory of a woman potentially surviving the ordeal, but possibly being able to vaginally birth future children – a debate that has continued even into the modern era.[26] It would take time, but his book and his arguments would finally gain traction in England during the nineteenth century, when these surgeries would become more commonly performed, with their life-saving power being more widely acknowledged.

For the sixteenth-century mother, however, a surgical birth would have been the stuff of nightmares. The oft-cited rumour that Henry VIII had commanded his own third queen's loss so that his prized son might be surgically and safely removed from her belly reinforces how tragic a caesarean was believed to be for a woman.[27] Legend and historical record had educated people of the sixteenth century on the subject of such surgical births, and although they were certainly not routinely performed, they were still regarded in fear. Take William Shakespeare's *Macbeth,* for example – first performed in 1606 and referencing the title character's enemy, Macduff. In the play, Macbeth is reassured by three witches that he cannot be killed by a man 'of a woman born'. However, when he learns that Macduff was 'from his mother's womb untimely ripped', he becomes aware of his gruesome fate. Macduff, having been born via caesarean section, was indeed able to kill Macbeth – a feature of his character and a reference to a commonly held belief at the time, that anyone born by this means was seen somehow as 'other'; perhaps even given certain special powers, as Classical Antiquity had theorised.[28] Shakespeare's writing on the subject would have had a certain shock value to his early Stuart viewers, at a time when the subject of caesareans was being hotly debated by medical professionals across Europe. One school of particularly religious thought had a severely negative view on these surgeries, not only because they were so often known to sacrifice the life of the mother, but because in doing so, they were thought to have the evil consequence of sinfully staining the resulting infant's soul.[29]

Therefore, if problems arose during the course of delivery, it was only the skilled midwife's quick hands and sharp intuition that had any hope of saving the mother and infant. And in the vast majority of cases, all ended well. From whichever position she pushed, the mother would safely deliver her infant into the waiting hands of the midwife, quickly to be wrapped in fresh, clean linen. From there, a quick and careful appraisal of the baby would begin, with the midwife 'tak[ing] notice of all the parts of it, and see[ing] all be right'. She would look immediately to the sex of the child and more often than not, a boy would garner higher praise. She would ensure that the baby was breathing well, clearing his or her nasal passages and mouth, if needed, and would soon after cut the umbilical cord, known as the 'naval string'.[30] Instruction on the subject dictated that the cord should be cut 'to a width of three fingers above the navel and tied'.[31] This cutting of the cord (far off yet from being the father's duty) also involved the inspection of the baby's navel. Particularly with firstborns, the number of wrinkles in the navel was believed to indicate the number of future children its mother might bear.[32] Likewise, the number of knots in the umbilical cord could predict the same thing – or at least, estimate the number of future pregnancies the woman might endure, whether or not those would all result in living babies.[33] The remaining stump of the cut umbilical cord was known to fall off naturally within three or four days of the birth, after which the caregiver would be instructed to treat the navel with 'ashes or red lead tempered with wine'.[34]

Immediately following a successful birth to a breathing, crying infant, the baby would be rubbed vigorously with acorn oil – a small amount wiped around the eyes – and then washed gently in warm water to remove the vernix.[35] At some point – usually within minutes of delivery – the mother would also birth the placenta (also known as the 'afterbirth', or as they often referred to it in the sixteenth century, the 'womb-cake').[36] In the majority of births, this delivery would require little assistance from the midwife and would tax the mother far less than had the birth of the infant. Following the baby's washing (while wrapped snuggly in linen), he or she would be dressed in a soft shirt and an absorbent 'breech-cloth' (the sixteenth-century version of a nappy) would be fastened securely with pins. Then, long, narrow strips of linen known as 'swaddling bands' would be wrapped tightly around the baby in order to keep the limbs straight and to ensure that they grew correctly.[37] Finally, he or she would be placed securely into a cradle so that attention could be focused on the mother. But there was also a contemporary argument for immediate bonding time between mother and baby, with *The Expert Midwife* (published in 1637) instructing:

> Many say that the child being washed and wrapped in his swaddling clothes, before he suck the breasts or take any meat, must be laid by his mother, lying in her bed, on the left side near the heart first of all; for they think, as they are persuaded, that the mother doth attract and draw to her all the diseases from the child, and that she doth expel and void again by the flux and issue of her womb what evil soever she hath attracted, without any hurt to herself.[38]

Whether or not the infant was afforded some close moments with its mother prior to being set in the cradle, a particularly Catholic midwife would commonly make the sign of the cross over the infant, sprinkle it with salt, and place a coin into its hand before laying it down.[39] In the years following the advent of the Protestant Reformation in England, such traditional Catholic practices were likely used less and less following births. But, however the child was finally placed into its cradle for a swaddled rest – preferably in a dark, shadowed place, so as to closely resemble the womb – it was then time for the midwife to focus on the new mother's care.[40] Common practice instructed on the application of animal skins to the exhausted woman, such as 'newly-flayed sheepskin' around her back to keep her warm, or a 'hare skin covered in the animal's blood' on her belly (for two hours in winter, but only one in summer). This particular practice was thought to help the womb heal. In a similar effort to assist the womb after birth, a linen pad was sometimes inserted into the woman in order to repel the uterus upwards and into its appropriate place once again.[41] Her stomach would be wiped with St John's Wort, and she would be encouraged to lie still in bed but advised not to sleep for at least four hours following the birth. She would be covered securely with comfortable sheets, and perhaps fed spoonfuls of nourishing broth by her gossips.[42] It is most likely that around this time, the anxious husband would have been notified of the birth, perhaps firstly with the announcement of the baby's sex, followed by a report on both the baby's and mother's health.

The recovering new mother, similar to her baby, was instructed to rest in a dark, comfortable place, free of loud noises, bright lights, or cold drafts, which were known to be harmful to the weakened womb.[43] The exact duration of her resting period would certainly have varied greatly depending upon her social class, her husband's ability to keep the household running, and the amount of help she had around her. A lower-class mother might expect a few days or less in bed before she needed to return to her pre-birth work and schedule, while an aristocratic or other high-born lady was more likely to enjoy weeks or even months of such recuperation. And indeed, such rest was deemed necessary by medical professionals and midwives of the period, with even preachers acknowledging 'it is a long time after [childbirth] that they recover their former strength'.[44]

It was well known that a woman would be expected to bleed following the birth for some period of time, though even Sharp's writing is ambiguous on the expected duration. First, she writes that 'a woman delivered of a Boy, must continue in her purification thirty-three days, and for a girl sixty-six days'. She then references the teachings of Hippocrates, writing that 'a woman must continue purging her blood forth so long as the child was forming in the womb that is thirty days for a Male and forty-two days for a Female'. In fact, she acknowledges that neither estimate should be taken at face value and that no woman should expect to be able to predict the exact amount of time she might bleed following childbirth. Breastfeeding, for example (a topic that will be explored in depth in the following chapter) was one notable factor that could influence the length of postnatal bleeding. In Sharp's words, 'women that give their own children suck, have their purgations not so long as those that do not'.[45]

Many details regarding a woman's recovery from childbirth were a matter of social, cultural, and religious debate – such as how long she was considered unclean or 'green' (a reference to her postnatal 'chlorotic pallor').[46] In general, the contemporary consensus was that after twenty or twenty-five days, the mother was safe from post-birth complications such as puerperal fever ('childbed fever' was used as an umbrella term covering a number of possible postnatal infections) or life-threatening haemorrhaging. A full month's recovery was thought to be more than adequate time for her to heal from an uncomplicated birth, though this, too, varied depending upon the source. Officially, the Church decreed that thirty days' recovery was satisfactory after birthing a boy, though a girl's birth would require closer to sixty days, due to the toll that female babies were known to take on their mother's bodies.[47] During these thirty-to-sixty days, the Church also forbade sexual relations between man and wife, though the reality of how many couples abided by this rule is difficult to pinpoint.

What ultimately followed the recovery period for new mothers was an official church service, which differed in its meaning before and after the start of the Protestant Reformation in England. Prior, in the first half of the sixteenth century, the 'churching' ceremony of a new mother was seen by some as a means to cleanse her body from its impure state – though this is a matter of some controversy and debate, as it is unclear exactly how women of the period viewed this ritual (or if they in fact believed themselves to be 'impure' as a result of giving birth).[48] Traditionally, in this Catholic service, the priest would have met the new mother, flanked by her midwife, gossips, husband, and perhaps friends and family, and not allowed her to enter the church until after she had been sprinkled with holy water.[49] This evolved – certainly after the start of the Reformation, and possibly before – to become a service with thanksgiving at its centre, that was also a happy social occasion. The 1552 version of the *Book of Common Prayer* (in a significant deviation from its predecessor from only three years prior) did not mention holy water, veils, or candles in the reformed service at all.[50] In this service, thanks was given for the woman's safe delivery, whether or not it had resulted in a healthy, living infant. The presiding officiant would proclaim the following words to end the service:

> O Almighty God, which hast delivered this woman thy servant from the great pain and peril of childbirth: Grant, we beseech thee (most merciful father) that she through thy help, may both faithfully live and walk in her vocation, according to thy will in this life present; and also may be partaker of everlasting glory in the life to come: through Jesus Chris our Lord. Amen.[51]

The occasion marked the end of the new mother's period of 'greenness' – her time of healing, isolating and regaining her strength.[52] If she was not breastfeeding her infant, this would also signify the resurgence of her sexual relationship with her husband, as well as her return to society.[53]

Though the focus of this chapter, and indeed this entire book, is on the most often seen case study of Tudor motherhood – that being a married woman, a successful delivery resulting in a healthy mother and infant, and the going forth into childrearing and mothering for years to come – it must at least be briefly acknowledged that these circumstances were certainly not always the reality for every sixteenth century woman. The unmarried young woman who had unintentionally become pregnant would have fared very differently throughout pregnancy and birth than those described throughout these chapters. Many would have found ways to abort their pregnancies long before the time for labour arrived and many more who allowed their pregnancies to continue would have birthed alone, perhaps in their place of work, privately in their homes, or even outside where no one would witness them. Some might have attempted to raise babies born out of wedlock by themselves or with the help of willing family members, but others resorted to desperate and often horrible measures. Jane Little of Middlesex, for example, who went into labour in 1593, had concealed her forbidden pregnancy for nine months before running out of her lodgings to labour alone in a field and give birth to a baby girl. There, she buried her baby alive before returning home, hoping to rid herself of the problem of an unwanted child. But her crime was soon discovered when the baby's body was found. Jane was later sentenced to hang for her crime.[54]

The severely negative stigma attached to illegitimacy in the Tudor period was the tragic cause for a surprisingly high rate of infanticide during the sixteenth century. The mother was usually the perpetrator of such crimes, through any means necessary, likely due to her helplessness, desperation, and the sure knowledge that her life would be ruined if the shame of her misconduct was uncovered. Terrible examples from the period live on in Elizabeth Norton's *The Hidden Lives of Tudor Women* which details a number of ways in which women dispatched their babies in an effort to save themselves. As it turned out, this was often an effort in vain, resulting in the mother's imprisonment and ultimate execution. In a less macabre alternative to an unwanted pregnancy, an unmarried woman lacking resources or support to care for a child might have seen her pregnancy through, given birth privately, and handed the new baby over to somebody else, in secret. This might have been to a Church authority, trusted confidante, or even a known midwife – anyone who could have been entrusted to see the baby safely into caring hands. It must have been a hopeless and devastating situation for any woman to find herself in, whether her unexpected pregnancy had come from a torrid love affair, or (sadly, as was not uncommon) a sexual assault. In any case, the pressures and desperate decisions facing an unmarried, pregnant woman in the Tudor period are difficult to fathom.

On a final, exceptional note to close this chapter, it should be acknowledged that while the death rate among infants in Tudor England has been over-dramatised throughout the centuries, the deaths of newborn babies certainly did occur in the birthing chamber, and with far more frequency than the deaths of mothers. Unfortunately, they occurred often enough that midwives were granted permission by the Church to baptise babies who would be certain to die before they would be able to be brought to church for a true baptism – which would normally have occurred either on the day of birth or within a day or two following.[55] Unbaptised children, in the eyes of the Church, were barred from entering Heaven – a thought too painful and horrible to accept for the majority of people during the period. So, if a newborn was still breathing during the birth or immediately following it, but the midwife knew it was likely to die, she could perform a simple baptism and the child would be named, thus ensuring its soul's place in Heaven.[56] The words of this makeshift baptism would be similar to: 'I baptise you, [name], in the name of the Father, the Son, and the Holy Ghost'.[57]

While these exceptions to the typical story of Tudor birth are difficult to write and read about, it is necessary to pay some attention to the plights of these women and babies, even as this book spotlights the traditional, most common Tudor woman's path into and through motherhood. In the vast majority of cases, the new sixteenth-century mother would have given birth to a healthy infant, recovered within the expected timeframe, and taken part in her churching ceremony after the allotted time. If she was fortunate, she would have a doting husband who was overjoyed at the birth and diligent in his care and attention to his newly healed wife. So would begin the journey of motherhood for this new Tudor woman – who would likely again in another year or two's time face the entire ordeal of pregnancy all over again.

Chapter Ten

Nursing and Nursemaids

Until the mid-sixteenth century, newly born babies would be whisked off to church either immediately following the birth, or within a couple of days. This was understood to be one of the most critical first actions taken with a new baby, with messages immediately sent to both the local parish priest, as well as those whom the new parents wished to name as godparents. Great weight was placed on the choosing of these three required godparents, two of whom would be of the same sex as the baby and one of the other.[1] These people were expected to hold a prominent role in or have some significant impact on the infant's life – whether by the giving of their name to the child (as was the case of godfather Thomas Cromwell to the newborn son of Ralph Sadler in the mid-1530s), or by bestowing upon the child gifts, favours, employment opportunities and valuable connections in later life. As such, Tudor parents gave significant thought to whom they would name as godparents to their children, and when the time of the child's baptism came, it was expected that those three named individuals – as well as the midwife and father – would accompany the baby to church. The mother, well-deserving of her rest, would remain at home for the event.[2]

How a baby was named in Tudor times was not quite so simple as the mother and father merely choosing a name that they agreed on, although sometimes, perhaps, that was all it took. More often, a name bestowed on their child would link him or her to members of the family, as in the case of royalty, when King Henry VII chose to name his firstborn son Arthur, in homage to the long-ago great King Arthur, from whom he claimed his family had descended. In the case of Princess Elizabeth – daughter to King Henry VIII and Anne Boleyn – the name was a nod to her paternal grandmother, Elizabeth of York (and perhaps her maternal grandmother as well, Elizabeth Howard). In many cases, it was likely the father who named his children himself, but there are also many examples of godparents choosing to 'gift' their own name to their godchild, as was true for the London grocer, Richard Hill's children. Six of his seven children with wife Margaret were named for their chief godparents between 1518 and 1526.[3] Although it was not commonly done, there were instances where siblings were given the same name, likely due to godparents. Such examples include the two 'George' brothers of the Calthorp family in Norfolk, as well as the Allines in Warwickshire who boasted not only two sons named John, but also two daughters named Agnes.[4] In general, there was not a wide variety of names to be given in sixteenth-century England, although uncommon examples do exist. Most commonly, boys were named Henry, John, Robert, Thomas or William, while girls were often Anne, Elizabeth, Jane (or Joan) or Mary.[5]

Among the recognisably important tasks of naming and baptising the newborn, it should go without saying that feeding the baby – and determining exactly *how* to feed the baby – was a crucial step in newborn care. This was certainly a matter of some debate in the sixteenth century, but it was recognised by writers like Eucharius Rösslin that breastfeeding was both a source of superior nutrition and necessary bonding time between mothers and their babies. The Humoural Theory painted a direct correlation between blood and milk (menstruation and lactation) – effectively teaching that the lack of menstruation in pregnancy meant that the blood was nourishing the growing foetus while in utero, only to then be transformed into milk that would nourish the newborn baby from the woman's breasts. In the following century, this was further argued and explained in John Sadler's 1636 writing: 'so long as the woman giveth suck to the child, and hath store of milk in her breasts, her terms be of little or no quantity … forasmuch as the ebbing of the one is the flowing of the other'.[6] As such, it was well understood that breastfeeding would likely stall a woman's menstruation in the months following birth – but more on that in a moment.

New mothers were often encouraged to breastfeed their babies (with Thomas Cranmer even attempting to make it an official practice decreed by the Church of England in 1553). Gynaecological texts declared 'it shalbe beste that the mother give her chyld sucke herselfe, for the mothers milke is more convenyent and agreeable to the Infant than any other womans, and more doth it nouryshe it, for because that in the mothers belly it was wont to the same, and fed with it'.[7] The subject was not without its controversies and contradictions, however. The topic of colostrum – the thick, early milk first produced by mothers both during and quickly following pregnancy – was warned against even by Rösslin, who advised: 'it shalbe best that the chylde sucke not of the mother's breste by and by as soone as it is borne, but rather of some other womannes for a day or two, for because that the crème (as they call it) straight after the byrth, the first day in all women doth thycken and congile'.[8] It was unknown to medical professionals of the sixteenth century just how nutrient-dense and antioxidant-rich colostrum was for infants. Because it appeared different from the recognisable white, thinner milk that would be produced in later days following the birth, it was hotly warned against. Thus, many sixteenth-century babies likely drank little-to-no colostrum at all. And as the feeding of colostrum was discouraged and avoided by those who could heed the advice, recipes were written and passed around to 'make a womans mylke come and increase'. The following recipe was published by *The Secrets of Alexis*: 'Take the greene leaves of fennell, and make thereof a decoction, be it in Wine or water, whereof yee shall give the woman drinke, as well at her meales as otherwise, as often as maie bee, and she shall be abundant in milk'.[9] Meanwhile, the newborn baby did not go without nourishment for those first few days of life. Instead, a wet nurse would have assisted – in either a formal arrangement or a more casual one, perhaps through a currently lactating friend or family member.[10] This was one situation that benefitted from the fact that so many women in the sixteenth century were often pregnant or nursing.

Poorer women who were without much help in the days following their births would have nursed their babies with very little thought given to the matter, while among the most elite circles of society (particularly increasing throughout the latter half of the Tudor period) breastfeeding was seen as unfashionable, unclean, and unbecoming of a woman.[11] In these circles, it was much more common for new mothers to hire a wet nurse – a lactating woman who would nurse and nurture the child on the mother's behalf. As with the choosing of godparents, the choosing of a wet nurse was of the utmost importance, particularly because it was popularly believed that breastmilk passed along the characteristics of the nursing woman to the infant. Great thought and care needed to be placed on choosing a morally 'wholesome' nurse, as *The Byrth of Mankynd* instructed. Guides and manuals were written to assist a woman in selecting just the right type of woman to nurse her baby, focusing on such qualities as her 'good colour and complexion' (indeed, there was a fear that a wet nurse of darker skin might confer her complexion upon a naturally white infant).[12] It was also advised that a wet nurse must only be hired after two months 'at the leaste' had passed since having given birth herself. Crucially, she should also have given birth to a baby of the same sex as the one for which she was being hired to nurse.[13] This particular direction gives some indication that physicians and midwives understood (or at least assumed) that breastmilk was uniquely formulated by women to meet the needs of individual babies, with the baby's sex being just one such distinguishing feature. Writers like Rösslin had much to say about the qualities necessary in a wet nurse and the consideration that one must take in this critical decision. In short, it was certainly not something to be taken lightly.

But neither was the hiring of wet nurses universally acknowledged as the 'correct' course of action for new mothers. Again, popular medical advice decreed that a mother should nurse her own baby and even Rösslin wrote his advice on choosing a wet nurse only in the case 'that the mother can not geve the Infant sucke her selfe, eyther for because of sicknesse, or that her brestes be sore, and her mylke corrupted'.[14] He makes no mention of a woman simply choosing not to breastfeed her baby because she thought it was unfashionable or beneath her. But indeed, this was often the reason for a wealthy mother of aristocratic, noble, or royal status to choose a wet nurse – though even more often, the choice was not even hers to make at all. While it was understood that breastfeeding typically delayed the return of a woman's menstrual cycle, it was not uncommon for her husband to be the one to have a strong preference for hiring a wet nurse. The simple reason: to beget more children and at a quicker pace.[15] In fact, this was probably one of the most influential details regarding whether or not a wet nurse was hired. While sixteenth-century men and women may not have fully understood the mechanics behind lactation's natural contraceptive effects, they could certainly see for themselves that, in many cases, another pregnancy could not occur until well after a mother had weaned her child. And in a period when medical guidance directed to breastfeed babies for at least a full year (oftentimes much longer), this was not acceptable to many husbands who were in want of more children.[16] Therefore, a great number of women would have had little choice in the matter.

But one notable critic of the hiring of wet nurses – aside from Erasmus, who in 1526 referred to non-breastfeeding mothers as 'half-mothers' – was noblewoman Elizabeth Clinton, Countess of Lincoln.[17] Born in 1570, she published a treatise titled *The Countess of Lincoln's Nursery* in 1622 for her daughter-in-law Bridget, in which she detailed the 'duty, which all mothers are bound to performe'.[18] Pleased with the decision of her daughter-in-law to breastfeed her own children, the countess lamented her own choice of having hired wet nurses for her sixteen children, acknowledging that it was 'the expresse ordinance of God that mothers should nurse their owne children'.[19] Referencing biblical examples of breastfeeding women – such as Eve, Hannah, Sarah, and the Virgin Mary – she asked pointedly:

> The mothers then that refuse to nurse their owne children, doe they not despise Gods providence? Doe they not deny Gods will? … Oh impious, and impudent unthankfulnesse; yea monstrous unnaturalnesse, both to their own natural fruit borne so neare their breasts, and fed in there owne wombes, and yet may not be suffered to sucke their owne milke.[20]

Noting some popular societal reasons for her contemporaries choosing not to breastfeed their own children – 'that it is troublesome; that it is noisome to ones clothes; that it makes one looke old…', she called such complaints out as 'unchristian' and 'unmotherly'.[21] In fact, she argued to the contrary that women who breastfed their babies were *more* beautiful and youthful than those who did not, because they were 'sure of God's blessing'.[22] The treatise is filled with vehement objections to what the countess knew to be the 'fashionable' decision of foregoing breastfeeding, and as she roundly chastised such women, she regretted that she had been 'overruled by anothers authority and partly deceived by somes ill cousell' (presumably that of her husband) when it had come to feeding her own children.[23] As such, she wrote that she had since worked to 'redeeme [her] peace … studying how to shew double love to my children, to make them amends for neglect of this part of love to them, when they should have hung on my breasts, & have beene nourished in mine owne bosome'. Acknowledging her own self-proclaimed error in hiring wet nurses, she saw it as her Christian duty in later life to encourage younger mothers to choose differently.[24]

But criticism came from the other direction as well, as no mother, even in the sixteenth century, has ever been quite able to escape the judgements of others when it comes to how she feeds her baby. In 1598, Anne Newdigate – the daughter of one knight and wife to another – received a letter from her disappointed father expressing his disapproval of her decision, likely because it reflected poorly on the family's status. 'I am sorry that you yourself will nurse her', he wrote – his sentiments echoed by the baby's own godfather.[25] Midwife, Jane Sharp agreed with the Countess of Lincoln's viewpoint, however, writing that 'the usual way for rich people is to put forth their children to nurse, but that is a remedy that needs a remedy… because it changeth the natural disposition of the child, and oftentimes exposeth the infant to many hazards'. She certainly did not mince words on the topic, noting that 'multitudes pretend weakness when they have no cause for it, because they have not so much love for their own…'.[26] Still, she had her own guidance for those who insisted upon hiring wet nurses for their babies, whether or not she agreed with the decision. Echoing the writings of Rösslin, she deemed a good constitution and good complexion to be keys ('if a Nurse be well complexioned her milk cannot be ill; for a Fig Tree bears not Thistles: a good Tree will bring forth good Fruit').[27]

Poor milk quality was the most critical concern, and with good reason, as contemporary professionals attributed 'sharp milk' to cause anything from cradle cap (or 'scalles of the heed') to deteriorating illness and death in infants.[28] Specifically, a wet nurse should have a sanguine complexion, without a squinted eye or misshapen nose, without 'black ill-favoured Teeth, or with stinking breath'.[29] The list of requirements went on (borrowing heavily from other writers on the subject) and ultimately proving the point that for a family who could afford to be choosy, the selection of an adequate wet nurse was no simple or quick task. The last will and testament of Lady Anne Cobham, who died in 1558, gives some insight into the importance placed on breastfeeding by the gentry class – and perhaps also the expectation of payment for a good quality wet nurse. While it is impossible to know from this document how she felt about her own family members nursing their babies or not, her will stipulated that money should be left to her daughter-in-law for the purpose of nursing her child.[30] We can assume that this meant she was leaving money to pay for her grandchild's wet nurse – and if it was important enough to bequeath money for such a purpose, we can also assume that this was a very important facet of childcare in Lady Anne's eyes.

Well into the seventeenth century, it remained common knowledge that poorer folk were far more willing to breastfeed their own babies, while mothers of higher social status and wealth were most commonly using wet nurses.[31] But even among these women, the mechanics of wet nurse usage would have looked different depending on the circumstances. For members of the highest aristocratic circles, the chosen wet nurse likely moved into the family's residence during her employment. This was, of course, mostly out of convenience for the mother, who would not need to travel in order to have her infant fed. Instead, the baby's care would have been largely overseen by a staff of nurses and attendants (all living under the same roof), and the wet nurse would have been a part of the 'team' of women charged with caring for him or her. A nursery, furnished appropriately with – at the very least – a cradle and adequate storage for linens, candles and clothing, would have been set up somewhere in the home, along with lodging for the nurses, which was provided along with their salaries.

For royalty, the set-up was mostly the same, but infants were generally sent away from the royal court, usually to a manor house nearby. There, a team of nurses would assemble to see to the baby's daily care – to include the wet nurse, whose salary averaged around ten pounds per year at the beginning of the Tudor period (nearly seven thousand pounds today).[32] In addition, there would be a 'dry nurse' who oversaw general nursing duties, as well as a few additional 'rockers' – assistants in the nursery whose duties included rocking the baby's cradle. All were managed by a lady of senior status and authority, such as Lady Margaret Bryan, in the case of Henry VIII's children, Prince Edward and Princess Elizabeth.[33] The baby's nursery and attendants might have relocated throughout the year to be near to court and whichever palace the royal parents were currently residing but time spent between baby and mother would ordinarily have been quite limited. In fact, quality time between an aristocratic or royal mother and her baby largely depended on her availability and schedule, as well as her own interest and was oftentimes a rarity. Between her own duties to her husband, her household, and perhaps her court, the business of baby-making *was,* at a certain point, truly a business rather than a tender, nurturing relationship, regardless of what the royal mother herself might have desired. Indeed, as a result, the bond between babies and their wet nurses could instead be very strong, even exceeding that of the maternal bond. This was generally the closest and most loving relationship that a royal baby would have.[34]

More often for the general populace, however, a family would send their baby away to stay with their chosen wet nurse, which was by far the most economical option. This came with its own challenges, however, as it was not uncommon for a wet nurse in need of money to take on too many babies at once. In such cases, neglect, hunger, and illness among the infants was possible which may have contributed to the series of sharp chastisements from the Tudor medical community throughout the period, who argued that babies fed by wet nurses were more likely to die from lack of care or disease.[35] But for those who chose (or had little choice in) the arrangement, proximity and location of the wet nurse mattered. Often, if the family lived in a more urban, crowded area such as London, they might have chosen a wet nurse who lived in the healthier air of the open countryside so visiting their baby was no quick or easy task.

Records and diary entries from the period indicate that monthly or bimonthly visits were probably the norm among such families – and fathers were known to take a vested interest in visiting their children just as mothers did. Much depended upon where a family lived and how much they could afford, but one example of this arrangement was

Dr John Dee – Queen Elizabeth I's astrologer – whose babies were sent just short distances from his home in Mortlake to Barnes and Petersham (1½ and 2½ miles away, respectively). In his case, the fee to send babies to the wet nurses' care came to an average of 6 shillings per month between the 1570s and 1580s (roughly 60 pounds per month today). His wife visited their children at the wet nurse's house about once a month, when she also paid the woman for her services.[36] Other writing from the period, such as *The Gentle Craft*, written by Thomas Deloney in the 1590s, references the cost of a wet nurse at around sixteen pence per week (or ten pounds today).[37]

Though a relatively uncommon predicament, it surely did occur that Tudor mothers who desired to breastfeed their own babies were met with challenges and impediments, yet found themselves unable to employ the services of a wet nurse for one reason or another. Infections such as mastitis (or 'milk fever' as it was known during the period), challenges with low milk supply, or common injuries and discomforts such as nipple-cracking might all have contributed to a mother's need to look elsewhere for her infant's nutrition, though her lack of resources may have prevented her from hiring another woman's assistance. In such cases, she may have turned to alternative food sources – what we in the modern day call baby formula. Nothing nearly so sophisticated or scientifically concocted as what is available today was accessible to sixteenth-century families, but certain alternatives to breastmilk did, in fact, exist. One recipe was known as 'pap' – a mixture made of animal's milk (typically goat's milk, as it was easier for babies to digest than cow's milk) and a starch such as breadcrumbs, as well as a little sugar for sweetness. A second option was a nearly identical blend using broth instead of milk, called 'panatta'. Both of these were viable alternatives to a family desperate to feed their baby, and were relatively simple and inexpensive to make. They were often fed to babies using 'pap boats' – small pewter bowls with narrow spouts – or with spoons, though one English painting dated 1593 depicts a baby grasping a feeding bottle, indicating that some sixteenth-century version of the modern day bottle certainly existed.[38]

While certainly innovative, and no doubt lifesaving for a number of babies who might otherwise have gone hungry during the period for a number of possible reasons, the challenge with this method came with proper and safe food storage. Both of these posed a significant threat to infants. In an era when the importance of cleanliness of utensils and food storage containers was not well understood, such concoctions could easily have become contaminated with bacteria. This was especially true for babies born in the heat of summer, when the absence of refrigeration was particularly problematic. This unhealthy situation could be made even worse when pap or panatta was stored in pewter, which contained lead (a metal with toxicity levels that the Tudors could not yet have understood). It is little wonder why there was a pervading attitude during the period that 'spoon-fed' infants were far more likely to die than were those who were breastfed.[39]

There was nothing quite paralleling the modern day breast pump for nursing mothers who needed to express excess milk, especially in the case of an infant who had trouble effectively nursing. Issues such as tongue and lip ties were no doubt present among sixteenth-century babies, though medical understanding of such conditions (and remedies for them) were understandably lacking. Mothers in such situations where their babies had trouble nursing and could not effectively drain their breasts would have been in desperate need of relief. They would have taken great efforts to avoid 'milk fever' – the infection caused by stagnant milk that was known to cause severe illness and even death. Hand expressing was one option (and probably the most common) though more extreme remedies included older children sucking milk out of the mother's breasts to alleviate her distress or illness. Still more extreme was the case of puppies doing the job, in what must surely have been a significantly desperate measure to relieve a particularly uncomfortable mother.[40] Though living in the following century, Anne Archer was one woman who turned to a puppy for help when her baby failed to successfully latch to her inverted nipples. Because the puppy also struggled to alleviate the situation, both she and her husband feared that breastfeeding was doomed to fail. Thankfully, attempts with the puppy were short-lived and her own infant was soon able to nurse without trouble.[41]

With the exception of poorer families, the vast majority of baby care would not have been taken on by the mother. However, this does not mean that wealthy, busy mothers were completely disinterested in their babies' wellbeing. Pierre Erondelle, who wrote *The French Garden* in 1605, described such a mother's care in the overseeing of her wet nurse's duties. He describes her as watching the nurse wake her infant son, lifting him out of the cradle to undo his swaddling bands before washing him. The mother wonders after the baby's condition, asking if there are fleas in the room, if his fingers are flea-bitten, and how many teeth he currently has.[42] Still, despite her curiosity, a mother like the one described by Erondelle might have had little physical contact with her babies, as evidenced by his description of her merely watching the nurse's hands-on care. And though he does not depict a strained relationship between mother and wet nurse in his writing, contemporaries noted that there was often a tension and rivalry between the two women.[43] While entrusting the expert infant care to her hired team of nursemaids, both the mother and her husband would have supported the arrangement in other ways – financially, of course, but also by providing the baby and nursery with fine furnishings, clothes, and toys.

Poor families, on the other hand, would undoubtedly have been more hands-on – at least if the mother was breastfeeding her babies at home. While physical attention and maternal bonding was most prevalent among these families, the quality of their resources was understandably less than those of higher status. Cradles, for instance, might have been simply a box or basket on the floor, or in some cases, non-existent. Herein was a challenge and warning faced by poorer, breastfeeding mothers, which those who hired wet nurses were likely never confronted with. It was the subject of co-sleeping with their babies – an act that had been deemed taboo and dangerous by the Church for centuries, due to the risk of an adult rolling on top of a sleeping infant. In fact, a century earlier, one church had specifically warned families against this 'harmful' practice until their children were old enough to say *'Ligge outer'* – or 'Lie further off'.[44] So serious was this subject taken that offending parents who had accidentally smothered their babies were forced into their local churches for formal admonishment by a priest, and godparents were charged with the solemn duty of ensuring that such accidents would not occur.[45]

On the sad subject of infant mortality, it must be noted that this rate was tragically high, though certainly more prevalent due to infections and illness rather than co-sleeping with parents. Unfortunately, towards the end of the sixteenth century, an estimated seventeen per cent of babies were dying within their first year of life.[46] Boys, for some reason, were slightly more likely to succumb to infantile illness than were girls – and the result of either tragedy was devastating to parents. For the many mothers and fathers who had to endure the loss of their infant children, it was customary that, where possible, no expense was spared at the baby's burial and memorial. Wealthier families were, understandably, better positioned for elaborate coffins (versus simple shrouds) and tomb memorials with heartfelt inscriptions, but poorer families did all they could to honour their deceased babies and bury them where they too would one day be buried.[47] The illustrations of swaddled children on tombs are sad reminders of the frequency of infant mortality in the sixteenth century and we modern readers would be misguided to think of it as anything less than an utter tragedy to Tudor families. Regardless of how numerous and frequent such deaths might have been, they were no doubt felt just as deeply as at any other time in human history.

Just as Tudor mothers and fathers were relatable in their parental grief, so were they relatable in how adorable they found their babies. Parents were charmed with their infants' coos, smiles, and first words (delighting in hearing 'mama' for the first time, similar to any modern mother).[48] Contemporaries noted the 'sweet baby-talk' of infants (and possibly of mothers, too), and how amusing it was to hear babies and young toddlers attempting to emulate their parents' speech.[49] The amount of time spent between mother and baby during the first months or years of his or her life would certainly have varied greatly depending on the family's situation and distance would have been necessary in the case of wet nursing until the baby was weaned. This could have been around a year old, as general guidance dictated, or upwards of three to four years. By this time, as family statistics from the period suggest, the typical Tudor mother would likely have already become pregnant again and perhaps welcomed another baby or two into the family in the meantime.

Chapter Eleven

'Infancy' and Young Childhood

Life, as those living in the sixteenth century understood it, could be defined in stages of time known as 'ages of man'. There were seven of them, made more famous by William Shakespeare, but known to men and women since medieval times (and in fact, with origins yet again in ancient Greece). In his play *As You Like It,* Shakespeare popularised the notion of these seven life stages – known as the infant, the schoolboy, the lover, the soldier, the justice, the retiree, and the infirm.[1] As he described these stages in his character Jacques' famous speech, 'All the world's a stage', he would have expected his audience to be familiar with the seven ages and to find relevance with them – more so if they were male than female, of course. Infancy, understood by modern readers to comprise the first year of a baby's life, was largely discussed in the previous chapter, though the Tudors viewed this stage of life quite differently. Far from making up only the first year of life, infancy was thought to last seven years – far beyond 'babyhood' as we now recognise it. Shakespeare described this period of time through Jacques as the time when a child is 'mewling and puking in the nurse's arms' and this perhaps demonstrates the level of immaturity and dependency with which these young children were viewed at the time.[2]

'Infants', as the Tudors considered them, were not yet old enough to be entrusted with much responsibility, and often not yet to be educated, though as will be explored in this chapter, that depended upon the social class of the family and child. It should, in fact, be mentioned that much more about sixteenth-century parenting and childhood has been written about through the centuries with an emphasis on upper-class or royal families. This is largely because personal diaries, letters and formal family records were much more easily maintained and retained in such families – not to mention the fact that a great number of lower-class individuals were illiterate and could not keep such records at all. Therefore, we as modern historians have fairly little first-hand evidence of family life from poorer, less educated parents and children. Still, assumptions and inferences can be made with the scant evidence available, while these chapters must naturally take a more focused look at childhood and child-rearing in wealthier families of the Tudor period. This is a regrettable – yet hopefully understandable – limitation of studying generalised family life of the sixteenth century.

The period of time between birth and age 7 – the first age – was a time for growth and development, and was often spent largely in the care of a nurse or nursery staff. Royal babies and young children during this time were frequently referred to as being raised 'among the women' – a reference to the women hired to oversee their care.[3] For a mother, these years of her young child's life could have looked remarkably different, depending on her circumstances. If she was breastfeeding, and therefore keeping her child close to her most of the time, she might have done so well into what we now refer to as the toddler years – until her child turned 3 or 4. Jane Sharp noted that 'a year old is sufficient to most children', though she had seen 'some in England that have kept their children sucking near four years' – so there was a great deal of variability here.[4] Alternatively, if the family was paying for the services of a wet nurse, they may or may not have decided to wean the baby closer to that one-year mark, simply for the financial benefit. But in wealthier families where the cost of a wet nurse mattered less, the time spent between mother and baby might have been minimal for the first few years of the baby's life – even beyond the time that his or her mother might have given birth to another baby. Weaning would have coincided with the natural progression of introducing solid foods to the baby – or rather, mushy foods, often pre-chewed by the mother or nurse.[5]

Teething could begin, as in children today, within months of life, and was often seen as a time of great distress or even danger for babies. Writing in the following century, John Pechey referenced children who had died of the 'breeding of teeth', due to the often severe symptoms accompanying them.[6] Teething remedies existed throughout the period, such as offering a baby a candlestick to chew on, or even an animal's tooth securely attached to a cord. One Tudor example exists with the infant Prince Edward (the future King Edward VI), who was gifted a wolf's tooth for this purpose with funds provided by Thomas Cromwell, on behalf of the prince's father, King Henry VIII.[7] No doubt, many mothers and nurses would have also known how to create soothing herbal concoctions and ointments to rub onto their babies' gums and alleviate pain. One example was written in the second book of *The Byrth of Mankynde* advising the mother to rub the infant's sore gums with her finger, then 'annoynt the same gummes with ointment made of hennes grese, hares brayne, oyle of camomell mixt with honye'. Another option, Rösslin wrote, was to mix 'turpen tyne tempered with honye, then take water, and in it sethe camomell and dyll, the which water beynge hote: pour it on the chyldes heade, holdynge it a fote above the heade'.[8] The expected efficacy of such remedies is hard for us to know, but the concerned Tudor mother would likely have taken any medical advice at her disposal, if aware that her child was suffering from teething pain.

It is important to note, however, that many women of the period would have lacked published resources or been unable to read them altogether, and would have relied on the advice of female friends or family members in such matters. Regardless, she would have likely taken whatever help she could get – whether written or verbal – if her child was ill or in pain. In fact, there was known to be a great deal of compassion from the typical Tudor mother to her young children, regardless of what medical resources she had available to her. The medieval poet, Alexander Barclay, wrote of the early Tudor housewife in *The Ship of Fools,* describing her as hugging and kissing the children and babies all around her, 'delous[ing] them and comb[ing] them', and noting that she 'puts butter on their necks to soothe dry skin'.[9]

While 'infancy' in Tudor England was a time for growth and taking care of young children, it was also a time for these young children to learn how to interact with the world around them. Older babies and young toddlers would learn to walk, for example, using a remarkably similar training apparatus to our modern day walker. A 1499 illustration in the encyclopedia *De Proprietatibus Rerum* depicts seven figures exemplifying the seven ages of man, with the toddler standing in a 'walking frame' – a four-sided structure on wheels that a toddling infant might have leaned against for support while learning to walk.[10] 'Leading strings' – long pieces of fabric or ribbon attached to a child's clothes – were yet another training apparatus for young walkers, held by an adult who walked behind them, as a means of guiding and supporting.[11] The 'learning' done by young children in this age is not to be confused with true education, which did not traditionally begin for another few years. But contemporaries of the period writing about parenthood recognised the great value that mothers had in the teaching of their young children. Juan Luis Vives had written during the first half of the Tudor period, 'that age [childhood] … taketh her first conditions and information of mynde by such as she hereth, or seth by her mother. Therfore, it lyeth more in the mother than men wene, to make the conditions of the children'.[12] Following the Reformation, William Gouge had echoed this sentiment, writing that 'while the children are young, their mother is most in their sight … what they learn in the younger years, commonly they learn of their mothers'.[13] Young children could learn virtually anything about their world by observing their mothers, but writers of the period stressed the importance of teaching two very critical things even at this young and tender age: good manners and godliness. Hugh Rhodes, who amended the existing *Book of Nurture, for Men, Servauntes, and Chyldren* in 1545, started his writing with the following statement:

> There is fewe things to be underst[ood] more necessary then to teache and governe Children in learning and good manners, for it is a hye service to God, it getteth favour in the syghte of men, it multiplyeth goods, and increaseth thy good name, it also provoketh to prayer by whiche Gods grace is obtained, if thus they bee brought up in virtue, good maners, and Godly learning.[14]

Good manners – particularly reverence and respect for elders – were paramount in a young child's behaviour, with parents (and any 'elder' being deemed the child's 'betters'). Rhodes advised caretakers about 'rebuking ydle talke and stammering, as [a child's] uncomly gestures in going or standing'.[15] In short, young children were not meant to be too familiar or comfortable with their parents or any authority figure around them. Rather, they were expected to speak appropriately and courteously, and to adhere to their parents' or guardians' instruction as to how to physically conduct themselves. Rhodes went on to further emphasise this point: 'Unto your Elders gentle be, against them say no harme. If youth doe evill, their Parents sure reape this reporte full soone'.[16] At mealtime, for example, children were expected to be silent unless spoken to, and thus invited to speak.[17] In the mornings, when rising from bed, they were required to bow or kneel before their parents in greeting and await their blessing.[18] These were, of course, rather high bars to set for a toddling 2- or 3-year-old, and some degree of leniency and understanding was most likely allowed for children so young. But the foundations for good manners and adherence to the authority of elders were certainly set from a very tender age, as is clear from contemporary writings on parenting.

From the time a child first began to speak words, he or she was likely taught to pray. With godliness – and the firm aim of raising children to be good Christians – as a top priority of Tudor parenthood, there was little more important to a mother and father than instilling prayer and scripture into their young child's life. This would, of course, in certain cases, have been left more to the duty of the child's nursery staff, but no matter who the authority figure was, it would have been paramount to his or her early education and daily upbringing. Prior to the Reformation, there was no formal requirement for parents to bring their children to church regularly, at least up until their confirmation (an occasion which had no specific age minimum, but often occurred somewhere near the onset of puberty).[19] Still, many children would have accompanied their parents to Mass on Sundays, while also learning the central role that religion played in their home life. Three essential prayers for them to learn – in Latin, of course – were the Lord's Prayer, the Ave Maria, and the Apostles' Creed. In the latter half of the Tudor period, the Ave Maria would no longer be compulsory for children to recite, being replaced by the Ten Commandments, with all prayers then being taught in English.[20]

Upon rising and going to bed, blessings would be given by parents, and before meals, children (particularly boys) would be taught to say grace from a young age – a tradition popularised in the fifteenth century and carried into and throughout the Tudor period. Following the Reformation, mandatory thirty-minute catechism classes were offered to children by the priest of every parish at a frequency of at least every six weeks, as ordered by the 1549 *Book of Common Prayer*.[21] In general, prior to this transition from Catholicism to Protestantism in England, the majority of a child's religious upbringing and education could be taught at home by a pious mother, but this shifted in the latter half of the century to a more church-focused education. Prayer and familial conversation surrounding scripture and godliness existed at home, without question, but the emphasis on church attendance and catechism class was increased. Still, religious requirements were far stricter for child members of the royal family, and even some of the aristocratic elite, than they were for the typical population. It was not uncommon for these children to be required to attend Mass daily in either a parish church or a private family chapel and, as they were afforded the luxury of being more literate than most of the population, they might also have been expected to pray the Liturgy of Hours each morning.[22]

The Tudor mother, apart from either overseeing the early education of her young children, or managing that of her children's employed nurses, would have also had the duty of making or providing clothes. This task would have likely taken up a great deal of time for the typical sixteenth-century housewife, as it was customary for a Tudor mother to hand-make the vast majority of her family's garments. In wealthier families or more exceptional circumstances, clothes could also be ordered from local tailors. Following the immediate months of infancy, a baby's clothes became more complex than the simple swaddling bands first administered soon after birth. Once the bands were no longer needed (usually around eight or nine months of age), clothes for an older baby typically consisted of long petticoats, meant both to protect the knees during crawling, as well as to allow easy access for breech-cloth changes.[23] Clothing items specific to a young girl or boy would not be necessary for some years, and the universal gown-like garment was intended with practicality in mind. Depending on the social class, of course, the child's clothes would have varied widely – from a simple smock or petticoat, to coats with detachable sleeves, bib-aprons, caps, and even chains hanging from the neck to indicate status – though many of these garments and accessories would likely only have been seen in paintings of aristocratic children, rather than being worn in daily life.[24] It is reasonable to assume that any Tudor mother who might have provided handmade petticoats for her own babies and toddlers would have had to make multiples for each child, and thus a significant amount of her time may have been spent on this task. A wealthier mother (or perhaps one who simply preferred not to make her children's clothes) would instead have allocated necessary funds to the nursery, so that adequate clothing could be purchased.

Perhaps the primary concern of Tudor mothers as it related to their children was the risk of illness and injury, as a great number of children were known to die in their first several years of life. Exact statistics on infant and young childhood deaths are impossible to come by, due to records that either have not survived the centuries, or were never created in the first place. But one estimate states that roughly one-fifth of Elizabethan children failed to reach their tenth birthday.[25] Many authors and medical professionals of the sixteenth century wrote on the subject of avoiding such a fate for their own children – their work largely only available to mothers of more elite classes, and therefore probably unread by the majority of sixteenth-century society. But the sheer number of resources available to literate mothers who had the means of obtaining the information illustrates the vast amount of concern placed on babies' and young children's health. *The Byrth of Mankynde* is just one example, with its entire second section devoted to common childhood ailments and their remedies – everything from constipation to chapped lips. Thomas Elyot's *The Castle of Health* also focused on childhood health, with a particular emphasis on diet and nutrition, and Thomas Moulton's 1540 publication *The Glass of Health* provided additional remedies for common illnesses and complications. In 1544, Englishman Thomas Phaer took another critical step by translating *The Regiment of Life,* written by Frenchman Jean Goeurot – a compendium of common bodily diseases that were known to affect adults. Having seen here a clear gap in paediatric writing and attention, Phaer gave the work a more child-focused perspective, adding it to further writing of his own – namely, *The Boke of Chyldren.*[26]

This groundbreaking work was the first English-written book centred solely on paediatrics and dismissing the commonly held notion that 'there is no cure to be ministered unto [infants] by reason of theyr weaknesse'.[27]

His writing covered an enormous range of topics, from the oft-debated subject of infant breastfeeding to forty different ailments and conditions for which a caretaker or mother might seek help. A great number of these were purely medical in nature, such as 'the palsye', 'consumption', 'fevers', and 'burnyng and scaldyng'. The amount of attention paid by Phaer to specific ailments can give us some indication as to the most frequently encountered medical issues in children during the period. For example, he lists four remedies for cankers in a child's mouth, five remedies for pain in and around the ears, and sixteen different remedies for issues related to the stomach, such as gas pains and vomiting.[28] But other sections of the book focus on childcare topics remarkably familiar even to the modern day parent – like 'terrible dreames', waking from sleep ('watchyng out of measure') and 'pyssyng the bedde'.[29] What a goldmine of information this must have been for sixteenth-century parents, if only they had access to it! The first of its kind for English speakers, it provided remedies for something as common as nightmares in young children, with Phaer acknowledging that 'oftentymes it happeneth that the child is afrayde in the slepe, and somtymes waketh sodaynlye and sterteth, sometime shryketh and tembleth'. Fascinatingly, he attributed these terrible dreams to 'stynkynge vapoures out of the stomacke into the fantasye and sences of the brayne' – which could be recognised by the parent from the child's foul breath in the middle of the night. This, he suggested, could be remedied by:

> … a lytle hony to swallowe, and a lytle pouder of the seedes of peony, and sometimes tryacle in a lytle quantitie with mylk, and to take hede that the chylde slepe not with a full stomake … and … not to rocke it moche, for overmoche shakynge letteth digestion and maketh the child manye tymes to vomyte.[30]

This particular instruction regarding rocking the uneasy child gives some insight into the nurturing care expected in a young child's mother or nurse. Too often, we modern readers might falsely assume a coldness in mothers of a distant historical age, but Phaer's writing paints a much softer picture – that of a Tudor mother administering a sweet tincture to her child, before rocking him or her (gently) back to sleep, free of the 'stynkynge' stomach vapours which had caused the bad dreams in the first place.

Waking from sleep – or 'watchyng out of measure', as Phaer wrote it – came with a much more controversial remedy, as modern readers would view it. He did aptly recognise the importance of good quality sleep in an infant or young child: 'wherefore whan it is depryved of the naturalle reste, all the whole bodye falleth in distemper, cruditie, and wekenes'. His proposed catalyst for interrupted or poor sleep was often 'corruption of the milke, or too moch aboundans', which would upset the infant's stomach, create poor digestion, and allow unpleasant fumes and vapours into the head and brain, 'wherof the child can not slepe but turneth and vexeth it selfe with cryeng'. The suggested remedy was to anoint the baby's forehead and temples with the oil of violets mixed with vinegar and to put a drop or two into the nostrils. Even better (and more dangerously, as we know now), acquiring the 'syrupe of poppye' (opium) and allowing the child to lick it before making a plaster to apply to the temples, would also induce sleep. Two other recommendations regarding poppies – either stamped with rosewater and mixed with breastmilk and egg whites, or combining the poppy's seeds and oil with the oil of lettuce to make a topical ointment – were suggested for the baby to 'receyve hys natural slepe'.[31] We know now that these remedies essentially suggested drugging children to sleep with opioids, but the Tudors certainly did not comprehend the dangers or ill-effects of these ingredients at the time.

Regarding 'pyssyng the bedde' ('pissing' being the usual sixteenth-century term for urination, and therefore not the crude or offensive slang known today), Phaer acknowledged that this was a problem seen equally in 'wel olde men as children'. Due to the 'debilitye or virtue retentive of the reynes or blader', urine was known to 'issueth out, either in theyr sleepe or waking against theyr wylles, havyng no power to retayne it whan it commeth'. His remedy for such an inconvenience was once again dietary, and he offered a few different suggestions – all regarding the avoidance of fatty meats, and the use of powder in one's meat and drinks. One suggestion was the brining and powdering of a plucked chicken, to be eaten two-to-three times a day. He noted that the 'stones

This family portrait, painted around 1567, depicts Lord William Brooke, 10th Baron Cobham, with his wife Elisabeth Brooke, six children, a woman who has been tentatively identified as the baron's sister and a few family pets. This is a classic example of the family portraiture that was popularised during the Tudor period. Most strikingly, it includes a Latin inscription that reinforces the focus on a woman's fertility within noble family lines: 'God grant that the line of Cobham beget many offspring such as Joseph'. (Master of the Countess of Warwick, *c.*1567; Courtesy of Wikimedia Commons, Public Domain)

Anne Hopton, first married to Henry, 3rd Baron of Wentworth, was mother to Thomas, Henry and Jane, all painted here with her in 1596. This portrait was likely commissioned by her second husband, Sir William Pope of Wroxton, whom she had married the previous year. The purpose of the portrait was perhaps meant to celebrate her fertility, as she is depicted here as being newly pregnant by her second husband, while posing beside the children she had already produced. (Marcus Gheeraerts the Younger, *c.*1596; Courtesy of Wikimedia Commons, Public Domain)

This 1562 portrait of Catherine Carey, Lady Knollys is a beautiful example of a noblewoman embracing the pregnancy fashions of the Tudor period. It gives us some insight into the garments worn by women who were expecting – most notably, her open coat fastened with adjustable ties, which revealed her growing bump and could likely have been worn throughout her pregnancy. In addition, she is clothed in a silver gown, often signifying chastity. With her husband Sir Francis Knollys, Catherine produced sixteen children. (Steven van der Meulen, *c.*1562; Courtesy of Wikimedia Commons, Public Domain)

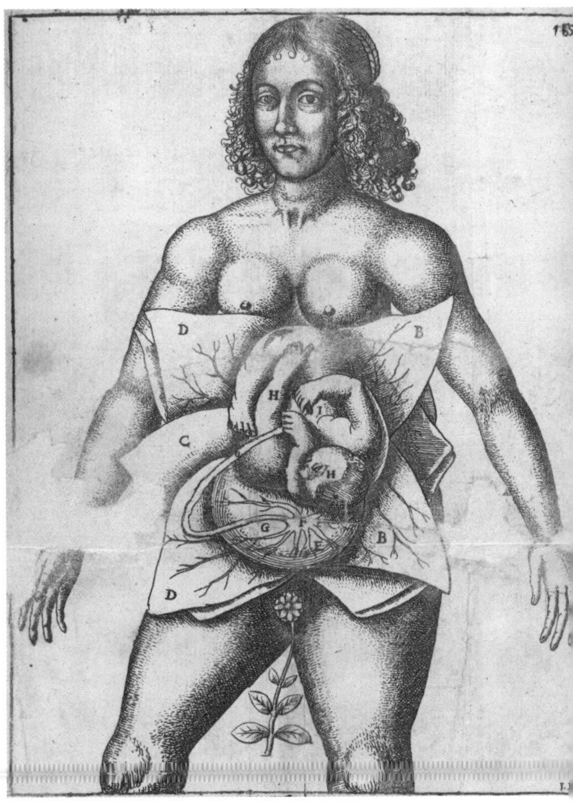

Jane Sharp, a notable midwife of the seventeenth century, wrote *The Midwives Book,* which was published in 1671. It was a remarkable addition to pregnancy and midwifery manuals of the period, most of which had previously been written by men. In it, she wrote of female anatomy, best practices during pregnancy and childbirth, and infant care. This popular illustration from the book details a woman ready to give birth — her uterus in bloom. (Wellcome Library, London, *c.*1671; Courtesy of Wikimedia Commons, Public Domain)

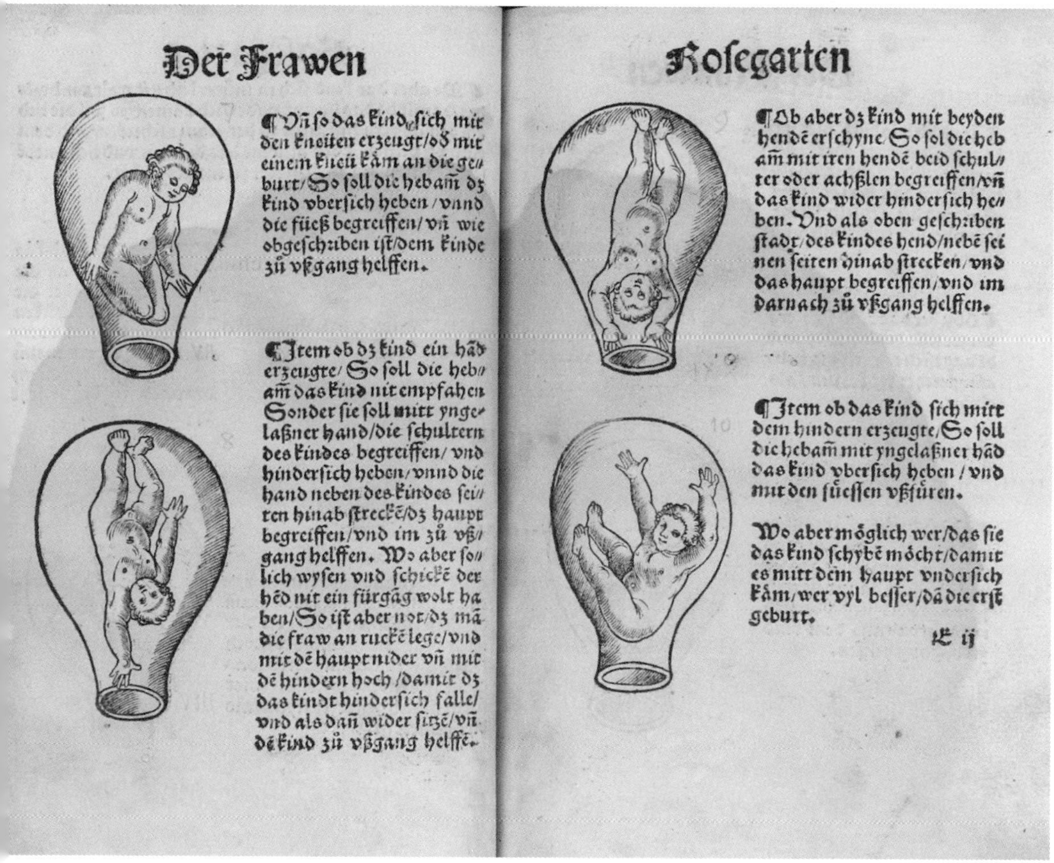

Der Frawen Rosegarten

¶ Vñ so das kind sich mit den knoiten erzeugt/od mit einem knew kām an die geburt/ So soll die hebam̄ dz kind vbersich heben/ vnnd die füeß begreiffen/ vñ wie obgeschriben ist/dem kinde zů vßgang helffen.

¶ Item ob dz kind ein hād erzeugte/ So soll die hebam̄ das kind nit empfahen Sonder sie soll mitt yngelaßner hand/die schultern des kindes begreiffen/ vnd hindersich heben/ vnnd die hand neben des kindes seiten hinab streckē/dz haupt begreiffen/vnd im zů vßgang helffen. Wo aber sollich wysen vnd schickē der hēd nit ein fürgāg wolt haben/So ist aber not/dz mā die fraw an ruckē lege/vnd mit dē haupt nider vñ mit dē hindern hoch /damit dz das kindt hindersich falle/ vnd als dañ wider sitzē/vñ dē kind zů vßgang helffē.

¶ Ob aber dz kind mit beyden hendē erschyne. So sol die hebam̄ mit iren hendē beid schulter oder achßlen begreiffen/vñ das kind wider hindersich heben. Vnd als oben geschriben stadt/des kindes hend/nebē seinen seiten hinab strecken/ vnd das haupt begreiffen/vnd im darnach zů vßgang helffen.

¶ Item ob das kind sich mitt dem hindern erzeugte/So soll die hebam̄ mit yngelaßner hād das kind vbersich heben / vnd mit den füessen vßfüren.

Wo aber möglich wer/das sie das kind schybē möcht/damit es mitt dem haupt vndersich kām/wer vyl besser/dā die erst geburt.

E ij

First published in German in 1513, Eucharius Rösslin's *Der schwangern Frauwen und Hebammen Rosengarten* was translated and expanded upon by Richard Jonas and Thomas Raynalde in later decades and published in England as *The Byrth of Mankynd.* It was immensely popular, as it described the female body, pregnancy, and childbirth in more detail than had ever been available to the public. These womb illustrations, showing the various positions that babies were believed to take while in utero were included in the publication, as were many further diagrams of female anatomy. (Eucharius Rösslin, *c.*1513; Courtesy of Wikimedia Commons, Public Domain)

In this portrait of an unknown pregnant woman during the late sixteenth century, maternity fashions are once again on display. Similar to Catherine Carey, this sitter is wearing an ornate silver gown to indicate her chastity. Her bump is boldly displayed, as is the smile in her expression, to emphasise her pleasure and pride in her condition. Pregnancy portraits such as these (at least among the nobility) grew in popularity and frequency throughout the Tudor period and were especially common during Elizabeth I's reign. (Marcus Gheeraerts the Younger, *c*.1595; Courtesy of Wikimedia Commons, Public Domain)

The Tudor birthing chamber was a place dominated by women. Many labouring mothers, like the one pictured here, were medically assisted by an experienced midwife, while they were comforted and supported by a team of attendants hand-picked for the occasion. This image, which comes from Eucharius Rösslin's 1513 publication *Der Rosengarten*, depicts a typical birth room scene, with the mother sitting on a 'woman's stool' while being checked by her midwife. Meanwhile, one of her attendants comforts her during the process. (Eucharius Rösslin, *c*.1513; Courtesy of Wikimedia Commons, Public Domain)

This peculiarly shaped chair, known as the 'woman's stool', was introduced in England in the sixteenth century, though it was utilised more by labouring women of the seventeenth century. Designed with a horseshoe-shaped cutout in the seat, it was meant to allow the labouring woman to deliver from a sitting position, where a waiting midwife would be able to catch the infant. This was only one of many positions taken by women when delivering their babies during the period. (Wellcome Library, London, *c.*1513; Courtesy of Wikimedia Commons, CC BY 4.0 Deed)

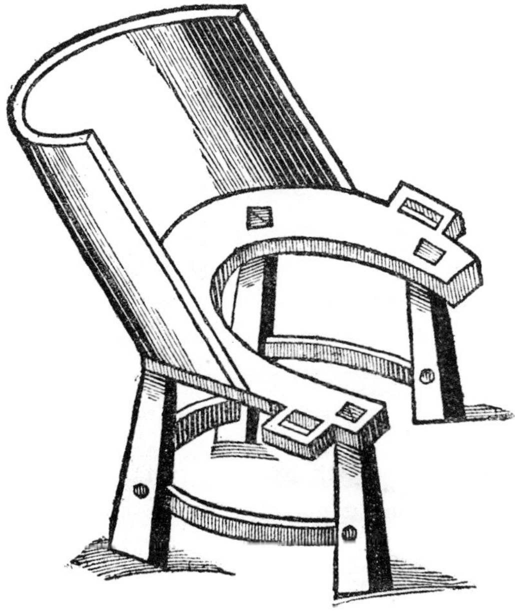

FIG. 228. — Chaise obstétricale, d'après Eucharius Rhodion et A. Paré.

This 1513 painting depicts the birth of the Virgin Mary, providing an intimate look at the goings-on of a birthing chamber around this period. The new mother is waited on and comforted by her attendants, while her midwife cares for the newborn infant, perhaps bathing and preparing to swaddle her. This would have been a familiar scene for most Tudor women, who would likely have been surrounded by trusted female companions for the event. (Wolf Traut, *c.*1513; Courtesy of Wikimedia Commons, Public Domain)

This funeral brass for Anne Astley (nee Wood) from 1512 is an example of the honour and recognition placed on women who passed away during childbirth. The inscription (translated from Latin) reads: 'Pray ye all for the soul of Ann a Wode, the second wife of Thomas Astley of Melton Constable, Esquire, who on the Day of Saint Agipitus the Martyr brought forth into birth a boy and a girl and after the danger of bringing forth she suddenly migrated to the Lord, in the year of Christ the most blessed the one thousandth five hundredth and twelfth'. (J. Guffogg, Blickling, St. Andrew's Church, 2019; Courtesy of Wikimedia Creative Commons, CC BY 4.0 Deed)

The Cholmondeley Ladies portrait, believed to feature sisters Mary and Lettice Cholmondeley, is an early seventeenth-century example of family portraiture that reinforced status as well as fertility. All four of the sitters in this portrait contain subtle differences in their appearances that slightly distinguish them from one another, but their societal rank is evident by the style of their dress and finery. Though the purpose of this portrait remains a mystery, it is possible that the placement of two sisters beside each other with their newborn babies was meant to reinforce their family's fertility. (Unknown Artist, British School, *c.*1600–1610; Courtesy of Wikimedia Commons, Public Domain)

This fascinating portrait, titled 'A Visit to the Wet Nurse', offers a detailed and intimate glimpse into life inside a Tudor home and the interaction between a mother and her infant. It depicts the visitation of a mother to her wet nurse's home, where the nurse holds the baby. Meanwhile, the visiting mother bends down to greet him or her as the baby is held towards her. In cases like this, where babies were sent off to be boarded at a wet nurse's residence, visits from mothers and fathers might have been infrequent (perhaps monthly) and would have also served the purpose of paying the wet nurse for her services. (Marten van Cleve the Elder, *c.*1572; Courtesy of Wikimedia Commons, Public Domain)

There were situations during the Tudor period, much like today, when infants could not be fed by a nursing mother or even a wet nurse, perhaps due to medical complications or a lack of resources. In such instances, sixteenth-century versions of the baby bottle were used, as pictured here in this 1593 portrait of a finely dressed baby. She holds what appears to be a wooden bottle with a spout, while she is dressed in a bib, apron, and collar befitting her social class. This is one of a few different apparatuses used as an alternative feeding vessel for babies, and one of very few illustrated examples that exist to this day. (Unknown Artist, English School, c.1593; Courtesy of Wikimedia Commons, Public Domain)

Lady Catherine Grey holds her eldest son, Edward Seymour, Lord Beauchamp for this intimate miniature portrait of a Tudor mother and her infant child. Painted in 1562, this portrait offers a somewhat more familiar and sentimental feel compared with other family portraits of the period. The sitter's finery and dress are on full display, lest anyone should question their rank, but in addition to these details are the physical touch between Catherine and her son. She holds him in her arms, while he has his arm resting against her chest. (Levina Teerlinc, *c.*1562; Courtesy of Wikimedia Commons, Public Domain)

In 1555, Lady Catherine Willoughby fled Queen Mary I's Catholic England along with her second husband Richard Bertie, her infant daughter Susan, and her daughter's wet nurse. This seventeenth-century illustration depicts the four of them fleeing together, reinforcing the importance of wet nurses and their placement within a noble family's employment. So valuable and hand-selected was this individual, that she was brought along by her employers even when they exiled themselves to Europe for four years. (Unknown Artist, 17th Century; Courtesy of Wikimedia Commons, Public Domain)

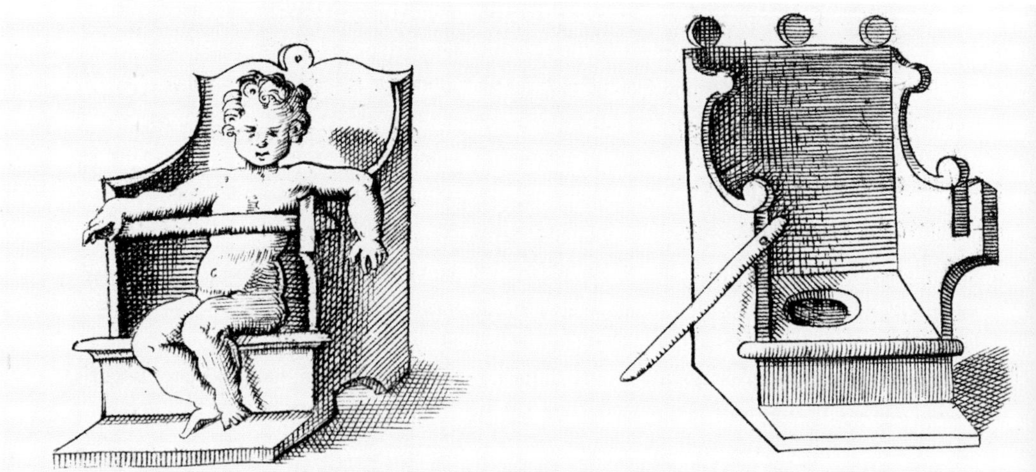

Hardly any information exists to this day about toilet training toddlers during the sixteenth century, but this fabulous illustration from 1577 shows a young child sitting on what appears to be a toddler training toilet, giving us some insight as to what this milestone may have looked like. This small lavatory includes a safety bar to keep the child securely seated, so as to prevent them from falling out and injuring themselves. (Wellcome Library, London, *c.*1577; Courtesy of Wikimedia Creative Commons, CC BY 4.0 Deed)

Similar in structure to the child's lavatory, this 1627 portrait of the infant Susanna de Vos displays an infant's chair, clearly used in this instance for eating. It appears to contain a solid seat and tray, which would have kept the young child secure while they ate, as young Susanna is doing here. Although this portrait is of Flemish origin, rather than English, it can be assumed that some similar apparatus existed in England for children of the period. (Cornelis de Vos, *c*.1627; Courtesy of Wikimedia Commons, Public Domain)

This image, taken from a 1920 instructional book titled *Mother and Child*, depicts a fifteenth-century mother feeding her infant with a wooden spoon. It offers valuable insight into how some women of both this period and the Tudor period fed their babies alternatives to breastmilk. Here, the mother is spooning broth from a bowl – perhaps 'pap' or 'panatta', which were both early forms of modern day baby formula. In cases where mothers had challenges breastfeeding their infants, such alternative food sources were valuable options, even as they were deemed potentially dangerous by some critics. (Hans Memling, 1920; Courtesy of Wikimedia Commons, Public Domain)

This cradle, often referred to as the 'Henry V Cradle', has been the subject of long-standing debate regarding its actual origins. It has been alleged that, rather than being used for the fourteenth-century royal infant, it may have been constructed during the following century, placing it closer to our Tudor period. In any case, the cradle, which is now housed by the Royal Collection, offers a valuable example of one such piece of furniture that would have been built and used for a royal or noble baby. Such nurseries also generally staffed a nursemaid whose title was 'Cradle Rocker', with a job description that was probably self-explanatory. (William Edward Gray, 1912; Courtesy of Wikimedia Commons, Public Domain)

Barbara Gamage, Lady Sidney and Countess of Leicester, poses here in 1596 with her six children – two sons and four daughters. The boys are almost indiscernible from the girls, due to the similarity of young children's garments. This is another portrait that would have served to reinforce Barbara's impressive fertility to the viewer – a matter of great pride for the family. In fact, she would go on to have another four children with her husband Robert Sidney, 1st Earl of Leicester. (Marcus Gheeraerts the Younger, *c.*1596; Courtesy of Wikimedia Commons, Public Domain)

This portrait of Frances, Lady Willoughby and her son, Francis, Lord Willoughby of Parham, is tentatively dated between 1618 and 1620. It presents a mother and son of substantial social status, with the young Francis bedecked in clothes to signify his rank while he also grasps a tennis racket. Such a portrait (especially if it was the only one painted of Lady Frances' likeness during her life) would have served as a valuable and sentimental legacy item for her son – perhaps the only likeness of her for which he could remember her by. (Paul van Somer, *c.*1618/1620; Courtesy of Wikimedia Commons, Public Domain)

This fabulous Flemish painting, titled 'Children's Games', offers a fascinating look into the many games and activities enjoyed by children during the sixteenth century. Painted in 1560, it features dozens of popular pastimes – everything from leapfrog to playing shopkeeper, and allows us to see how children of the period engaged with their peers and enjoyed a bit of fun. (Pieter Brueghel the Elder, *c.*1560; Courtesy of Wikimedia Commons, Public Domain)

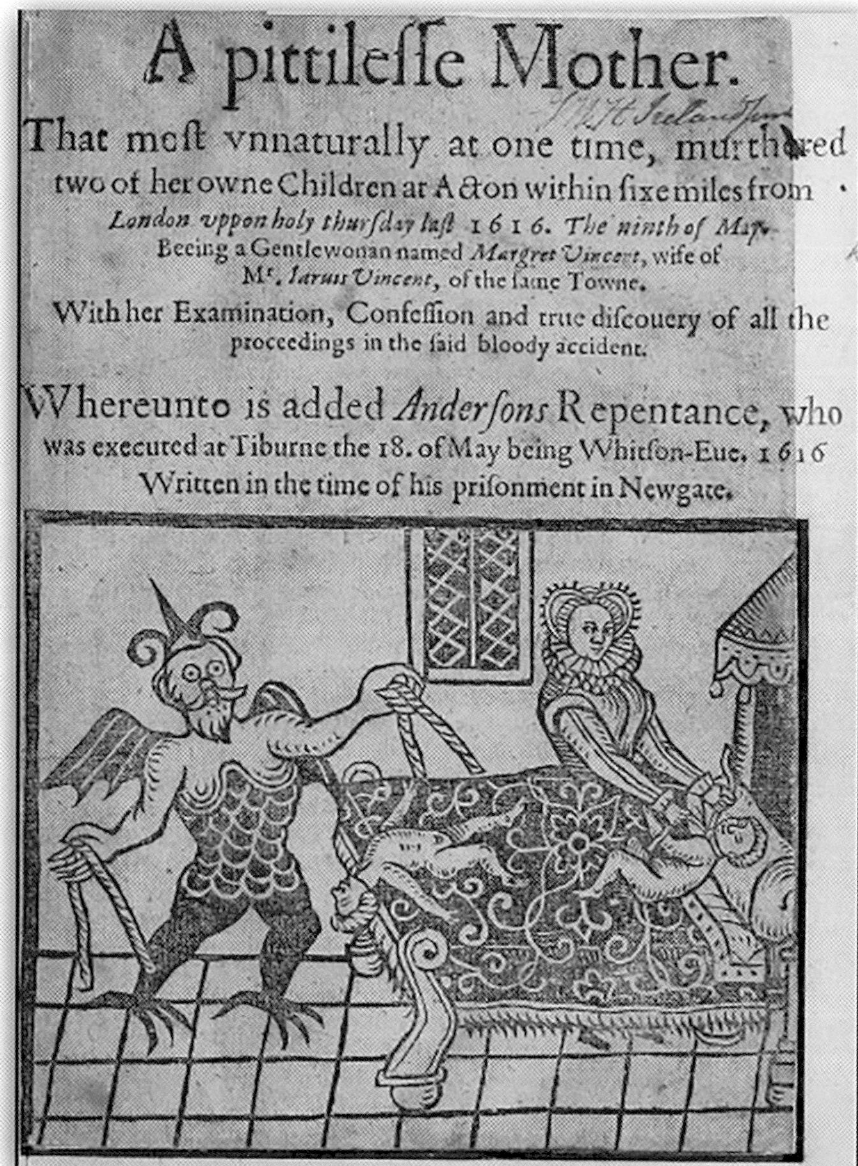

A pittileſſe Mother.

That moſt vnnaturally at one time, murthered two of her owne Children at Acton within ſixe miles from *London* vppon holy thurſday laſt 1616. The ninth of May. Beeing a Gentlewoman named *Margret Vincent*, wife of Mr. *Iaruis Vincent*, of the ſame Towne.

With her Examination, Confeſſion and true diſcouery of all the proceedings in the ſaid bloody accident.

Whereunto is added *Andersons* Repentance, who was executed at Tiburne the 18. of May being Whitſon-Eue. 1616 Written in the time of his priſonment in Newgate.

This pamphlet titled ‘A Pittilesse Mother’ was published in 1616 and details the tragic account of a mother who murdered two of her young children after a religious disagreement with her husband. The cover text reads: ‘A pittilesse Mother that most unnaturally at one time, murthered two of her owne Children at Acton within sixe miles from London uppon holy thursday last 1616 the ninth of May. Beeing a Gentlewoman named Margret Vincent, wife of Mr. Jarvis Vincent, of the same Towne. With her Examination, Confession, and true discovery of all the proceedings in the said bloody accident.’ (Unknown Author, *c.*1616; Courtesy of Wikimedia Commons, Public Domain)

The Valmarana family portrait, – while Italian, not English – depicts yet another beautiful example of a noble family of the sixteenth century. The mother and father, dressed in dark colours, are surrounded by their eight children who appear to span the ages of infancy through teenagerhood. In addition to the variety of garments and colours illustrated, we see several facial expressions and activities that everyone is engaging in, from the mother who holds her infant, to the child riding his hobby horse, and the teenage girl who is reading. Portraits such as these are fascinating insights into the potential family dynamics and structure of the period. (Giovanni Antonio Fasolo, Unknown Date; Courtesy of Wikimedia Commons, Public Domain)

This portrait depicts the family of Edward, Baron Windsor, who stands with his wife, Katherine de Vere and their four children. The elderly woman on the right has not been positively identified, though it is likely that she is either Edward's mother or perhaps the children's nurse. In either case, her importance to the family unit is noteworthy, given that she was included in this portrait. (Unknown Artist, *c*.1568; Courtesy of Wikimedia Commons, Public Domain)

Queen Elizabeth I's famous Chequers Ring is perhaps the most curious piece of surviving jewellery from the Tudor period. Believed to have been worn regularly by Elizabeth – even at the time of her death – it features two portraits within its ornately embellished locket compartment. Elizabeth's own profile is easily recognisable, but the second sitter's identity has been a matter of some debate. Some believe it to depict Elizabeth's mother, Anne Boleyn, perhaps signifying a connection and sentimentality for the mother she barely knew. Others have argued that it is more likely to be Elizabeth's fourth stepmother, Katherine Parr, with whom she shared a close connection for a time. Either way, the clear value that Elizabeth placed upon the ring perhaps proves an emotional and nostalgic connection she had shared between herself and a maternal figure. (Ann Longmore-Etheridge, 2009; Courtesy of Wikimedia Commons, Public Domain)

of an hedgehogge poudered is of the same virtue'. As a third dietary alternative, he recommended eating goats' claws dredged in powder, either crushed into a drink or consumed in pottage.[32] No behavioural guidance was offered (such as any specific toilet training practice) but rather Phaer's cure for bed-wetting focused on strengthening the bladder through specially prepared food. Presumably, toilet training was utilised by parents of sixteenth-century England, though scant information about their practices and methods exists today. We do have evidence of toddler toilets from the sixteenth century, however, thanks to a 1577 illustration of a small child on a training lavatory, complete with a safety bar that could hold the child securely in place.

This first age – a time of social learning, physical development, and the introduction of manners and faithfulness – was a vitally important time in a child's life. During these formative years, a sixteenth-century mother might have been hands-on in her child's development, or she may have overseen his or her care from a comfortable distance, perhaps as she simultaneously gave birth to another child or two. Much of her time would have been occupied with seeing to her children's needs, whether by financially providing for them or by supplying her own handmade clothes, nursery items, or toys. Still, a great deal more of her time (depending on her circumstances) might have been taken up with household tasks such as cooking, cleaning, or work – such as physical labour like tending fields or completing administrative tasks for her husband's business. A great deal of variety existed in the Tudor age for women of all social classes, so it is impossible to pinpoint the exact routine of a mother during the period, or how much she would have been physically involved in the early upbringing of her children. As is the case with many social topics of the Tudor (or any historical) period, virtually every aspect of a mother's involvement, attention, and knowledge of her young child's daily life depended on her social class, financial situation and overall lifestyle.

Chapter Twelve

Daily Life: Discipline and Play

Although it would have varied widely depending on the family, as well as the child's age, Hugh Rhodes provided a general guideline as to the typical expected daily schedule for a child in the Tudor period. He wrote to the Tudor child: 'Ryse you earely in the morning, for it hath propertyes three: Holynesse, health, and happy welth, as my Father taught mee. At syxe of the clocke, without delay, use commonly to ryse, and give God thanks for thy good rest when thou openest thyn eyes'.[1] Following the morning prayer, the child should blow their nose (always into a handkerchief, never a sleeve) and 'purge … other filthy things lyke case, thou knowest what I mean'.[2] They were then instructed to make their beds, sponge their clothes and clean their shoes before dressing for the day. Before greeting family members, their hands and faces should be washed, and finally, 'When that thy parents come in sight, doe to them reverence: Aske them blessing if they have bene long out of presence'.[3]

While all of this might have been the Tudor child's morning routine, the mother's morning would have looked quite a bit different. Sir Anthony Fitzherbert wrote specifically in *The Boke of Husbandry* (prior to the Reformation) of how a wife should rise and tend to the house in the morning. First, waking around four in the morning during the summer months, she should 'lyfte up thy hande' and make the sign of the cross, reciting her prayers – the Pater Noster (Our Father), Ave Maria and the Apostles' Creed. Following her prayers, she should 'swepe thy house, dresse up thy dyssheboard (dishboard), and sette all thynges in good order within thy house'. If she was a farmer's wife, she would be responsible for milking the cows before turning her attention to her children – to 'take uppe thy children and araye theym'. Once her children were clean, dressed and ready, she could return to the kitchen to prepare breakfast for the family.[4] Breakfast would be served a few hours after waking, perhaps around six o'clock, or shortly after the children woke. In 1577, William Harrison wrote that the English ate only twice a day, skipping breakfast entirely – except for children ('you hungry stomach[s] that cannot fast till dinnertime') – but this appears not to have been wholly true for the entire population, given other contemporary evidence.[5] Depending on the household and the family's resources, this meal could have consisted of simple bread and ale, or it might have included fried bacon, eggs, kippers, or porridge.[6] In wealthier families, it might have been more lavish and served by cooks and servants, rather than by the mother. This too, however, was known to vary, as the breakfasts of the Earl of Northumberland's two sons reportedly consisted only of 'basic household-bread, a small loaf or manchet of fine wheat bread, beer, and chicken or mutton bones'.[7] But for the majority of sixteenth-century society, the Tudor housewife would have prepared the meal, perhaps with some help from servants, and it would have been a sit-down affair for the whole family, perhaps minus her husband, whose workday often started around five o'clock, with a break for breakfast during the work morning.[8] Still, a dutiful and loving Tudor wife who had risen for the day around the same time as her husband, might have packed breakfast for him before he left home for the day.

Once the day had begun for the Tudor family, young children (prior to the age where they would begin any formal education) could likely expect to spend time with their mothers or nurses, engaging in a range of activities that depended, as with anything, upon their means and circumstances. Across social classes, however, there was an emphasis upon working on good manners. Courteousness and deference to parents and authority figures was paramount in the upbringing of young children, as a wide range of Tudor authors insisted. Parents (particularly mothers) were instructed by experts of the time period to avoid 'boorish' habits in their children, such as rudely squinting their eyes, picking their noses, or speaking with their mouths full.[9] Boys were to be taught differently from girls, of course, as the two sexes were very seldom treated the same. Parents should impress upon their sons to be bold and outgoing (while still always polite to elders), while girls should be meek and quiet in all that they did – to emulate the 'pleasant sobernesse that should be in a woman', as Sir Thomas Elyot put it.[10] Both boys and girls would have been taught the most basic gestures of respect – those of bowing and removing one's cap in a boy's case, and curtseying in a girl's – by the time they were about 4 or 5 years old.[11] They would be expected to refer to their parents as 'Sir' and 'Madam', and to rise from sitting whenever an elder entered the room.[12]

There were consequences for failing to adhere to such teachings, and for children engaging in any bad or discourteous behaviour. However, some writers of the time – such as Erasmus, writing in 1532 – described the lack of manners among children born of 'churls', 'carters', and 'ploughmen'.[13] He contrasted this with the good manners and respectability of children brought up among the elite. Similarly, William Harrison, a clergyman who wrote *The Description of England* in 1577, noted that children brought up in poorer families entirely lacked those critical qualities of manners and godliness. He went on further to write of English women as a whole – first commenting on their beauty and 'good proportion of limbs', but quickly deteriorating into harsh judgement of those women among the lower classes.

> This nevertheless I utterly mislike in the poorer sort of [women], for the wealthier do seldom offend herein, that, being of themselves without government, they are so careless in the education of their children (wherein their husband also are to be blamed), by means whereof very many of them, neither fearing God, neither regarding either manners or obedience, do oftentimes come to confusion, which (if any correction or discipline had been used toward them in youth) might have proved good members of their commonwealth and country by their good service and industry.[14]

The opposite was argued, however, by those who viewed the household servants employed in the houses of wealthy families as the culprits in teaching children poor manners – and even worse, foul language. Elyot specifically warned about this, noting:

> … we daily hear, to our great heaviness, children swear great oaths and speak lascivious and unclean words by the example of other[s] whom they hear, whereat the lewd parents do rejoice, soon after, or in this world, or elsewhere, to their great pain and torment.[15]

Others agreed with Elyot, such as an Oxford schoolmaster in the 1490s, who chastised careless parents with the following complaint: 'If [the children] happen to call the dame [mother] "whore" or the father "cuckold" (as it lucketh), they laugh thereat and take it for a sport, saying it is kind [natural] for children to be wanton in their youth'.[16] Assertions such as these, however, should be approached the same way one would approach a generalised view of today's parents and their supposed tolerance of children's swearing and disrespect. Were some sixteenth-century mothers and fathers more lenient in this regard? Probably, as we can infer from contemporary evidence, as well as our modern knowledge that no two sets of parents are identical in their morals or their teachings to their children. Respect for elders and an emphasis on courteous speech was, by and large, the golden rule for children in the Tudor period but as with anything, 'bad' behaviour was tolerated differently in different households likely up and down the social ladder.

It was necessary, many Tudor authors wrote, that parents should utilise proper discipline – often to include a fair amount of corporal punishment – on their children in order to attain proper behaviour. An early example of this teaching is in William Caxton's translated version of *Aesop's Fables* in 1484, just before the dawn of the Tudor period. The fable titled 'A Younge Thief and his Mother' opens with the line, 'He whiche is not chastised at the begynnynge is evyll and pervers at the ende'. It goes on to describe a story where a young boy begins to steal items and bring them home to his mother. Instead of chastising and disciplining him, she 'toke them gladly'. When he grows older, he is caught for his thieving and sentenced to hang. His mother – present at the gallows and weeping in distress at her son's conviction – catches his attention and he asks the justice for the opportunity to speak to her. When she is led towards him, he leans in as if to whisper something in her ear, but swiftly bites her nose instead. The justice is appalled, berating him for the action, to which he replies:

> My lords ye have no cause to blame me therefore, for my moder is cause of my deth. For yf she had wel chastised me, I had not come to this shame and vergoyne. For who loveth wel, wel he chastyseth. And therefore chastise wel youre children … that ye falle not in to suche a [case].[17]

This notion that parents must correct their children's unwanted behaviour from a young age was even popularised in contemporary entertainment during the period, such as in the Elizabethan play *July and Julian,* which featured 'a mother beating her daughter for failing to carry out some instruction'.[18] Corporal punishment was well documented by diarists and those who kept family records, such as Dr John Dee. He wrote the following about his 7-year-old daughter on 1 May 1589: 'Katharin by a blow on the eare given by her mother did bled at the nose very much, which did stay for an howre and more; afterward she did walk into the town with nurse; upon her coming home she bled agayn'.[19] Such punishments may have been meted out just as often by fathers as by mothers, and the degree to which they was administered, as well as their frequency, would have had great variability depending on the family. Just as it would be today, it is impossible to assume a generalised view of punishment and discipline in a sixteenth-century family, as parents' styles would naturally have differed, just as with the subject of swearing, already discussed.

On the subject of corporal punishment, it must be noted that there were parents during the Tudor period who took violence to an extreme with their children – even to the point of murder. One well-known example written in the early seventeenth century was the case of the 'Pittilesse Mother', Margaret Vincent, who strangled two of her children, aged 2 and 5, while her young infant was boarded away from home with a wet nurse. In this instance, the catalyst for murder was not misbehaviour from her children, but rather a religious disagreement that Margaret had had with her husband, regarding how the children should be educated. According to the contemporary scholar, John Chamberlain, the 'fanatical'

Catholic Margaret had been 'urged by her husband to conform her self, and to have her children otherwise educated, [but] she tooke this course to rid them out of the world rather then to have them brought up in our [Protestant] religion'.[20] The author of a 1616 pamphlet titled *The Pittilesse Mother,* which detailed this crime, admonished Margaret (who hung for her crimes) and lamented her children by writing:

> … by their own mother, who by nature should have cherished them with her own body, as the pelican that pecks her own breast to feed her young ones with her blood. But she, more cruel than the viper, the envenomed serpent, the snake, or any beast whatsoever, against all kind, takes away those lives to whom she first gave life.[21]

The vast majority of mothers during this time period would likely never have committed the crime that Margaret Vincent had and they were also far less likely to do so if they were married. As tragic as it was, most of the murders of children committed by their parents were by unmarried mothers, and usually quite soon after the birth – a crime known as neonaticide.[22] However, it is difficult to know exactly how many married mothers (and fathers) might have committed such a crime in a similar manner to Margaret, because the deaths of these children were much more likely to be attribute to accident. As Catherine Damme and Barbara Travitsky have uncovered and written about, 'it was the conflation of illegitimacy and infant death, or the use of undisguised violence that led to legal action, and to records'.[23]

Thankfully, such tragic instances were by no means normal during this period and indeed, most mothers would likely have only used corporal punishments against their children when deemed absolutely necessary (again, with variability). We know, for example, that some mothers wept and wailed when discovering that their own children had been beaten by their schoolmasters, let alone if hit at home. These women 'complaineth of the cruelty of teachers', according to the same Oxford schoolmasters who had complained about parents before, and as far as he was concerned, these mothers pampered and pandered to their sons at home.[24] Would they also have been the same mothers who beat their own children into submission? If we are to believe Erasmus and Harrison, such punishments were more likely to be seen among the upper classes, but according to Thomas Elyot and the Oxford schoolmasters writing in the 1490s about the pampered sons of wealthy families, the opposite was true. In fact, it is impossible to say with certainty who was more likely among Tudor parents to harshly discipline or utilise corporal punishment with their children but we have plenty of evidence to suggest that it happened, and with a frequency that most likely made it a relative 'norm' in Tudor parenting.

Mercifully however, although many Tudor parents practised harsh discipline with their children, they also valued and embraced the importance of fun and play. Childhood was not only to be a time of education and discipline, however important those things were. It was also meant to be an age for games, silliness and some degree of being carefree. Even Sir Thomas More emphasised this in his youth during the 1490s, with painted cloth illustrations paired with verses that demonstrated nine 'pageant verses'. The first one, called 'Childhood', displayed a young boy playing with a top and scourge, with the words:

> I am called Childhood, in play is all my mind, To cast a quoit, a cokstele and a ball, A top can I set and drive it in his king; But would to God these hateful books all Were in a fire burnt to powder small; Then might I lead my life always in play, which life God send me to mine ending day![25]

A top appears to have been a popular sixteenth-century toy for young children, as further evidenced by a character in the 1522 drama *The Worlde and the Chylde,* who also plays with a top.[26] As Thomas More's subject points out – and much like children of the modern day – it was likely a commonly expressed desire by children to play rather than to complete their schoolwork and until about the age of 7, this was acceptable and encouraged by caretakers. Younger children were often provided with toys, manufactured and priced to suit nearly any family's needs. There was everything from the aforementioned top to the simple cup and ball, to tin toy animal figurines. For younger babies, rattles were a commonly-gifted toy, while older children might have received hobby horses and dolls – the latter of which had already been around for centuries but was expanded upon in mid-sixteenth-century Germany with the advent of elaborate doll houses and accessories.[27] Toys were crafted from a variety of materials – from animal bone to wood, and even rags and straw, in the case of dolls made for poorer children. These items might have been hand selected and purchased by mothers and fathers – or even handmade – and gifted to children as a mark of affection. Among royal nurseries, it was likely more common that the king and queen (or their right-hand men) would have supplied the funds necessary to shower their fortunate children with the finest toys that money could buy. No matter the social class, toys were essential for Tudor children.

Just as important as toys, however, were games. Playfulness was seen and experienced by children in a multitude of formats and across all social classes, whether structured – as in a group of boys playing Blind Man's Bluff – or free-form, such as a young girl and boy playing make-believe with a mock bridal procession and ceremony. One of the best examples of this type of imaginary play comes again from Dr John Dee, who wrote in his diary on 22 January 1582 that his son 'Arthur Dee and Mary Herbert, they being but three yere old the eldest, did make as it wer a shew of childish marriage, of calling ech other husband and wife'.[28] Even the popular 'rock, paper, scissors' game had its sixteenth-century version for children.[29] Many recognisable games existed throughout the period, as evidenced by the extraordinary 1560 Dutch painting 'Children's Games' by Peter Brueghel, which depicts more than two hundred children involved in about eighty different games popular during the period. This painting is a remarkable resource, as it provides such an insightful view into some of the many games and activities enjoyed by sixteenth-century children. There are those riding each other like horses, rolling hoops across the village path (a game known as 'hoop trundling'), leaping over each other in the recognisable 'leapfrog' game, playing make-believe shopkeeper and customer, and more. The painting shows a sense of frivolity and merrymaking that we sometimes forget must have been customary to childhood, in a general sense, throughout any age of history. Game-playing and toy-wielding is nearly as natural to a child as is breathing, and it is refreshing to see that it appears this was the case even in the sixteenth century.

Of course, there were also those who sought an educational aspect to children's games, as the Spanish philosopher, Juan Luis Vives, clearly did. He emphasised that 'well-bred' girls were better off being entertained by 'chaste tales' and activities that would educate and better themselves for later life. Dolls, he argued, were akin to idolatry, and likely to teach a young girl to value fashion and finery over more humble and respectable things. In his view (and likely many others), it was better to disguise lessons in caring for a household or doing meaningful tasks with simple objects and games, which would allow the children to have fun, while not realising that they were also learning valuable skills for the future.[30] This is not far off of even some modern day parenting advice – to conceal useful, educational tasks with an enjoyable game that accomplishes two tasks at once. With this in mind, it is easy to imagine a Tudor mother utilising such tactics to teach her own young children to be helpful and knowledgeable within the household. Perhaps she used dolls to show a daughter how to assist in the care of her infant siblings (a task which was probably quite useful in standard, large sixteenth-century families) or maybe she created games that could assist with tidying up or preparing a family meal.

Songs and rhyming verse certainly had their place in Tudor England, with some of today's recognisable nursery rhymes having their origins – or some version, at least – in the sixteenth century. 'Three Blind Mice' is one such example, published in 1609 by the musician Thomas Ravenscroft with the lyrics: 'Three blind mice, three blind mice / Dame Julian, Dame Julian / The Miller and his merry old wife / She scraped her tripe, lick thou the knife'.[31] Children would likely have heard most songs such as this one at home, probably from mothers who sang to them. There would be no recognisable body of popular nursery rhymes until the eighteenth century, which proves that any rhyming verses used throughout the sixteenth century and still identifiable (in some form) today, must have been sung with some regularity by Tudor families. Similarly, short rhyming vignettes similar to the well-known 'Jack and Jill' (not recorded until the eighteenth century) existed among Tudor families and were probably used to entertain children. One example contained the following verse – predictably macabre, as nursery rhymes often are: 'Tom a lin and his wife, and his wife's mother / They went over a bridge all three together / The bridge was broken and they fell in / "The Devil go with all", quoth Tom a lin'.[32]

In cases where fathers were perhaps away from the home on travel or business, there is evidence of Tudor mothers updating their husbands through letter writing about their children's welfare. One excellent example is that of Margery Paston to her husband John, who was away from their Norwich home in January 1486. She wrote, 'To my mastyr, John Paston, be this delyvird', and proceeded to update and ask him about a number of things, including his welfare. Halfway through the brief letter, she wrote, 'Syr, your chyldryn be in goode helle [health], bellsside [blessed] be God'.[33] It is a short update that gives very little away about their children's wellbeing (they had at least two children under the age of 10 at this time), but it indicates that literate mothers had an interest in keeping their husbands abreast of the goings-on at home, at least as far as their children's health was concerned. As discussed in the previous chapter, the health of children and their avoidance of life-threatening diseases was one of the primary concerns of sixteenth-century parents.

To return to the daily schedule of a Tudor mother, however her day had been spent – and whether it was she or her hired staff who had seen to the children's welfare and entertainment for the day – she would likely have had to prepare a midday meal ('dinner') to be served somewhere between ten o'clock and noon; the earlier being the more fashionable dinnertime for aristocratic families, with lower classes eating a bit later. This was the largest of the daily meals – likely to be hot, if resources allowed for it, and with the most variety of ingredients. The Tudor housewife likely would have spent some time preparing this meal while her young children played, or if they were old enough, they may have assisted her. Once again, the poorest families might only have dined on bread, as they had for breakfast, but more fortunate families could have enjoyed a selection of roasted meats, fish, fruits and vegetables (more likely among the aristocracy), or most commonly, pottage – a thick soup consisting of vegetables, grains, and sometimes meat.[34] It is worth noting here that adults living England were generally expected to follow the religious rules around fasting, meaning they avoided eating meat every Friday of the year, as well as the vigils of forty different annual religious festivals and three 'Ember days' every quarter.[35] Children, however, were exempt from the requirement of fasting until they reached puberty – and sometimes even later – though different households would have had different views as it related to preparing their children for adulthood and fasting. In cases where the family employed cooks who catered to the dietary needs of adults, it is likely that children were taking part in fasting as well, regardless of official Church requirements.[36]

Roughly five hours after this midday meal – between four and five o'clock – the Tudor mother would need to prepare and serve the final meal of the day – supper – with enough time to eat and clean by the natural light of the day. This meal would have been lighter than dinner, perhaps consisting of porridge either made with milk or water. Lucky townspeople with disposable income also had the option of purchasing pre-cooked meals as takeaway suppers, which they could then eat at home with their families. And for a mere five per cent or so of the population, supper could be a repeat of the elaborate dinner affair, with an array of meats, vegetables, fruits and herbs, all meticulously prepared and elegantly served by household staff.[37] However it was enjoyed, supper would likely be the last family gathering of the day before evening prayers were said and children were shuffled off to bed, often with one very recognisable element that modern readers will appreciate.

Bedtime stories – and the general concept of mothers entertaining and settling their children to bed with storytelling – was probably just as familiar in Tudor times as it remains today. Stories are, and have always been, essential in childhood, and it appears from contemporary sources that this was no different in the sixteenth century. Whether or not a mother was literate, she could certainly tell her children stories – as could her husband, for that matter. The Clifford family, for example, chose to do this by passing down a familial story to their children, telling of their ancestor, Henry Lord Clifford, and how he had convincingly concealed himself as a shepherd boy during the Wars of the Roses some decades prior.[38] In fact, it is likely that many families did exactly this, though more often, they probably told of their ancestor's great achievements such as notable accolades, grand adventures, and military victories. Thus, these stories would serve dual purposes: firstly, to entertain and excite their children, while simultaneously engraining the triumphs of their ancestors into their offspring, likely with the hope that they would be known and told for generations to come. We can also safely presume that a great number of fictional stories were told, such as the tales of Robin Hood and King Arthur, both of which we know to have been cherished legends (the latter being somewhat believed by many) throughout the Tudor period.[39] Of course, biblical stories would also have been popular, probably more so after the 1530s, when the Bible was regularly read in English during church services, and parents could more easily repeat those stories to their children at home.[40]

Shakespeare's *The Merry Wives of Windsor* show us another way that Tudor parents used storytelling, apart from entertaining their children or lulling them to sleep. In this play, two wives – Mistress Ford and Mistress Page – recount the terrifying story of Herne the Hunter, a phantom hunter who supposedly haunts Windsor Great Park. The pirated version of the play notes that 'women to affright their little children say that he walks in shape of a great stag'.[41] Their full, frightening description in the play is as follows:

> There is an old tale goes that Herne the Hunter, Sometime a keeper here in Windsor Forest, Doth all the wintertime, at still midnight, Walk round about an oak, with great ragged horns, and There he blasts the tree, and takes the cattle, and [makes] milch-kine yield blood, and shakes a chain in a most hideous and dreadful manner.[42]

Frightening stories aside – and hopefully not being told before sending children to sleep – parents would have imposed a bedtime that was shortly after dark, often with more than one child being assigned to the same bed, once they were out of nursery.[43] Perhaps taking into account the guidance of Thomas Phaer in avoiding nightmares in children, a wise sixteenth-century mother would have made sure that her children had not eaten too much during the evening hours and that she did not rock them too fervently prior to bedtime to ensure that those pesky stomach vapours remained firmly in place.

Chapter Thirteen

Educating Sons and Daughters

When a child reached the age of about 7 years old – the age of 'adolescence' – it was often time for him or her to begin attending school, though no actual legal requirement for this existed in Tudor England.[1] According to Shakespeare, this was the time of the 'whining schoolboy with his satchel and shining morning face, creeping like a snail unwillingly to school'.[2] Parents could, and often did, choose to send their children off for some formal education around this age, however, because there was a myriad of benefits for both the child and the family as a whole. For one, learning to read – one of the critical skills taught in sixteenth-century classrooms – was essential in order for anyone in the period to improve his or her station in life. Boys who might grow up to be gentlemen would often be expected to hold some public office or take a job that required the writing and reading of documents, while children of both sexes would someday (perhaps) need to keep accurate accounts of household expenses, employees' salaries, family diaries and other similar records. Secondly, a family's ability to pay for their children's formal education of any kind was a sort of status symbol in Tudor England and of high value in terms of the family's reputation within the community.

Just the ability to pay pennies for a family's children to learn to read set them apart from those who could not afford to do so, and this alone was likely to make it worthwhile for a number of sixteenth-century mothers and fathers to scrounge together the money necessary. Even a 'free' education during the period (as some schools did not charge for attendance) would have cost a family money, simply in terms of the clothes their children were expected to wear, as well as their school supplies. One record for Richard Fermor, the son of an

Islington gentleman, shows he was required to have purchased 'a Greek grammar, a text of the Latin author Sallust, a pen, an inkhorn, paper, and a satchel to carry his books'. This reportedly cost his parents 6s. 8d. – the equivalent of approximately fifty-seven pounds today.[3] As such, it likely goes without saying that formal education was far more common among the middle and upper classes, while the majority of lower-class children were more likely to learn all that they needed to know about life and work from their parents, and they often began labouring from quite a young age.[4] Unsurprisingly, formal education was also far more likely to be sought out for boys than it was for girls.

Often, for the youngest of students needing only to learn to read, education could be done at home by a literate parent – usually a mother who had adequate time to devote to the task during the day. In wealthier households, the job might fall to a hired governess or tutor. This was indeed the case for royal children, whose households were generally staffed with a variety of tutors covering a number of different subjects around the time they turned 7. But for parents who fell in between these two options – those who were either illiterate themselves or lacked the time and resources to teach their own children the basics of elementary education – a formal teacher or school was required. Still, these teachers and 'schools' did not always look as one might expect. The act of 'sending one's children to school' could have been as basic as sending them next door to the literate textile worker, who could build in breaks throughout his day in order to instruct his pupil.[5] The cost of hiring such a teacher was relatively low and the type of instruction offered could vary between girls and boys, as parents deemed appropriate. A seamstress who was willing and able, for example, could take in young girls as pupils to learn spinning, sewing, or lacemaking.[6] Girls could, and certainly did, learn to read during the Tudor period, though with far less frequency than boys, and often only if they were among the upper classes of society. By the 1530s it was becoming more and more fashionable for the nobility to begin educating their daughters (generally at home, either by their mother or a hired governess), making it more likely that they might at least be able to read, and perhaps write, alongside their male counterparts. Still, records of female education in general across the Tudor period are sparse when compared to that of males.[7]

As for the age at which children were taught to read, it seems likely that this had actually begun around the age of 4 or 5, and that waiting too long to learn was a source of embarrassment for some children. One boy named Edward Herbert (later Lord Cherbury), born in 1583, for example, complained in his autobiography, 'my friends did not think fit to teach me so much as my alphabet until I was seven years old'.[8] The reason for this, according to him, was an affliction of the ears, which 'ceased' at the age of 7. Then, as he wrote, 'my schoolmaster in the house of my said lady grandmother began then to teach me the alphabet, and afterwards grammar, and other books commonly read in schools'.[9] Based on his writing, it is likely that more children learned to read during the Tudor period on a timeline more recognisable to children today. Reading, in general, was taught to children before writing.[10] Up until the Reformation had taken its firm hold over much of everyday English life, after the 1550s, a child would have first learned the alphabet, and reading in general, in Latin. The first reading materials probably given to a child to master were religious texts, or more likely the psalms from the Bible itself. As prayer and scripture had been used to teach a child to speak, so too could they be used to teach that child to read – and these books were obviously an easy enough resource for any mother, family member, or neighbour to reach for when tasked with teaching a child.[11]

While reading was arguably the most important subject taught to sixteenth-century children, other subjects – such as arithmetic – were common as well. The range of academic subjects branched out widely the further up the social ladder a child was, with royal children learning everything from philosophy to French to the natural sciences. While still a prince and heir to his father King Henry VIII, the young Prince Edward was instructed in a wide range of subjects, including philosophy, the liberal sciences, Greek and Roman classics, and geography – not to mention such gentlemanly subjects like etiquette and fencing.[12] His sister who was close in age, Princess Elizabeth, learned similarly to him by both her own tutors and the ones they both shared. She certainly learned reading and penmanship, as well as foreign languages, as she and Edward frequently wrote to each other in order to practise what they'd learned, as well as to engage in a little sibling rivalry.[13] Among those of slightly lower status, business skills were also taught – presumably mostly to boys – in order to prepare them to be successful in their future professional endeavours. By and large, the nature and breadth of academic subjects available to a child during the period depended greatly upon what his or her parents needed them to learn, and the resources and financial backing they were able to put toward that education.

Though Princess Elizabeth is an example of a well-educated Tudor girl, the subject of female education was debated among experts and academics. There were those who held the opinion that young girls should only be taught what was absolutely necessary for them in order to maintain a household, provide food and comfort for their future husband and attend to their wifely duties. Many questioned whether it could even be harmful for girls to be taught too much – particularly as it related to Latin and Greek languages. Richard Hyrde, who contributed to a translation of Erasmus' *Treatise on the Paternoster* in 1524, wrote of this mindset, though he himself disagreed with it. He wrote:

> I have heard many men put great doubt whether it should be expedient and requisite or not, a woman to have learning in books of Latin and Greek … Alleging for their opinion that the frail kind of woman, being inclined of their own courage unto vice and mutable at every novelty, if they should have skill in many things that be written in the Latin and Greek tongue … it would of likelihood both inflame their stomachs a great deal the more to that vice that men say they be too much given unto of their own nature already.[14]

Decades later, Thomas Becon wrote a contrasting perspective to this mainstream fear of female education. He considered it primarily a biblical duty for her to be well-learned, acknowledging that she should first and foremost be taught 'to be sober-minded, to love [her] husband, to love [her] children, to be discreet, chaste, housewifely, good, [and] obedient to [her] husband'.[15] But in order for her to be educated in virtue, he argued that she must be taught to read, at a minimum. This would benefit both herself and her entire future family as she would one day be at the helm of her own children's religious upbringing. In fact, he asked the pointed question, 'Can any thing be more necessary or godly in a Christian commonweal, than to bring up maids and young women virtuously, and to teach them?'[16] He therefore pushed for the building of female schools to be built in every town, guided by 'honest, sage, wise, discreet, sober, grave, and learned matrons', because as he further questioned:

> If it be thought convenient, as it is most convenient, that schools should be erected and set up for the right education and bringing up of the youth of the male kind, why should it not also be thought convenient that schools be built for the godly institution and virtuous bringing up of the youth of the female kind? Is not the woman the creature of God so well as the man? And as dear unto God as the man? Is not the woman a necessary member of the commonweal?[17]

Here, he even made an acknowledgement that mothers were often the ones instructing their children, when he asked, 'Can the mothers bring up their children virtuously, when they themselves be void of all virtue? Can that woman govern her house godly which knoweth not one point of godliness? Who seeth not now then, how necessary the virtuous education and bringing up of the woman-kind is?'[18] It was a convincing and impassioned argument from the former chaplain of Archbishop Thomas Cranmer, though even he acknowledged that some differences should remain between boys' and girls' education. Certain subjects were less likely to be needed by girls, though he stopped short of proclaiming them 'dangerous' for them, as previous writers had.[19]

Ultimately, girls were often afforded a basic education, but were prohibited from attending most grammar schools along with the boys (geared for children ages 7 and up), and especially universities (for those aged around 18 and up).[20] Even these, however, were not available to every boy, regardless of how bright he might have been, or how keen he would have been to further his education. For the vast majority of sixteenth-century children, basic elementary education was more than enough to get by in adulthood. Higher education, such as grammar schools and universities, were reserved only for those who had the status and the means to afford them and girls were almost universally barred from attending, even when they were more academically inclined than their male peers.[21] Richard Mulcaster, who wrote in the 1580s on the subject, actually went so far as to recognise how quickly and well girls tended to learn, even when compared to their male counterparts. He noted: 'We see young maidens be taught to read and write and can do both with praise; we hear them sing and play and both passing well; we know that they learn the best and finest of our learned languages to the admiration of all men'. When beginning this writing, however, he pointed out that he would first address the education of boys, because 'naturally the male is more worthy'.[22] It might have been somewhat progressive thought for the period, but it was surely slow progress, nonetheless.

Prior to schools being readily available to girls as they were for boys, it was largely up to the mother to provide a basic education for her daughters, even as she might have sent her sons off for more formal instruction outside of the house. Of course, the circumstances here varied but most women, especially of the upper classes, were likely able to teach their daughters the basics of 'reading, religion, sewing, embroidery, music, dancing, and cooking'.[23] One notable example of a mother-educated young woman was that of Rose Hickman, the daughter of a London merchant. She recalled that her mother had sent for reformist texts from the continent in order to instruct her three daughters about the new religion, and how she 'used to call me with my two sisters into her chamber to read to us out of the same good books very privately for fear of trouble because these good books were then accounted heretical'.[24] Other daughters of Tudor women recalled the sources used in order for their mothers to teach them to read, notably the Bible, or later in the century, John Foxe's *Acts and Monuments* and other similar religious works.[25]

Reading and needlework appear to have been two of the most critical skills afforded to young girls, if they were given the opportunity for an education at all. Lucky ones of higher status might additionally learn to write, but the majority of them would almost certainly not have been taught subjects such as science, math, or politics. The primary purpose of their education, no matter how extensive or lacking it might have been, was to prepare them for life as dutiful Christian wives and mothers, while their brothers were often simultaneously preparing for futures as businessmen, politicians, or other such professions. Even so, village schools did exist for girls as well as boys, even if they were not quite as numerous. These were often run by religious men – an example being one school in London, run by a priest named William Barbour between 1504 and 1515. He took in a total of thirty students, primarily focusing on religious doctrine.[26] Somewhat surprisingly, co-educational schools also existed, though it is difficult to say how common they were throughout the country. The majority of teachers in these schools were male, but some learned women acquired their own teaching licenses and ran schools of their own.[27]

The typical school day in Tudor England had to mirror the parents' working day, with early beginning hours – six o'clock in the summer, or seven o'clock in the winter – and ending the day around five or six o'clock in the evening. Breaks from learning were had, such as a breakfast break a couple of hours after lessons had begun, followed by another around eleven. At some schools, where the children's homes were within close proximity, children were afforded the opportunity to return home for the midday meal before resuming afternoon classes for another few hours.[28] In the case of boarding schools, where parents would have had to send their children away to live and learn in the same place, daily trips home for meals were obviously impossible, so children would eat together. Again, if children were within walking distance of their school, punctuality mattered, and any tardiness (or worse, truancy) was cause for punishment – often taking the form of a beating by the school master. As such, mothers would often accompany their children on the walk to school, or send a servant to accompany them, to ensure that they arrived safely and in time for lessons.[29] Any corporal punishment that might have been meted out against children during the school day (not uncommon during the period) would likely have been noticed by mothers in the evening, perhaps when washing or changing clothes. These punishments had often been administered with either a ferule or palmer (flat strips of wood, or spoon-shaped instruments meant to smack the hands) for minor infractions, or a bundle of twigs called a birch. This secondary punishment was reserved for greater offenses, and typically carried out by the schoolmaster himself, as opposed to prefects. In these cases, another pupil would have needed to hold the offending student still while his shirt and drawers were pulled aside – the birch then being struck against his bare bottom.[30] In either case, such punishments would have certainly resulted in visible wounds, which were likely shocking to a great number of mothers. And as seen in the previous chapter, such discoveries were often met with her tears and distress, which might have then led to confrontations with the offending teachers.

Schoolmaster, Nicholas Udall, of Eton, between 1534 and 1542, was one notorious example of a harsh disciplinarian with his students. His brutality was recalled by former student Thomas Tusser, who later went on to become a poet. He wrote, regarding Udall:

> From Paules I went, to Eaton sent,
> To learn straight waies, the latin phraies,
> Where fiftie three stripes given to mee, at once I had:
> For fault but small, or none at all,
> It came to pas, thus beat I was,
> See Udall see, the mercie of thee, to me poore lad.[31]

Even so, school was not entirely a source of trepidation and dread for sixteenth-century students. In fact, it was likely much the same as it is now for modern children – a time to socialise with peers, engage in some amount of youthful fun, while also needing to attend to the serious business of the school day. All of this was done while hopefully avoiding getting into too much trouble. As Shakespeare referred to the school-aged child 'creeping like [a] snail unwillingly to school', the fellow Elizabethan, Francis Segar, also described them at the end of the school day – of 'running like a heap of bees … whooping and hallooing as in hunting the fox'.[32] With these descriptions in mind, it is easy to imagine a child very much like those of today, running excitedly home after a long day of lessons.

What might have awaited them at home was likely a prepared supper, as well as the opportunity for some play and recreation, and depending on the age, some household chores or additional domestic lessons. Girls, especially, might have been required to spend a few hours after the school day working on their needlework or taking instruction from their mothers in some other similar skill. She might also have been expected to assist in preparing supper, or cleaning up afterwards, while her brother might have been called to assist his father with some manual labour before preparing for bed. The Tudor family's daily life was recognisable in some of these ways, as parents aimed to prepare their children from a very early age how to be constructive, contributing members of their families. And this was with good reason, for as we will see in the next chapter, even these young, school-aged children were not far off from beginning their working lives.

Chapter Fourteen

Parenting the Adolescent

The period of time in which a sixteenth-century mother would have raised, and perhaps educated, a school-aged child, as discussed in the previous chapter, could have spanned several years. Her daily life – attending to her household duties, perhaps working alongside her husband, caring for her children, accompanying them to and from school, and preparing meals – might have looked largely the same from day-to-day, and lasted from the time her child was around 3 or 4 until they reached the age of adolescence. As it should be clear by now, her circumstances within these many years would have looked remarkably different, based on a number of factors, such as her job (if she had one), the daily responsibilities required by her class and social status, whether or not her children were attending grammar school, boarding away for their education, or living at home, and finally – perhaps most critically – how many pregnancies she had endured or was in the process of enduring. It mustn't be overlooked that the typical Tudor woman was likely pregnant every other year or so, which might have resulted in eight-to-twelve pregnancies within her childbearing married years, on average.[1] Caring for children and perhaps seeing to their educational and foundational needs as they approached adolescence, while also continuing to birth children and care for infants throughout those years, would have taken an understandable toll on the average woman. Perhaps it should come as little surprise then, that around the onset of puberty, children were often sent out of the home to pursue the next chapter of their lives – that of service and work.

Of course, Tudor mothers and fathers were not sending their children away simply because they were overwhelmed by the chaos of a bustling household, many mouths to feed, and near-constant pregnancies – though one might forgive them if that were the case. Sending their children into the homes and service of others, in fact, was the expected path for the majority of families across social classes, for a number of important reasons. For one, a lower-class boy whose future was not destined to include boarding school or a university education, would have been required to begin working and earning a living as early as possible. In fact, it was only a small minority of children who would go on to higher education during the Tudor period, so entering the workforce was considered the norm for most of the young population as they approached their teenage years. Thus, the age of apprenticeship began around the onset of adolescence, when he could learn from a tradesman, shopkeeper, farmer, or merchant and begin his servitude and on-the-job training. Yeomen, or wealthier farmers, could employ teenage boys as farm servants, who were able to help with agricultural tasks and the caretaking of livestock, and this might set him up well with the skills he would one day need in order to establish his own career and support himself in the future.

Girls, likewise, could enter the homes of other older women of similar status, in order to fine-tune their domestic skills and improve upon all that they had learned at home under their own mother's tutelage. They could also be hired alongside their male peers by farmers, for house work and dairy production.[2] Another option for them, of course, was to begin their lives as servants in the households of gentlemen.[3] This was by no means an undesirable or frowned upon position to hold for a girl during the period, because the skills she would learn as a servant would certainly benefit her in later years. As a future wife, she would also be expected to 'serve' her husband and to be experienced with house care and domestic duties.[4] In fact, young men in search of a bride in later years were advised to look first at her 'capacity to work rather than riches', even if that meant she was a 'servant in some degree'.[5] This proves the importance of such female skills, and that there was certainly no shame in servitude. A mother sending her daughter off to work as a servant would likely have been glad that she was gaining valuable life experiences and training to become a successful housewife. But whatever the circumstance or work opportunity, for boys and girls starting around the age of 10 (perhaps slightly older), it was time to begin the transition into adult life. A Salisbury parish list from 1533 reveals that one-third of young women that year were in service, as well as half of the men.[6]

The aristocracy and nobility also had much to gain for their children by securing a place for them in another household of similar status, because those children would broaden their own social circles and perhaps acquire themselves a patron. This patron could be someone who might later introduce them to various career opportunities, marriage prospects, or perhaps simply act as a valuable contact for them to call upon, should they need to in the future.[7] Henry Lord Stafford, son of Henry VIII's former friend, the later executed Edward, Duke of Buckingham, is a great example of a father who arranged exactly such positions for his own children. His son, also named Henry, was sent to the household of Thomas Wriothesley for a time, before later transferring to the home of Edward Seymour, Duke of Somerset. In both of these cases, Stafford's heir was in close proximity and serving some of the most notable names and high-ranking men in England at the time. His younger brother, Thomas, served another grand figure – Sir William Paulet, the Lord High Treasurer and Lord Keeper of the Great Seal. He, too, was a fine example of a Tudor man to emulate for the young Stafford. Their sisters were dispersed among the households of notable noble women, such as the Countess of Salisbury, the Duchess of Norfolk, the Countess of Arundel, and the Dowager Queen Katherine Parr, widow of Henry VIII.[8] In all of these houses, the Stafford girls would have humbly served their mistresses along with a number of other serving girls, while simultaneously observing and learning how these grand women ran and structured their households. Such a hands-on education was vital for their own future marriages and homes, as they would hope to one day emulate all that they had learned. Of course, for the upper crust of society, the most coveted of all households to send daughters to serve in was that of the queen of England, as well as those of other notable ladies of the court. Understandably, such positions were difficult to come by.

One young lady who desired exactly this job was young Katharine Bassett, daughter of Honor Grenville, Viscountess Lisle. While serving in the household of Lady Eleanor Rutland in 1539, she wrote the following to her mother, beseeching her help in the matter:

> Madame, the cause of my writing to your ladyship is, that we hear say that the King's Grace shall be married, and my

> lord and lady as yet doth hear no word of their coming up to London. Wherefore I desire your ladyship that ye will be so good lady and mother unto me as to speak that I may be one of the Queen's mades, for I have no trust in none other but your ladyship to speak for me in that cause.[9]

In response, Lady Lisle made the request of both the Countess of Rutland and John Norris, both of whom told her to be patient, as neither the king nor queen were appointing maids to the household at that time.[10] After further contacting a woman referred to as 'Mother Lowe' by the Countess of Rutland, Lady Lisle's connections and correspondence were finally successful. Katharine Bassett was promoted to Anne of Cleves' household sometime in 1540, though Anne was no longer the king's wife by this time.[11] In any case, this collection of surviving letters between mother and daughter, from a highly connected and esteemed family, demonstrates the strings pulled and favour sought by Lady Lisle to help Katharine into a coveted position at court. Similar situations of mothers assisting children into employment opportunities undoubtedly existed across social classes, but not all of them would have been so formal or successful as the above example.

In fact, positions at the royal court in general were quite limited, though opportunities abounded for young people among all social classes to work and learn in that environment. An account from 1471–2 (just prior to the advent of the Tudor Dynasty) lists around fifty young people as serving in the royal household, ranging widely from high-to-low status. At the highest end, there were young noblemen known as 'henchmen', who were gaining a nobleman's education along with their aristocratic peers. These young men learned manners, social skills, sports, and foreign languages, likely alongside the heirs to the throne. Below the henchmen were choristers, who were trained in the royal chapel to play and sing holy music. Some of these, depending on the pitch required in their voices, would have been prepubescent, while others were teenagers. Finally, there were the lowliest of child workers in the royal household – the servants, who staffed virtually every department.[12] A similar structure of childhood employment can be seen in the great households of the nobility – an example being Henry

Algernon Percy, Earl of Northumberland, who in 1512 had employed around thirty young people to serve himself and his family.[13]

The practice of sending one's children out of the home for work experience, and in a sense, a furthering of their education, was commonplace among sixteenth-century families in England, and for yet another recognisable reason. Modern parents might be able to attest to the fact that children (particularly teenagers) often respond better when instructed by adults who are not their own parents. This appears to have been understood and appreciated in Tudor times as well, as argued by Jeremy Goldberg of the University of York. He acknowledged that while parents could teach their own children certain things, '[children could] learn other things and different things and more things if [they got] experience of being trained by someone else'. This belief was echoed even in other parts of Europe, and throughout the medieval period leading up to the sixteenth century. Fourteenth-century Italians had acknowledged that unruly teenagers often needed to be sent away to 'another country … or close friends' because it was believed that while he remained with his own parents, 'he will not mend his ways'.[14] But no matter how universal some of this reasoning and understanding had been, or for how many years the practice had been known and utilised by parents, the act of sending one's children away from home at such a young age was met with criticism by some outsiders. A Venetian ambassador writing around 1500 wrote home to his employers in Italy with a particularly scathing report of this practice, saying:

> … having kept [their children] at home till they arrive at the age of seven or nine years at the utmost, [parents] put them out, both males and females, to hard service in the houses of other people, binding them generally for another seven or nine years. And these are called apprentices, and during that time they perform all the most menial offices; and few are born who are exempted from this fate, for everyone, however rich he may be, sends away his children into the houses of others whilst he, in return, receives those of strangers into his own. And on inquiring their reason for

> this severity, [the parents] answered that they did it in order that their children might learn better manners.

He further offered his view of sixteenth-century English parents in general, saying they had 'a want of affection' towards their own children, and that he believed 'they do it because they like to enjoy all their comforts themselves'.[15] He went on to say that he might have forgiven the English parents their 'want of affection' in sending their children away, if only they would one day bring them back home at the end of their apprenticeships, but this was not the case. Rather, he said, 'they never return, for the girls are settled by their patrons, and the boys make the best marriages they can, and, assisted by their patrons, not by their fathers, they also open a house and strive diligently by this means to make some fortune for themselves'.[16] He insisted that Tudor parents preferred to house other people's children rather than their own during this life stage, as they could get away with feeding those children less while simultaneously working them harder than they would their own.[17]

While this paints a rather bleak picture of Tudor parents and the way they viewed and assisted their own children through such transitional years, it must be noted that this ambassador got quite a few things wrong in his assessment. Nicholas Orme, who has written extensively on sixteenth-century children and their upbringing, has pointed out that this author 'set the age for leaving home too low'. He cites the fact that the historical record reveals that very few children left home before the age of 10 – and more likely 15.[18] Also, the Venetian author neglected to recognise the many benefits that these children could gain by being exposed to other families, and the personal and professional connections they were likely to acquire. Marriage prospects were, indeed, a driving force behind sending adolescents (beyond the onset of puberty) to an employer who might play the role of matchmaker and arrange for a union that the child's own parents would have been unable to achieve. And even when marriage was not the primary concern – when work experience, instead, was paramount – the arrangement was beneficial, in that it likely introduced children to work that differed from that of their own parents. Farms were staffed with young male farm hands and servants, artisans hired young apprentices, and inns and bakeries were staffed with young women.[19] Up and down the social ladder, Tudor children were exposed to a range of employment opportunities meant to benefit *them* first and their families second, unlike the Venetian ambassador's negative interpretation.

Of course, it must be acknowledged that children's employment could also often be used by parents to help make ends meet. This was true in particularly dire circumstances, such as the sad case of Alice Reeded. A 40-year-old mother of four in 1570, her husband had left her with the children (including an infant that she was still breastfeeding), and she was obliged to learn how to spin wool in order to make her rent and put food on the table. As she did so, she sent her two older children – a 14-year-old daughter and 9-year-old son – out into the workforce to earn money spinning fabric. In this case, the children's work experiences were directly meant to keep their struggling family afloat and support their impoverished lifestyle. A similar case was that of the widow Anne King, who also spun cloth and had her 17-year-old daughter out working to help finance the room they rented together.[20] This was probably a very common story throughout sixteenth-century England, particularly for mothers who had been abandoned or widowed by their husbands and now needed their children to step up and start financially contributing.

How such employment and apprenticeship arrangements came to be depended on the family's connections, or lack thereof. Many families might have organised a plan for their child's employment with a friend or acquaintance, or even another family member. Wealthier families were known to occasionally house a relative of lower social class, as a 'favour' to his or her parents and a way of enlarging the young individual's connections. In this sense, there was a route available to such a youngster for improving upon the social class he or she was born into, and this might have been a lucky break. Another alternative to finding employment for young people was at a 'hiring fair', held throughout many villages and cities for employers to find potential servants and workers.[21] There, young men looking for work might be accompanied by their parents and lined up to wait for employers to approach and recruit them.

It should be noted that, although this chapter has discussed employment opportunities for adolescents (such as household servitude) as well as apprenticeships, these were two very distinct things. The reason that they are grouped together in discussion here is simply due to the typically similar ages that sixteenth-century children began each of these life experiences. In general, child servants were hired on a very limited basis, typically only serving their masters for a year or so before moving on to a new opportunity. These were also very often only verbal agreements, rather than contractual ones.[22] This type of limited, less formal service was not necessarily a career starter, either. It was unusual in the Tudor period, for example, for a young servant girl to remain a servant after she married and started her own family, though the skills she learned while employed as a servant would be useful in her future life.[23] Rather, this type of work experience was seen as a transitional period – a way of gaining knowledge, perhaps making a little money, and hopefully forging meaningful connections and references for the future. For a great many parents and their children, the hope was also that marriage matches might be made – or at least, introduced.

An apprentice, however, was contractually obligated to his employer – typically a craftsman, shopkeeper, or merchant – for at least a handful of years, with the full expectation that he would become proficient in the skill or trade that he was learning, and thus begin a true career of the same sort.[24] Every child that left home as a teenager in order to find work, therefore, was not an 'apprentice' unless it was formally agreed upon and sanctioned by the law, as there were restrictions on who was allowed to hire apprentices and under what conditions. Once a young person (typically a boy, but sometimes girls) entered into an apprenticeship, their master acted as their legal guardian and parent in many ways. In fact, this was true for both apprentices and servants alike. In either case, the child's mother and father no longer provided financially for their care or offered them any real parental attention once they left home. An example of this in a Tudor servant is the 19-year-old Elizabeth Barton, who was employed as a household servant in 1525 by a gentleman named Thomas Cobb. Shortly after her employment began, she fell seriously ill and it was Cobb, rather than herself or her parents, who paid for her food and medical care while she recovered, even as she could perform none of her household duties.[25] It was the same situation for an apprentice, where one of the master's primary duties was to provide care and comforts for his employee.

Both of these arrangements came with a set of clear expectations and rules, though in the latter's case, these rules were written and signed upon by both employer and apprentice. The expectation of good behaviour in an employee or apprentice was a given and punishments (often corporal) were known to be meted out by masters and employers. Grace Sharington wrote, 'I have seen my father [Sir Henry] with his own hands (for example's sake) scourge a young man naked from the girdle upwards, with fresh rods, for … a saucy and irreverent behaviour towards us his children', before dismissing him from employment.[26] An example of the explicitly written expectations of behaviour during an apprenticeship is the employment contract for William Johnson of Kingston-upon-Thames, who became an apprentice tailor to Robert Paltock in 1566. His contract stipulated the following:

> The tailor was to teach him all his craft, hiding nothing, and provide him with lodging, food, drink, clothes, and shoes appropriate for a servant. He undertook to make small payments to Johnson during the first seven years, and wages of 30s. in the eighth. In return, Johnson promised to keep his master's secrets and not to waste or lend his master's goods without permission. He was forbidden to play with dice, cards, or unlawful games; to visit taverns or ale-houses except with his master's leave, to engage in fornication with any of his master's household, or to leave his employment or marry without consent.[27]

Girls were only occasionally apprenticed during the sixteenth century, with numbers quite low in London, and only slightly higher in other towns around England. Most often, female apprentices were taught skills such as dressmaking and instructed by the wives of their masters. An example is Helen ap Richard, who was apprenticed by a master seamstress in Bristol in 1542, contracted to the typical seven years of work and on-the-job training.[28] Much less frequently were young women apprenticed and taught by men, though it did happen on occasion. Girls who took part in apprenticeships were usually meant to learn the 'art of housewifeship', as skills that fell under this umbrella set them apart from males. Cooking, cleaning, sewing, and caring for a home were (as we have previously discussed) the most pressing lessons a young Tudor lady could learn. But as a fair number of girls would grow up to support their future husbands' businesses, they were sometimes taught these skills as well. Least often were the apprenticeships for girls in male-dominated trades, though they were seen on occasion throughout the period.[29]

Though apprenticeships generally consisted of long, gruelling days of work consistent with those of adults, they were invaluable to a youth as he or she entered the workforce. The successful completion of such an apprenticeship would, in many cases, set a young man (now likely in his late teens, or even twenty) up for a mature entry into his community as an adult citizen, or 'freeman'.[30] He would be seen as a skilled and competent worker in his field and able to begin his career immediately. This meant that if a Tudor mother's son left home around the age of 12 or 13 to begin his apprenticeship, he would very likely never return home as the completion of his apprenticeship contract would mark the beginning of his independent, adult life. Of course, this probably came with a fair bit of variability depending on the family and individual situation, but it is striking to consider that adolescents would have left their parents' homes at such a young age, perhaps never to return. Compared with the general age of independence for children in the modern era (typically around 18), this difference is profound. Tudor mothers parted with their children far earlier than we modern mothers do, assisting them in finding work opportunities and living arrangements outside of the family home around seven to ten years earlier than the youth of today.

So, what did sixteenth-century mothers do once their adolescent children were out of the house gaining work experience? First, it mustn't be forgotten that the average mother would likely have had other younger children still to attend to – perhaps several. The ages of her children might have spanned so significantly that while she had one 13-year-old entering an apprenticeship and leaving home, she was preparing to give birth to yet another baby. By this time (likely around the age of 40) she would have been at or nearing the end of her childbearing age, but might still have been in the throes of pregnancy and childbirth for another few years. Second, while she tended to whatever other young children remained in her care (as well as seeing to her household and wifely duties and perhaps her own job responsibilities), she might also have been housing adolescents other than her own. If she had a particular skill that she was able to impart upon a teenager of another family, then someone else might have sent her their child to be trained, taught, and housed – while she had sent her own child of a similar age away for the same purpose. This was certainly not always the case (every Tudor family did not necessarily take in another couple's teenage child), but it should be acknowledged that it was a possibility. If she had taken on a pupil, apprentice, or employee – or if her husband had – then she would have had the same responsibility to feed, house, and clothe him or her, just as she did her own children. Doing so might have reinforced her sentimentality towards her own teenage children who were no longer at home. We can assume that a great many mothers would have certainly maintained correspondence with their adolescent children who had moved out. But of course, this would only have been possible if both she and her children were literate and able to write letters to one another.

Based on medieval accounts, the process of leaving home for a teenager was often a painful and traumatic one, with one medieval letter stating: 'For all that was to me a pleasure when I was a child, from three years old to ten … while I was under my father and mother's keeping, be turned now to torments and pain'.[31] This experience might often have resulted in the adolescent wanting to keep in touch with the parents left behind, though the frequency with which this was actually done is difficult to know. Travelling to visit one's parents might also have been difficult, if not impossible, once the adolescent left home, depending on how far away they had been sent. The most fortunate cases might have been those where a child was sent to a nearby neighbour or resident within the same town as their own family, so frequent visits between parents and children could be possible. But for many, this was likely not the case.

Though these are not English examples, letters from sixteenth-century Nuremberg, Germany offer glimpses into the correspondence received from mothers and their children who had left home to start apprenticeships during the period. One of these letters, written by Michael Behaim in the 1520s, living and apprenticing far from home in Milan, complained to his mother about how he was being made to sweep the floors at his master's business, rather than actually learning the trade he was meant to be taught. Another 14-year-old son of the same family later in the period, named Friedrich, also wrote to his mother from school. In his letter, he asked her to send him goods 'to keep up appearances with his peers, and wondered who would do his laundry'. In response, his mother sent him three shirts, along with the warning that 'they may still be a bit damp so you should hang them over a window for a while'. She even suggested that he use the sack for his own laundry, offering motherly wisdom and practical advice even from a distance.[32] Like any good mother would want to do, she provided for him as best she could even while he was employed and housed by a master.

A later example, this time from England, returns us to the well-known and influential Paston family, specifically to Lady Katherine Paston. She wrote to her son, William, while he was away at Corpus Christi College at the University of Cambridge on 11 June 1624, and though the letter is lengthy, it is worth quoting nearly in full, as it is an exceptional example of a mother's concern for her son while he was away from home. It begins with the salutation, 'To my very wellbeloved sonne William Paston,' and continues:

> I doe much desire to heer how you doe, I hope you have received my late letters written to mr Roberts and you:/ take heed to your selfe good child, that I may here a good report of your Civill and kinde behaviour towards all. But cheeffiy [chiefly] have an espetiall care to fear and serve god: lett it be the first and last thinge you thinke of and then be sure the blesinge of the almighty will preserve you in all your ways.

Predictably, Lady Katherine's 'chief' concern for her son at university is that he is taking his faith seriously and commending himself to God. This goes along with the theme of sixteenth-century parenthood that we have covered in previous chapters – that raising children to be God-fearing good Christians was the single most important duty as a mother. She goes on to add further practical advice and motherly wisdom: 'Take heed of frute of all sorts if you eate any. Eate very moderately for to much ocation ofte times much sikenes'. She then mentions that she is sending 'a pece of gowld for a token' before signing off, 'thy most Lovinge Mother, Katherine Paston'.[33]

These letters detailed above offer fascinating examples of motherly words of affection and advice during the period regarding the washing of dirty laundry and taking care not to overeat. Countless other similar letters exist in the exceptionally preserved collection known as the Lisle Letters, detailing daily life, childrearing accounts, and correspondence between parents and children during their years apart. These are written much the same as the above example between Katherine and William Paston, and give further insight into the regular updates and well-wishes they received from each other.[34] We can be sure that many other similar letters were sent by concerned mothers missing their children, whether they were away for work or school. Though the majority have been lost to history, viewing examples such as these remind us modern readers of the humanity and familiarity shared between mothers and their growing children from centuries ago. Their cares and concerns were not so different from those of today. This evidence shows that they tried to offer support, love and care to their adolescent children however they could during this transitional period, if only they had the means and literacy necessary to do so.

Chapter Fifteen

The Ageing Mother and Her Adult Children

A typical Tudor mother might have had many years of daily life consisting of the descriptions detailed in the previous several chapters, as her active childbearing years likely spanned between the onset of her marriage around her mid-twenties until she was between the age of 40 and 50. 'Old age' is difficult to define in sixteenth-century terms, as different people had differing perspectives. In general, it landed somewhere between age 40 and 60, with one medieval writer even pointing to 35.[1] In reality, the perception of old age probably had quite a lot to do with what the individual woman looked like as she approached age 40 and beyond. A life of hard manual labour, living and working in rough conditions, and perhaps a great number of pregnancies could have aged her outward appearance well beyond her actual years, causing 'age spots, facial hair, a stooped posture, and missing teeth', to say nothing of wrinkles, a worn complexion, and increased weight.[2] The degree to which each woman experienced these physical changes would have varied significantly, and might have played a role in how 'old' she was alleged to be by her peers.

Naturally, an obvious signifier of a woman's ageing body was the onset of menopause – the cessation of menstruation and the end of her fertility. Though the term 'menopause' was not used until the eighteenth century, the process by which the female body stopped menstruating in later years was understood by both men and women of the Tudor period. As is the case today, the age that a woman might have experienced menopause had some variability, but probably most often took place between the ages of 40 and 55, coinciding with the general understanding of 'old age'. In fact, many people during the period placed the onset of menopause right at the specific age of 49, based on the Hippocratic 'seven ages of man' theory, popularised by Shakespeare. The theory touted that man (and woman) reached a significant physical change every seven years. Roughly a century later, this would be expounded upon by a physician named John Friend, who wrote, 'The menstruous Purgation, or a flux of Blood issuing from the Uterus every Month, usually begins its Periods at the *Second Septenary,* and terminates at the *Seventh,* or the Square of the number Seven'. He noted, however, that there was inconsistency from woman to woman regarding this timing – that 'there are others whom it forsakes not at the forty-ninth; besides the relations we have of Women altogether free from it'.[3] It was not a singular event, but rather a gradual changing of a woman's courses (her 'flowers', 'terms', or whatever she chose to call them). The type of menstruation she experienced might have begun to change around the time she turned 40, as evidenced by letters on the subject, written by Lady Brilliana Conway, who lived from 1598 to 1643. An early modern physician noted these natural changes, explaining, 'Nature is always so kind to let [women] know' – through irregular menstruation such as abnormally heavy or even missed periods from month-to-month.[4]

To return to the Humoural Theory – the basis for which all bodily functions were understood during the sixteenth century – the period of menopause in an ageing woman was believed to be related to her body drying out. As such, she was believed to have less excess blood for her body to purge. This was explained by James Drake, who wrote in the following century:

> About the time of Puberty or Eruption of the *Menses* the Breasts begin to swell, and grow prominent, probably from a greater Afflux of Humours at that time, which not only fill the Vessels, but dilate the Substance of them; which Opinion is confirm'd by their shrinking when Age renders them unfit for Procreation, and their *Menses* deserts them.[5]

The drying-out of the ageing woman's body was, in a sense, a morphing of her femaleness into maleness, taking on an overall dryer constitution, and thus becoming more manly – which was even further emphasised due to things like facial hair that might have begun to appear as a woman aged. In fact, this phenomenon and belief was even noted by Shakespeare in *Macbeth*, who had Lady Macbeth begging the spirits to 'unsex' her – to remove her femininity as she tried to encourage her husband to murder King Duncan. 'Make thick my blood', she said. 'Stop up th' access and passage to remorse/That no compunctious visitings of nature/Shake my fell purpose.'[6] Clearly, as this play was first performed in the early Stuart Dynasty, Shakespeare believed his audience to be familiar with the concept of a woman losing her femininity – and perhaps some of her weakness and frailty – when she was no longer menstruating. This is striking because it creates an image of an ageing sixteenth-century woman who was now viewed less as a woman than she previously was, and there were certainly further implications to that, which we will explore later in this chapter.

It is important to note the great variability in age that a sixteenth-century mother might be parenting her adult children, and even reaching a new phase of parenthood – that of becoming a grandmother. First, though, was the ageing parents' involvement in their adult child's betrothal and marriage. Well before the births of grandchildren (in most cases) was the arrangement of marriages – or at least, hopefully, the approval and blessing of them. We have covered already how intimately acquainted most sixteenth-century parents needed to be in the plans for their children's marriages, because these unions affected a number of things, not least of all the family's financial status and placement within their society. And so, the cycle from chapter four continues here. Just as the typical Tudor mother would have likely had her own parents involved in the arrangement or blessing of her union, so would she now have the same jurisdiction over that of her own children – along with her husband, of course. We can assume that this was a period fraught with tension for many families during the period, perhaps in situations where the children and parents disagreed on the subject.

We must remember that many of these adult children – now in their early twenties, perhaps – had not lived with their parents in their family homes for several years. They had most likely been working, apprenticing, or attending university for around a decade by the time the notion of a marriage contract was first broached and this was oftentimes first forged by an employer or contact that had been made during this transitional period. Again, as with every topic within this book, this comes with a great deal of variability. Those of higher rank would have been approaching the age of marriage and perhaps would have already had someone starting to arrange matches made for them, well before those of lower status. They would also have had far less say in the matter, as a general rule. For most of the population, depending on the job situation, the employer's personal contacts (or own children, who may also have been of marriageable age), and a number of individual factors that are difficult to account for, potential marriage matches for young people might have been found either by their employer, their parents, or some other close relative. A mother's role during this period would likely have been to echo her husband's wishes regarding her children's marriage prospects. She might have been the primary parent corresponding with her children on the subject, but it would have often been her husband who was negotiating logistically and financially with potential suitors and their families. Things like dowries for daughters, as well as jointures, needed to be sorted out prior to any marriage contract and this was one area where we have evidence of a mother taking the lead.[7] One Devon woman in 1567 promised to provide for her soon-to-be-wed daughter 'twenty nobles in money, a bed, two brazen crocks, and six pewter vessels' to take along with her to her marriage.[8] Often, in the case of arranged marriages by parents, such negotiations would be discussed and agreed upon before the two betrothed individuals even met.

One example of this type of arranged marriage – much to the chagrin of the daughter and bride in question – was that of young Katherine Prescott in the early seventeenth century. At the tender of age of 12, it had been decided by her father, Henry Prescott, that she would marry the 15-year-old William Bower, who was 'of a very good estate'. But Katherine was not at all in favour of this plan. She exclaimed passionately that she would 'leape into a worke pitt and drowne her self before she married William Bower'. This did nothing to stir up sympathy from her father, however, who roughly threatened to withdraw all 'financial support and paternal blessing' for Katherine unless she consented.[9] On the other side of the coin, though, were the marriages that went ahead *without* parents' blessing and approval. Just prior to the Tudor Dynasty,

Margaret Paston and her husband John cut their daughter Margery entirely out of the family when she fell in love with and married their bailiff, Richard Calle.[10] In cases like this, where children had the gall to marry without their parents' involvement, mothers and fathers were often known to take action and try to undo the union. In doing so, they attempted to restore their authority over their adult children.

An example of this was the marriage of Thomas Thynne and Maria Audley, both aged 16 in 1594. Maria, who was serving at the court of Queen Elizabeth I that summer, met Thomas – the son and heir to a landowner and member of Parliament – at a Beaconsfield inn. They married on the same day they met, simply by repeating their own vows in the presence of witnesses in an above chamber of the establishment. But knowing that their respective parents were opposed to each other's families (due to a conflict that had spanned decades) and would therefore not approve of any marriage between them, they kept their union a secret the following morning when they went their separate ways – Thomas to Oxford; Maria back to court. This appears to have been a 'victory of love at first sight between two passionate teenagers', who eschewed the preferred order of things, as society dictated.[11] Thomas was even quoted as saying that he was 'no more afraid of his [father's] displeasure than Maria was of her mistress's [the queen]'.[12]

But when news broke of the marriage in early April 1595, it was primarily Thomas' mother, Joan Thynne, who leapt into a fury. She worked tirelessly to have the marriage annulled, specifically pointing to the fact that it had significantly damaged her family financially. For one, an adequate dowry had not been garnered from Maria's family – as she had expected £4000 – £5000 with any future wife of Thomas'. But she also pointed out that her husband, Sir John 'lost all benefit of his eldest son's marriage, and his daughters lost money which by this means was intended to be provided for them' (as their own dowries).[13] All this was essentially to say that Maria and her family would unfairly gain from this marriage beyond what would ever have been agreed upon by the Thynnes. Thomas was, after all, set to inherit the family estate of Longleat, where he could one day expect to earn £3000 per year.[14]

Joan was beyond disappointed with her son and for a time chose to keep the embarrassment of Thomas' betrayal a secret. She wrote to her husband, 'for the keeping of it secret here, doubt you not of it, for here is no mistrust of this matter'.[15] She expressed her hope that 'they may be divorced', while also expressing 'how hard is my hap to live to see my chiefest hope and joy my greatest grief and sorrow'.[16] It was no small thing for a son or daughter to go against their parents' wishes and marry without consent, yet even while Joan and her husband sought 'remedies' to the situation – arguing that Thomas and Maria could not be legally married because of their young ages – they were unsuccessful in their attempts to break apart the union. Following several months of costly lawsuits and bitter letters exchanged, Thomas and Maria set up their own household in a house provided by the latter's family. Joan Thynne never forgave them, despite Maria's attempts at reconciliation. Though unconfirmed, this story of star-crossed Elizabethan lovers and their parents' vehement rejection of the union has been suggested as the inspiration behind William Shakespeare's *Romeo & Juliet.*

A much more favourable (and common) situation, of course, was to have children marry according to their parents' wishes and negotiations, such as in the case of Bess of Hardwick's children. In 1580, she wrote to both her stepson and son-in-law, Gilbert Talbot, regarding the arranging of a marriage for her youngest son, Charles Cavendish, and a young woman named Margaret Kitson. She expressed her wish that 'the maryage … may be dyspatchte before Lent' and discussed the lands that would be settled upon her son and his new wife following the marriage.[17] Three years prior, she had written to Robert Dudley, Earl of Leicester, regarding his assistance in arranging a marriage for her widowed daughter, Elizabeth. She expressed her gratitude for his 'care to do good styll to me and myne, and theryn ys expressed your Lordship's honorabe[ll] providence now entended for my dowter [countess of] lennox yn maryage'.[18] This particular second marriage would never come to be, but the letter indicates the involvement of her mother – along with her impressive connections – in attempting to arrange for it.

Parents of the Tudor period expected to be able to negotiate such happy agreements before planning a public ceremony in a parish church. One family would often hold a reception of dinner and dancing at their own home following the wedding, though this depended on resources. Grand, royal weddings, such as that between Prince Arthur Tudor and

Catherine of Aragon in 1501, culminated in a week-long celebration of marriage, including jousting, banqueting, and courtly entertainment. For those couples of families much less well off, guests might have contributed to a 'bride ale' (a celebratory feast) on a smaller scale.[19] Overall, it was hoped for that the event was an agreeable and enjoyable one for both parties involved. Depending on the mother's age, it was altogether possible – even probable, depending on social class – that she might be watching her child marry and begin to have children of their own several years before she herself reached menopause and came to be considered 'old'.

To focus on Catherine of Aragon, and in particular, her plight in April 1502, when her husband, Arthur Tudor, passed away suddenly after only months of marriage, we see an example of a concerned royal mother advocating for her adult child. Upon hearing the news of her son-in-law's death, Isabella of Castile, along with her husband, Ferdinand of Aragon, expressed her 'profound sorrow' in a letter conveyed by the Spanish Ambassador, and insisted that because 'the Princess of Wales [Catherine] is suffering' … 'she must be removed, without loss of time, from the unhealthy place where she now is'.[20] A few months later, Isabella wrote once again on behalf of her daughter – this time to Ferdinand, Duke de Estrada – with the following sentiment:

> I, therefore, command you, because it is very necessary, that you press much for the departure of the Princess of Wales, my daughter, so that she may immediately come here. You must say that the greater her loss and affliction, the more reason is there for her to be near her parents, as well for her consolation, as on account of her age. For, you know that no other Princess ever endured more grief than the Queen-Princess, when she was widowed, or led such a sad and bitter life on account of the death of her husband as she did.[21]

Of course, much attention was also paid in these letters to the demands for restitution of Catherine's dowry, which had already been paid to the king and queen of England upon her marriage. But these letters also indicate a genuine concern for her welfare, and a real desire to have her home to bring her comfort in a time of need. Certainly, much hope and expectation had been centred on this political alliance and marriage, but for Isabella of Castile, the news brought to her in the months following her daughter's wedding was not the news of a royal grandbaby but rather, the sad news that her widowed young daughter of only 16 was in need of her advocacy.

A general estimation might be that the typical sixteenth-century mother would become a grandmother somewhere near the onset of 'old age' as it was loosely defined during the period, though this depended, of course, on the age that she had been when she married and started having children.[22] As discussed in chapter four, the average age for sixteenth-century adults to marry was much the same as it is today – somewhere in the mid-to-late twenties. But for aristocratic and noble circles, this life event was often pushed forward several years. The most common age range for girls of noble families to wed was between 13 and 16 years old – over a decade earlier than those lower down the social ladder (although this age range is debated among historians).[23] This means, of course, that the age one would likely reach grandparent status was quite earlier for those in the upper ranks of society, perhaps only around their mid-to-late thirties, versus the more usual forties or fifties.[24]

Take Margaret Beaufort as an example – the mighty mother of King Henry VII and 'mother' of the Tudor Dynasty. She had been married three times by the time she was 15 and gave birth to Henry at just 13.[25] As such, she was only 43 years old when she became a grandmother to Arthur Tudor, the son and heir to Henry and his wife, Elizabeth of York. As she lived to the relatively average age of 66 years old, she knew her surviving grandchildren – Margaret, Henry, and Mary – until they were 20, 18 and 13 respectively.[26] No wonder she remains one of our most notable examples of a sixteenth-century grandparent, by which we can try to understand the ageing woman's role in family life. Her life as both a mother and a grandmother were extraordinary by contemporary standards, as it was filled with political discord, intricate plotting, the surviving of a decades-long war, and assisting to navigate her own son to the throne of England, effectively ending the Wars of the Roses. Consequently, she also lived just long enough to see her grandson Henry VIII become king in 1509. And while the vast majority of women in the sixteenth century would not have experienced such a dramatic life as a mother and grandmother, there were likely plenty of them who mirrored Margaret at least in age and ability to know their adult grandchildren.

But what was the typical role of a Tudor grandmother? Just as is the case today, it is difficult to pinpoint a 'general' image of a grandmother in the sixteenth century, as her role and visibility in her grandchildren's lives depended on a number of things. For one, proximity was of the utmost importance. Depending on where her child and their spouse set up their own household, she may or may not have been within easy travelling distance. Marital households were often established through the husband's family, though certainly not always, as this depended on both families' financial situations and what they were able and willing to bring to the union. Sometimes this could take the form of a family home being bestowed upon a son and his new wife, or a purchased house that was gifted as a wedding present. In such a case, it can be argued that the maternal grandparents might have lacked proximity or ease of travel to visit grandchildren, but again, it is impossible to generalise. One thing that we do know from earlier chapters in this book is that a bride's mother would almost certainly have been invited to be by her daughter's side in childbed. As it was the custom for an expectant mother to be surrounded by female companions in the birthing chamber – both friends and relatives – her mother was likely always at the top of the list of those attendants most needed. In fact, just as the typical Tudor mother would have likely leaned upon her own mother's first-hand wisdom, knowledge, and advice about pregnancy and childbirth, she could now bestow the same favours upon her own daughter or daughter-in-law, if the relationship was close enough.

Beyond the birthing chamber, however, there was a skewed perception about grandmothers and elderly women in general during the period. Contrary to what might be expected – that elders in the sixteenth century would have been held close and protected by the younger generations, due to the risk of rampant diseases and dangers – the image of an old woman had, for centuries, been characterised and illustrated as 'dangerous, venomous, and contagious to children'.[27] This imagery was not helped at all by Shakespeare's description of old age – the seventh, final stage of life, which was characterised by 'second childishness and mere oblivion/Sans teeth, sans eyes, sans taste, sans everything'.[28] Of course, Shakespeare was likely describing a much older individual that the theoretical Tudor grandmother we are exploring here, but even a woman around the age of 50 would have been considered 'old' by the majority of the population. Depending on her diet, lifestyle, number of pregnancies and other health factors, she may well have lost a good number of teeth, have been experiencing some loss of eyesight, and been presenting with other outward signs of ageing. All of this made her – at least historically speaking – a figure to be feared and viewed with suspicion. In her youth, her regular menstruation had diluted the evil humours living within her. But with the onset of menopause, those humours (viewed as poison) were 'left to stew fetid in the body, with the worst toxins escaping malignantly through wrinkled eyes'.[29]

For this reason, 'poisonous' old women were feared to infect and endanger babies and children with a mere glance of their eyes. It is little wonder why so many old women were therefore accused of witchcraft and suspected of evildoing in the later sixteenth century and beyond. It also begs the question: How many elderly women and grandmothers were trusted around babies and young children, even their own grandchildren? Were there medieval beliefs about the dangers and evils of old age dismissed by young mothers who wanted their own mothers close by? Were they regarded as silly superstition and outdated stories meant only to frighten and shock? Certainly, there were grandmothers who were kept close to their families and played an active role in their grandchildren's lives. In fact, this was probably the majority of cases for women who lived long enough to see her children have children of their own, even sometimes taking the form of a shared residence. Probably most often occurring for widowed grandmothers, this living arrangement might have benefitted both parties involved, with childcare help provided by the grandmother, and bed and board provided by her child and his or her spouse. It would have been a recognisable arrangement even to modern readers, but although such a situation was likely common during the period, examples and contemporary evidence for it is unfortunately scant.[30] In fact, it is difficult to know virtually anything about the living situations, affectionate relationships and general lifestyles of Tudor grandparents – because such descriptions were not often revealed in written sources from the period. Our greatest resources for viewing multi-generational families and the existence of grandparents (and their living knowledge of grandchildren) are last wills and testaments. Unfortunately, these speak little-to-nothing of family bonds or descriptors of family life.[31]

The greatest examples that we have for the roles of grandmothers in their grandchildren's lives are primarily those of the royal families of the Tudor Dynasty and just before – and even among those, there are only a few. None of Henry VIII's three children procreated in their adult lives, and it was his and his children's reigns that made up the bulk of the Tudor Dynasty. Margaret Beaufort, as previously described, is arguably the most famous example of a Tudor grandmother, though her role in her grandchildren's life was likely more political than it was affectionate or 'grandmotherly'. This cannot be held against her, given the nature of her life and the political climate into which her grandchildren were born. Her primary goal had been to see her own son on the throne of England, and to see his heirs follow in his stead. A proud grandmother she surely was, but how affectionate or loving she was with her young grandchildren is impossible to know.

One of Margaret's counterparts and rivals for a time during the Wars of the Roses, Cecily Neville, is another example, and yet another driven by political ambition and a desire for her family to hold the crown. As the mother of King Edward IV, one of the last Plantagenet kings, she remained at court as the Dowager Duchess of York for at least part of her son's reign, and at least some of the births of his ten children by Elizabeth Woodville. In fact, she went a step further than most were able. She became a great-grandmother to Arthur, Margaret and Henry (children of Henry VII and Elizabeth of York, her granddaughter) all before passing away in 1495 – ten years into the dawn of the Tudor Dynasty. To become a great-grandparent in the Tudor period was certainly not something to be expected by the general population, though Cecily had, of course, been betrothed at age 8 and married at 14. She also lived to the grand age of 80 years old – not just old, but *exceptionally* old by contemporary standards. Most women could not hope to live nearly so long, or to see so many generations of her family come to be.

Yet another late fifteenth-century grandmother was Jacquetta of Luxembourg, mother of Elizabeth Woodville and great-grandmother of Henry VIII. Though she herself passed away at the more expected age of 55 or 56 (many years prior to her great-grandchildren's births), she had at least twenty-one grandchildren by her fourteen children during her impressive life. And to tie everything back together, she was also accused of witchcraft in her old age, around the age of 53, in 1469. This was, however, likely more to do with the political manoeuvrings of the time, rather than her wrinkled eyes and aged appearance.

Certainly, older women – specifically those beyond the age of fertility and into their post-menopausal years – were viewed far differently than women still within their childbearing years. Not only did their age and lack of menstruation deem them potentially frightening and dangerous to children, but for centuries it had also been claimed that such women had lost their ability to love. Andreas Capellanus, a twelfth-century author of a treatise titled 'About Love', had written centuries prior to the Tudor period the following:

> Age is a bar, because after the sixtieth year in a man and the fiftieth in a woman, although one may have intercourse his passion cannot develop into love; because at that age the natural heat begins to lose its force, and the natural moisture is greatly increased, which leads a man into various difficulties and troubles him with various ailments.[32]

Though written four centuries prior to the Tudor period, it echoes beliefs and sentiments shared by those in the sixteenth century. And although this quote is aimed at elderly people in general (both men and women), it is striking that women were deemed incapable of love a full ten years earlier than their male counterparts. This was almost certainly due to menopause, reinforcing the argument that a woman's chief purpose and value (from the medieval period on through the Tudor period) was her ability to procreate.

As she aged, it is no exaggeration to say that the sixteenth-century woman lost her worth. If she lived a similar lifespan to her husband, then perhaps she would at least enjoy his companionship (and if lucky, his respect and love), though the majority of women in the sixteenth century outlived their husbands by a number of years.[33] Maybe she would have been embraced by her married children and children-in-law, though this would certainly have depended on her proximity to them. The degree to which she would have known and interacted with her grandchildren is difficult to ascertain, given the meagre contemporary evidence available on multi-generational families for the population at large. Hopefully, she would be spared in her old age the fear of the younger generation due to her wrinkles and grey hair – and even worse, the damning accusations of witchcraft that too often accompanied that fear. Certainly, by viewing the elderly Tudor woman in this way, from all different angles from which she could have been judged and identified as she left her childbearing years behind, we are left with the greatest argument for the importance of her role as a mother during this period. No matter her role as an aged woman – whether happy grandmother or feared witch – without her fertility, she was less 'female'. She was no longer capable or worthy of romantic love because she could no longer bear children for her husband. All of this together paints a rather vivid picture of what it meant to be a woman in the Tudor period, to have her fertility dictate her very identity. It was, without question, one of the sixteenth-century woman's most crucial assets. Without it, as she aged, she was viewed as something else entirely.

Conclusion

A Mother's Legacy

The Tudor woman's life expectancy was short by modern standards, perhaps by a good twenty or even thirty years compared to women of today. If she was considered 'old' starting around 50, she may have only had another decade to live, on average – and what would her legacy be to her children when she passed on? This answer, as with most in this book, depended enormously on her social standing, financial status, and assets upon her death. If she had been an heiress – an aristocratic daughter, or at least married into a noble and wealthy family – then she might have left her children with an impressive array of sentimental items, books, clothes, and other material objects from her life. It was not her place to bequeath a family fortune, lands, or estates upon her sons and daughters – this was reserved for the men of the family (unless in the case of widowhood).[1] But much can be gleaned by examining the last wills and testaments of mothers, and how they dispersed their personal effects among their children and even grandchildren.

Lady Anne Cobham, who was mentioned in chapter ten as having left behind money for her grandchild's wet nurse, also left personal items, such as a gold ring and two of her best handkerchiefs, to her daughter. The daughter-in-law who received the money for the wet nurse also received Lady Anne's 'gown of wrought velvet furred with jennets' as well as 'a kirtle of purple velvet', and her son was left two handkerchiefs. The phrasing of the word 'best' in her will (as in the description of two of the handkerchiefs) might have signified her personal affection for the daughter who received them, and we see this in examples of other wills also. A woman named Amy Busby, for example, who passed away in 1581, directed in her own will that her daughter Katherine should be given 'my best russet gown and my best apron', while another daughter, Alice, was left 'my best kerchief', and yet another daughter, Jane, was given 'one kerchief, one smock, and my good petticoat'. Are the adjectives used in these specific instructions meant to indicate that Amy favoured Katherine and Alice by leaving them some of her 'best' items, while poor Jane was left only the 'good' petticoat? Perhaps this interpretation is a stretch – however, historian, Amy Licence points out that Amy Busby also left items to her son's wife, which completely lack descriptors of this kind. She specified 'my second gown, one smock and one kerchief' for her daughter-in-law, perhaps showing her clear preference for the daughters of her blood.[2]

However, perhaps too much should not be read into such wording. The lower-class Margaret Chadwell wrote in her will that she would leave her 'best black gown' to her daughter, Jane Hyll, along with another gown made of worsted.[3] Were these words simply descriptors of the gowns and nothing more? Did such adjectives also indicate a specific closeness between the mother and her children, that she expected they would know exactly which items were her 'best' ? Once again, using wills in order to interpret affection felt between family members is probably not best practice, but this type of wording does raise questions as to the meaning behind such descriptors. Ultimately, these wills prove more about the practicality of mothers (and fathers, too) in the passing down of their everyday items to their children. Well-made clothes, handkerchiefs and aprons would serve multiple generations well if they were properly kept and cared for, and the items specified in these wills shed light on the great value placed upon them, and also the significant care taken in determining which child received which items.

In the case of widowhood, a mother could bestow more than just her personal items and clothing to her children at the time of her death. Usually, her husband would have owned all of the household's property – to include virtually everything both inside and outside of the home. It was therefore not her responsibility or right to dictate where these items went at the end of her life unless her husband had already passed away. An example of one such woman is Elizabeth Denzie of Great Bourton, who died in 1602. In her will, she was able to leave her son, John, the vast lands of the family farm, dictating, 'my quartern of a yard land in the fields of Bourton, and all its lands, leys, meadows, pastures, common feedings etc.' Her daughter, Alice, was able to receive household items that she would certainly find useful in her own home, such as:

> ... nine pairs of sheets and a small sheet with an open seam, two tablecloths, two towels, four table napkins, three platters, two porringers, a saucer, the worse brass pan [there's that curious adjective again] a kettle, a loom, a cowl, a coverlet, a bolster, a winnow-sheet, and a blanket.

Her clothing appears to have been the least of her concerns, which makes sense given that she was responsible for the farm and all within it, without her husband. Whatever clothing she did leave behind was determined to be split equally among her three daughters.[4]

Royalty also had their sentimental items passed down from one generation to the next – tokens of affection from parents to children, as well as practical second-hand gifts to avoid wasting costly garments and clothing items. Of course, in the case of jewels and jewellery, they were also seen as status symbols and reminders of one's family wealth, prestige, and noble ancestry. For some of these items – such as the famous Chequers Ring worn by Queen Elizabeth I – their origin and meaning remain unclear to historians today. This particular piece does signify, however, without question, a certain sentimental importance and homage paid to a maternal figure. One of only a few surviving pieces of jewellery worn by the last Tudor monarch, this ring has been tentatively dated to the mid-1570s, when Elizabeth had already been queen of England for nearly two decades. It is ornately designed, with the jewelled lettering of 'E' and 'R' for 'Elizabeth Regina', held together by a mother-of-pearl hoop set with rubies. It is a gorgeous piece of jewellery, but the statement pieces are the two portraits contained within the ring's locket. Elizabeth's side profile is easily recognisable as the bottom portrait, but the figure above her remains the source of some scrutiny and debate even to this day.

The most prominent theory has argued that the young, French-hooded woman in the above portrait is Anne Boleyn, Elizabeth's mother. If so, then the sentimentality of this ring for Elizabeth is particularly interesting.

For one, Anne was executed by her husband, Henry VIII, when her daughter was only 2½ years old, so any memories that Elizabeth had of her mother were likely distant and vague, if they existed at all. Also, the means of Anne's death was cause for some danger and scrutiny, even decades after the event had passed. As she had been executed on the king's orders – and under the suspicion of adultery – the notion that Elizabeth would have continuously and sentimentally worn a piece of jewellery depicting her maternal bond would have been controversial. The ring would have been viewed as a reminder of the whispers of Anne's unfaithfulness and even, perhaps, Elizabeth's own questionable parentage. Whether or not this was on Elizabeth's mind, and if it would have deterred her from wearing a ring with her mother's portrait inside it, is something we cannot know.

We do know, however, that Elizabeth spoke very little of Anne during her own life, so the fact that the Chequers Ring was worn so prominently, even at the time of her death, speaks of a sentimentality that would be particularly interesting – if, in fact, the face is Anne's.[5] One theory to the contrary states that Elizabeth wore the ring bearing her mother's likeness, not because of any personal affection or nostalgia for her but rather as a stark reminder of the consequences of one wrong political move.[6] Yet another theory claims that the image isn't Anne's at all, but instead Elizabeth's fourth stepmother and Henry VIII's final wife, Katherine Parr.[7] In any case, this particular piece of Tudor jewellery paints a (possibly) very sentimental image of a grown English monarch fondly remembering the legacy of her mother (or mother figure). In other families, where mothers could have afforded to have their portraits painted, similar mementos might have existed for their children to keep and remember them by, though they were likely not quite so elaborate as Elizabeth I's ring.

More likely, the majority of families and children who had the resources would remember their parents through portraits that were displayed, not necessarily within hidden compartments of jewellery but framed and hung within the home. During the Tudor period, to have one's likeness sketched or painted was a coveted commodity and one that might have only been accomplished once in a person's lifetime – and again, only if they had the means to afford an artist's work and time.

For the average child, just one portrait of a parent – or both, if lucky enough – would have undoubtedly been a cherished keepsake, and may have adorned the walls of the family home for generations to come. Miniatures, or small portraits meant to travel alongside an individual, were often given as romantic gestures between courting partners, or spouses who were separated by work and travel. But similarly, it is easy to believe that such portraits would have been kept by children after their own parents had passed away, in a time when the deceased person's likeness may only have been captured by an artist's paintbrush a single time, if at all.

Along the same line as the individual portrait, Tudor family portraits were popular among the wealthy and elite, and grew in popularity throughout the period. Such portraits – again, possibly only being painted once in a family member's lifetime – captured so much more than the individual snapshot of a person. They were meant to convey the entire family life – husband, wife, and children and sometimes pets. They often also included symbolic family imagery that told a much greater story than what was immediately obvious to the viewer's eye. One of the most notable examples is the family portrait of William Brooke, 10th Lord Cobham, with his wife, sister and six children, painted in 1567. In this painting (which has already been mentioned in previous chapters), the children are holding a number of family pets, as well as eating food in front of the adults, who stand in the background.[8] The portrait tells much about the Cobham family through the sitters' styles of dress, as well as the food that adorns their plates. This was a status symbol for the family and its descendants, to be sure, and much more than a sentimental piece of artwork for which the children could remember their parents.

Another striking Tudor family portrait is that of Edward, Baron of Windsor, and his family, dated 1568. It is a similar arrangement of family members, with Edward and his wife, Katherine de Vere positioned behind their four sons – but here, instead of the children eating food at a dining table, they are playing games together. Chess and playing cards are illustrated, giving some insight into the pastimes of elite family members and their children.[9] But most notably in this portrait, there is another sitter behind the youngest son. Her identity has been questioned, with some historians pointing to a possible governess or nurse for the children, while others have argued that she might have been either Edward's or Katherine's mother, and the boys' grandmother.[10] She is clearly elderly, wearing a stern expression and clearly important enough to such a noble family, as to be painted alongside them. If she was a grandmother, this illustrates a sentimental maternal tie between generations within a Tudor family unit. If she was instead a nurse, her inclusion in the portrait points to another particularly sentimental attachment for the family. If she bore no blood relation to the other sitters, then she was clearly a beloved and appreciated maternal figure to the boys, and likely a great help to Edward and Katherine. In either case, the woman's presence in the de Vere portrait is fascinating and thought provoking.

Among those who could not afford portraiture of themselves for family members and future relatives – and even among those who could – perhaps one of the greatest legacies a mother (or any parent) could leave behind was a life story that was worth telling for generations to come. This was true for both the poor and rich, with Catherine of Aragon and her own mother's legacy as a prime example. Throughout her adult life, Catherine invoked the memory and lasting reputation of her mother, Queen Isabella I of Castile – in particular, her fervent and unwavering Catholic faith and fierce spirit. With Catherine having been 16 years old when she left Spain to marry Prince Arthur Tudor in England, she had spent more than enough years around her formidable mother to have learned much from her, and to gain a sense for her notoriety throughout Europe. Far into her adulthood, Catherine would lean on the knowledge she had of her own mother's successes as queen of Castile and consort to the mighty Ferdinand of Aragon. Though most of her life was spent away from her mother, her legacy was strong enough that it had a lasting impact on Catherine.

Her husband, Henry VIII, similarly held a sentimental attachment for his own mother, Elizabeth of York, who had passed away following childbirth when Henry was only 11 years old. As an adult, Henry allegedly admired the varying traits among his six wives that reminded him of his own mother, which indicates a particular fondness and nostalgia for the affectionate relationship he must have shared with her. We know that he had indeed mourned her upon her death, as evidenced by the *Vaux Passional* manuscript, held today in the National Library of Wales. One of the illustrations inside this book, thought to have once been owned by Henry VII, shows the 'presentation of a book to the King, who can be identified by his heraldic emblems'.[11] To the side of the illustration is a bed draped in black, signifying the death of Henry's wife, Elizabeth, with her son, the future Henry VIII, dressed in green and crying into his arms atop it.[12] In a most obvious tribute later in life – and one that was commonly used throughout the period – he named his second daughter (and only child by his second wife, Anne Boleyn) Princess Elizabeth, in his beloved mother's honour.[13] The evidence certainly suggests that his mother had left an impression on her son long after her death, as many mothers of the period likely did.

Evidence of lowlier children mourning their deceased parents throughout the sixteenth century is harder to come by, as is any remaining written record of how they remembered or spoke of them during their daily life. For this, we can only assume what we know to be true for the large majority of people, whether hundreds of years ago or in the modern age: that mothers made a significant impression on their children and were remembered in a variety of ways by them long after they were gone. Whether they were present, attentive mothers who had nursed, educated, disciplined, played and remained close and in touch with their children long after they had grown, or even if they had been more distant, removed, and occupied with other obligations required by their status, mothers left a mark. Sixteenth-century children, as they grew, would have had varying degrees of closeness with their mothers, but as evidenced by Henry Tudor's mourning at his own royal mother's passing, we should not assume that it was only the poor, fully hands-on mothers who garnered affectionate relationships with their children. After death, a mother was remembered through artwork, jewellery, clothing items, and trinkets left behind at her request. Her memory was enlivened through her children's storytelling and personal memories – perhaps for generations.

And for Tudor daughters in particular, the connection to lost mothers was especially poignant. In most cases, her mother would have instructed her in the many facets of daily life that made her a woman in society's eyes – everything from cooking and cleaning to letter-writing and childcare. If she had been lucky enough to have had her mother by her side during her own pregnancies and childbirths, then she would have been left with the memories of all the vastly valuable lessons her late mother had shared with her, not least of all how to bring life into the world (a distinctly *female* knowledge during the period). Undoubtedly, throughout her adult life as a housewife, businesswoman and mother in her own right, she would see traces of her mother in much of what she did, as it would have been her mother's duty to ensure that this was exactly the case. Perhaps she wore the gowns left behind, or wrapped her newborn baby in a blanket knit by her mother decades prior. Maybe she cooked for her own husband and children the familiar stew and pottage recipes from her own childhood and hung up the apron left to her in her mother's will before trudging to a child's bedside to recite a bedtime story or song that her own mother had used to comfort her long ago. Echoes of her mother were likely everywhere. And so, as she raised her own children, utilising the skills, lessons, tools, recipes, medicinals, songs and rhymes that had long ago been used on her, the cycle of Tudor womanhood – and motherhood – continued.

Notes

Introduction

1. Alison Sim, *The Tudor Housewife* (1996), p.2.
2. Sally Hales, 'We explore the lives of Tudor women' in *BRITAIN Magazine,* 21 October 2016, https://www.britain-magazine.com/carousel/lives-of-tudor-women/.
3. Barbara Harris, 'A New Look at the Reformation: Aristocratic Women and Nunneries, 1450–1540' in *Journal of British Studies,* Vol. 32, No. 2 (1993), p.90.
4. William Monter, 'Protestant Wives, Catholic Saints, and the Devil's Handmaid: Women in the Age of Reformation' in *Becoming Visible: Women in European History,* Renate Bridenthal, Claudia Kooz and Susan Sheard (eds.) (1987), p.206. (Cited in Harris, *A New Look at the Reformation*, pp.89–90.)
5. Dowries were required to be paid by the family in either case for a young woman, whether when marrying or when joining a nunnery and entering the religious life.
6. Harris, *A New Look at the Reformation*, p.95.
7. Marilyn Oliva, 'Aristocracy or Meritocracy? Office Holding Patterns in Late Medieval English Nunneries' in *Studies in Church History*, Vol. 27 (1990), pp.197–208. (Cited in Harris, *A New Look at the Reformation*, p.93).
8. Claire Cross, Noreen Vickers, *Monks, Friars and Nuns in Sixteenth Century Yorkshire* (1995), p.4.
9. 'Estimated Population of England and Wales, 1570–1750', A vision of Britain through time, https://www.visionofbritain.org.uk/census/GB1841ABS_1/6.

10. Christine Coch, '"Mother of my Contreye": Elizabeth I and Tudor Constructions of Motherhood' in *English Literary Renaissance,* Vol. 26, No. 3 (1996), p.431.
11. Jacques Jouanna, 'The Legacy of the Hippocratic Treatise The Nature of Man: The Theory of the Four Humours' in *Greek Medicine from Hippocrates to Galen: Selected Papers* (2012), p.335.
12. Julia Martins, 'What is the 'Wandering Womb?', Secrets of Women, 16 January 2023, https://juliamartins.co.uk/what-is-the-wandering-womb; Helen King, 'Once Upon a Text: Hysteria from Hippocrates' in *Hysteria Beyond Freud* (1993), pp.14–17.
13. King, 'Hysteria from Hippocrates', p.17.
14. Coch, 'Mother of my Contreye', p.426. This is particularly evidenced by the stark change in attitude towards women after menopause or in the case of a woman who had problems menstruating and was unable to demonstrate the clear indicator of fertility, which was expected of women at the time. This absence, or the ageing out of fertile years, made women appear less 'female' to the rest of society, as is discussed in chapter fifteen.
15. Lipscomb, 'Suzannah Lipscomb: Women, Sex and Power in the Sixteenth Century', YouTube, 28 June 2020, https://www.youtube.com/watch?v=TY5mrshQT3o&t=342s.
16. Linda A. Pollock, 'Embarking on a rough passage: the experience of pregnancy in early modern society' in *Women as Mothers in Pre-Industrial England* (1990), p.47.
17. Although written in the century following the Tudor period, Sharp's education and first-hand experience certainly stem from practices and knowledge shared by midwives of the sixteenth century and therefore still apply to a study of this period.
18. Kremer, 'What medieval Europe did with its teenagers', BBC News, 23 March 2014, https://www.bbc.com/news/magazine.
19. Alison Wall, 'For Love, Money, or Politics? A Clandestine Marriage and the Elizabethan Court of Arches' in *The Historical Journal,* Vol. 38, No. 3 (1995), p.514.
20. Jessica E. Godfrey, *Attitudes Toward Post-Menopausal Women in the High and Late Middle Ages, 1100–1400* (2011), p.30.

21. Jenny Keating, 'History of Adoption and Fostering in the United Kingdom' in *Oxford Bibliographies,* 28 May 2013, https://www.oxfordbibliographies.com

Chapter One – Sixteenth-Century Medical Theory: The Four Humours

1. Jouanna, 'The Legacy of the Hippocratic Treatise The Nature of Man', p.335.
2. Ibid., p.340–2.
3. Amy Licence, *Living Like a Tudor – Woodsmoke and Sage: A Sensory Journey Through Tudor England* (2021), p.291. The opposite of the 'bad mixture' known as 'dyscrasia' was the term 'eucrasis', also coined by Galen.
4. Jouanna, 'The Legacy of the Hippocratic Treatise', p.335.
5. *British Medical Journal 1888* (London, 1857), pp.312–13.
6. Jouanna, 'The Legacy of the Hippocratic Treatise', p.335.
7. Ibid., p.342.
8. Thomas Elyot, *The Castel of Helth* (1541), pp.4–7.
9. Jouanna, 'The Legacy of the Hippocratic Treatise', p.342.
10. Elyot, *The Castel of Helth*, pp.4–7.
11. Ibid.; Jouanna, 'The Legacy of the Hippocratic Treatise', pp.338–39.
12. Elyot, *The Castel of Helth,* pp.4–7; Jouanna, 'The Legacy of the Hippocratic Treatise', p.342.
13. Licence, *Living Like a Tudor*, p.292.
14. Ibid., pp.291–92; Angela He, 'The Humors and You! Medieval Health, Diet, and Humoral Theory', Bernard Becker Medical Library Blog, 31 August 2023, https://becker.wustl.edu/news/humors-and-you/.
15. Jouanna, 'The Legacy of the Hippocratic Treatise', p.342.
16. Licence, *Living Like a Tudor,* p.291.
17. He, 'The Humors and You! Medieval Health, Diet, and Humoral Theory', Bernard Becker Medical Library Blog, 31 August 2023, https://becker.wustl.edu/news/humors-and-you/.

18. Julia Martins, 'What are the "Non-Naturals"?', Secrets of Women, 1 August 2022, https://juliamartins.co.uk/what-are-the-non-naturals.
19. Emtiazy M.; Keshavarz M.; Khodadoost M.; Kamalinejad M.; Gooshahgir S.A.; Shahrad Bajestani H.; Hashem Dabbaghian F.; and Alizad M., 'Relation between Body Humors and Hypercholesterolemia: An Iranian Traditional Medicine Perspective Based on the Teaching of Avicenna' in *Iran Red Crescent Medical Journal,* 1 March 2012, https://www.ncbi.nlm.nih.gov/pmc/articles/PMC3372029/.
20. He, 'The Humors and You! Medieval Health, Diet, and Humoral Theory', Bernard Becker Medical Library Blog, 31 August 2023, https://becker.wustl.edu/news/humors-and-you/.
21. Elyot, *The Castel of Helth,* p.9.
22. Ibid., p.11.
23. John Partridge, *The Treasurie of Commodious Conceits* (1573), ch. vi, ch. xxxix.
24. He, 'The Humors and You! Medieval Health, Diet, and Humoral Theory', Bernard Becker Medical Library Blog, 31 August 2023, https://becker.wustl.edu/news/humors-and-you/.
25. Partridge, *The Treasurie of Commodious Conceits*, ch. lxv.
26. He, 'The Humors and You! Medieval Health, Diet, and Humoral Theory', Bernard Becker Medical Library Blog, 31 August 2023, https://becker.wustl.edu/news/humors-and-you/.
27. Partridge, *The Treasurie of Commodious Conceits*, ch. lxii, ch. lxiii, ch. lxv.
28. Licence, *Living Like a Tudor*, p.295.
29. Furnivall, F.J. (ed.) and Andrew Boorde, *A Compendious Regiment or a Dietary of Health* (1542), p.287.
30. State Letters & Papers, Henry VIII (August 1514). (Cited in Licence, *Living Like a Tudor*, p.296.)
31. Boorde, *A Dietary of Health,* p.293.
32. Ibid., p.229.
33. Martins, 'What are the "Non-Naturals"?', https://juliamartins.co.uk/what-are-the-non-naturals.
34. Boorde, *A Dietary of Health*, p.291, pp.289–90.
35. Ibid., p.244.

36. Martins, 'What are the "Non-Naturals"?', https://juliamartins.co.uk/what-are-the-non-naturals.

Chapter Two – Reproductive Anatomy of the Tudor Woman

1. Aradia Wyndham, 'The Byrth of Mankynde, 1540 | Book History', The Baby Historian, 7 February 2020, https://thebabyhistorian.com/2020/02/07/the-byrth-of-mankynde-1540/.
2. Ibid.
3. Suzannah Lipscomb, 'Suzannah Lipscomb: Women, Sex and Power in the Sixteenth Century', YouTube, uploaded by Oxford Festival of the Arts, 28 June 2020, https://www.youtube.com/watch?v=TY5mrshQT3o&t=342s.
4. Jean-Baptiste Bonnard, 'Male and female bodies according to Ancient Greek physicians' in *When Medicine Meets Gender* (2013), p.12.
5. Ruth Goodman, *How to Be a Tudor* (2015), p.269.
6. Coch, 'Mother of my Contreye', p.431.
7. Bonnard, 'Male and female bodies according to Ancient Greek physicians', p.16
8. Aretaeus, Francis Adams (ed.), *De causis et signis acutorum morborum (lib. 1)*, Tufts University ch. xi, http://www.perseus.tufts.edu.
9. Coch, 'Mother of my Contreye', p.431.
10. Goodman, *How to Be a Tudor*, p.269.
11. Plato, R.D. Archer-Hind, M.A. (ed.), *The Timaeus of Plato* (1888), [91 A-E] p.341.
12. King, 'Hysteria from Hippocrates', pp.25–6.
13. Ibid., p.26; Bonnard, 'Male and female bodies according to Ancient Greek physicians', p.16.
14. King, 'Hysteria from Hippocrates', p.31.
15. Hippocrates, *Nat. mul.* 8 and 7. (Cited in Bonnard, 'Male and female bodies according to Ancient Greek physicians', p.12.)
16. Julia Martins, 'What is the "Wandering Womb"?', Secrets of Women, 16 January 2023, https://juliamartins.co.uk/what-is-the-wandering-womb.
17. King, 'Hysteria from Hippocrates', pp.26–7.

18. Edward Jorden, *A briefe discourse of a disease called the suffocation of the mother* (University of Michigan). Early English Books Online Text Creation Partnership, 2011, p.5.
19. Ibid., p.1.
20. Ibid., p.5.
21. Ibid., p.23, p.2.
22. King, 'Hysteria from Hippocrates', p.26.
23. *Merriam-Webster Dictionary Online*, 'hysterical', https://www.merriam-webster.com/dictionary/hysterical.
24. Amy Kenny, 'Returning the Wandering Womb with "Fetid and Rank Smells"', The Recipes Project, 7 October 2018, https://recipes.hypotheses.org/10794.
25. It is worth mentioning that uterine prolapse is, in fact, a real medical condition, though, of course, not caused by any roving nature of the organ.
26. Aretaeus, *De causis et signis acutorum morborum,* ch. xi, http://www.perseus.tufts.edu.
27. Ambroise Paré, *The Workes of that famous Chirurgion Ambrose Parey, translated out of Latine and compared with the French,* T.H. Johnson (trans.) (1678), p.574.
28. Kenny, 'Returning the Wandering Womb with "Fetid and Rank Smells"', https://recipes.hypotheses.org/10794.
29. Alessio Piemontese, *The Secrets of Alexis: containing many excellent remedies against divers diseases, wounds, and other accidents* (1615), p.13.
30. Paré, *The Workes of that famous Chirurgion Ambrose Parey*, p.574.
31. Richard Jonas, *The Byrth of Mankynde* (London, 1540), fol. xx.
32. Christopher A. Faraone, 'Magical and Medical Approaches to the Wandering Womb in the Ancient Greek World' in *Classical Antiquity,* Vol. 30, No. 1 (2011), p.5.
33. Kenny, 'Returning the Wandering Womb with "Fetid and Rank Smells"', https://recipes.hypotheses.org/10794.
34. Martins, 'What is the "Wandering Womb"?', https://juliamartins.co.uk/what-is-the-wandering-womb.
35. L. Dean Jones, *Women's Bodies in Classical Greek Science* (1996), p.189. (Cited in Faraone, 'Magical and Medical Approaches to the Wandering Womb in the Ancient Greek World', p.5.

36. Ibid., p.4.
37. Ibid., p.5.
38. *Liber de sinthomatibus mulierum* 1, MS 173 (1300–25), fol. 246v. (Cited in Monica H. Green, 'From "Diseases of Women" to "Secrets of Women": The Transformation of Gynecological Literature in the Later Middle Ages' in *Journal of Medieval and Early Modern Studies,* 30 (2000), p.10.
39. Green, 'From "Diseases of Women" to "Secrets of Women"', pp.11–12.

Chapter Three – Flowers and Fertility

1. Green, 'From "Diseases of Women" to "Secrets of Women"', pp.13–14.
2. Barbara H. Traister, '"Matrix and the pain thereof": a sixteenth-century gynaecological essay' in *Medical History,* 35 (1991), p.440.
3. Sara Read, '"Thy Righteousness is but a menstrual clout": Sanitary Practices and Prejudice in Early Modern England' in *Early Modern Women: An Interdisciplinary Journal*, Vol. 3 (2008), p.1.
4. Helen King, *Hippocrates' Woman: reading the female body in Ancient Greece* (1998), pp.28–9. (Cited in Bonnard, 'Male and female bodies according to Ancient Greek physicians', 12.)
5. Etienne van de Walle, 'Flowers and Fruits: Two Thousand Years of Menstrual Regulation' in *The Journal of Interdisciplinary History*, Vol. 28, No. 2 (1997), p.186.
6. 'The History of Menstrual Hygiene', Simple Health, 12 March 2019, https://www.simplehealth.com/blog/a-history-of-menstrual-hygiene; The Merriam-Webster Dictionary dates the first English use of the word 'menstruation' to 1686.
7. Green, 'From "Diseases of Women" to "Secrets of Women"', p.13.
8. *King James Bible Online*, https://www.kingjamesbibleonline.org/John-15-2/.
9. Julia Martins, 'Flowers', CEMS KCL Blog (King's College London) 25 June 2021, https://kingsearlymodern.co.uk/keywords/flowers.
10. Ibid.
11. Ibid.
12. van de Walle, 'Flowers and Fruits', p.186.

13. Read, 'Thy Righteousness is but a menstrual clout', p.1; Bonnard, 'Male and female bodies according to Ancient Greek physicians', 12; van de Walle, 'Flowers and Fruits', p.186.
14. Rivière, Lazare; Cole, Nicholas; Culpeper, Nicholas; and Rowland, William (trans.), *The Fifteenth Book of the Practice of Physick: Of Womens Diseases* (1655), p.400.
15. Bonnard, 'Male and female bodies according to Ancient Greek physicians', 12.
16. Kate Aughterson (ed.) *Renaissance Women: A Sourcebook* (1995), p.61. (Cited in van de Walle, 'Flowers and Fruits', p.190.)
17. van de Walle, 'Flowers and Fruits', p.188.
18. Ibid., pp.193–94.
19. Traister, 'Matrix and the pain thereof', pp.449–50.
20. Piemontese, *The Secrets of Alexis*, p.210.
21. Ibid.
22. Ibid., p.211.
23. Nicholas Culpeper, *The Complete Herbal* (London, 1850), p.24.
24. Grueninger, Natalie (Host) 'Reproduction and the Female Body with Julia Martins', Talking Tudors Podcast (Episode 161) 19 June 2022, https://onthetudortrail.com/Blog/2022/06/20/episode-161-reproduction-the-female-body-with-julia-martins/.
25. Monica Green, 'Flowers, Poisons, and Men: Menstruation in Medieval Western Europe' in *Menstruation: A Cultural History* (2005), p.51.
26. Sara Read, *Menstruation and the Female Body in Early Modern England* (2013), p.105.
27. Ibid., p.106.
28. Ibid., p.113.
29. Green, 'Flowers, Poisons, and Men', pp.54–5.

Chapter Four – A Time to Wed

1. Nicholas Orme, *Tudor Children* (2023), p.219.
2. E.A. Wrigley and others, *English Population History from Family Reconstitution 1580–1837* (2010), p.130. (Cited in Orme, *Tudor Children*, p.31.)

3. Elizabeth Norton, *The Hidden Lives of Tudor Women* (2017), p.86.
4. Ibid., p.87.
5. Ibid.
6. Juan Luis Vives, *A Very Fruitful and Pleasant Book Called the Instruction of a Christian Woman* (1529), p.124.
7. Norton, *The Hidden Lives of Tudor Women,* p.85.
8. Ibid., p.87.
9. Goodman, *How to Be a Tudor,* p.266.
10. Norton, *The Hidden Lives of Tudor Women,* pp.85–6.
11. Stephanie Kline, *Edward VI: Henry VIII's Overshadowed Son* (2023), p.17.
12. Ibid., p.140.
13. During this period, an unconsummated marriage was hardly recognised as a marriage at all, and grounds for the legal – and relatively uncomplicated – dissolution of the union.
14. Vives, *Instruction of a Christian Woman* (1529).
15. Norton, *The Hidden Lives of Tudor Women,* p.87.
16. Lauren Johnson, *So Great a Prince: The Accession of Henry VIII: 1509* (2017), p.90.
17. Ibid.
18. Claire Kennan, 'Till death do us part? Divorce in medieval England' https://blog.nationalarchives.gov.uk/till-death-us-part-divorce-medieval-england/.
19. It should go without saying that offspring can, and indeed did, result from unhappy marriages as well as happy ones. Unhealthy and even violent marriages likely abounded in the sixteenth century, though statistics on such unions are difficult or impossible to gather.
20. Orme, *Tudor Children,* pp.217–18.
21. John Stow, *A Survey of London* (1603), pp.94–5. Later in the Tudor period, as evidenced by Vives' writing, the rise of Puritanism began to proclaim dancing as lewd and immoral, precisely because it was connected to the sexual energy of youth.
22. *Certain sermons of homilies* (1562). Early English Books Online Text Creation Partnership, 2011; https://quod.lib.umich.edu.
23. Orme, *Tudor Children,* p.220.

24. Ibid. Such government involvement included the punishment for the mother and/or father to care for the illegitimate child even if they did not want to, with imprisonment as a last resort for such offenses.
25. Goodman, *How to Be a Tudor,* p.264.
26. Licence, *Living Like a Tudor*, p.311; Ibid., p.310.
27. Goodman, *How to Be a Tudor,* p.284.
28. Norton, *The Hidden Lives of Tudor Women,* p.88.
29. Ibid., p.95.

Chapter Five – The Christian Duty

1. Edmund Tilney, *A briefe and pleasant discourse of duties in marriage, called the flower of friendshippe* (1568). Early English Books Online Text Creation Partnership, 2011; https://quod.lib.umich.edu.
2. Goodman, *How to Be a Tudor,* p.263.
3. Genesis 1:28, *The Holy Bible (King James Version).*
4. David Cressy, *Birth, Marriage, and Death: Ritual, Religion, and the Life-Cycle in Tudor and Stuart England* (1997), p.18.
5. Libby Howlett, 'A Long Winter's Nap', Agecroft Hall & Gardens Blog, 31 January 2023, https://www.agecrofthall.org/single-post/a-long-winters-nap.
6. French, Katherine L.; Smith, Katheryn A.; and Stanbury, Sarah, 'An Honest Bed: The Scene of Life and Death in Late Medieval England' in *Fragments: Interdisciplinary Approaches to the Study of Ancient and Medieval Pasts,* 5 (2016), https://quod.lib.umich.edu.
7. Goodman, *How to Be a Tudor*, p.286.
8. Jennifer McNabb, 'She is but a girl: Talk of Young Women as Daughters, Wives, and Mothers in the Records of the English Consistory Courts, 1550–1650' in *The Youth of Early Modern Women* (2018), p.91; Ralph Houlbrooke, 'Love and marriage in Tudor England' in *History Extra*, 10 February 2015, https://www.historyextra.com/period/tudor/love-and-marriage-in-tudor-england/.

9. Johnson, *So Great a Prince,* p.91.
10. Kline, *Edward VI*, pp.1–6.
11. Licence, *Living Like a Tudor,* p.309.
12. Goodman, *How to Be a Tudor,* p.269.
13. Licence, *Living Like a Tudor,* p.309.
14. *The Book of Vices and Virtues* (date unknown). (Cited in Licence, *Living Like a Tudor*, p.313.)
15. Goodman, *How to Be a Tudor,* p.269.
16. Lipscomb, Suzannah (Host) 'Sex & the Tudors with Dr Kate Lister', Not Just the Tudors Podcast (Episode 110) 5 May 2022, https://access.historyhit.com/not-just-the-tudors/videos/sex-and-the-tudors; Helen King, 'The clitoris – a brief history', The Conversation, 4 January 2023, https://theconversation.com/the-clitoris-a-brief-history-196817.
17. Goodman, *How to Be a Tudor*, p.268.
18. Ibid., p.267.
19. Grueninger, Natalie (Host) 'Reproduction and the Female Body with Julia Martins'; Kyra Kramer, 'Gingerbread Houses and Mulled Wine', On the Tudor Trail, 11 December 2017, https://onthetudortrail.com/Blog/2017/12/11/gingerbread-houses-and-mulled-wine.
20. Ibid.
21. Elyot, *The Castel of Helth,* p.39.
22. Boorde, *The Dietary of Health,* p.269.
23. Licence, *Living Like a Tudor,* p.293.
24. Piemontese, *The Secrets of Alexis,* p.135.
25. Ibid.
26. Ibid.
27. Sara Read, *Maids, Wives, Widows: Exploring Early Modern Women's Lives, 1540–1740* (2015), p.128.
28. Grueninger, Natalie (Host), 'Reproduction and the Female Body with Julia Martins'.
29. Licence, *Living Like a Tudor,* p.312.
30. Read, *Maids, Wives, Widows,* p.128.
31. Grueninger, Natalie (Host) 'Reproduction and the Female Body with Julia Martins'.

32. Goodman, *How to Be a Tudor,* p.269.
33. Norton, *The Hidden Lives of Tudor Women,* p.90.
34. Goodman, *How to Be a Tudor,* p.269.
35. Ibid., p.268.
36. Piemontese, *The Secrets of Alexis,* p.135.
37. Ibid., p.28.
38. Ibid., p.135.
39. Philip Barrough, *The Method of Physick, containing the causes, signes, and cures of inward diseases in man's body, from the head to the foote* (1624), p.180.
40. Goodman, *How to Be a Tudor,* p.268.
41. Barrough, *The Method of Physick,* p.180.
42. Ibid.
43. Pollock, 'Embarking on a rough passage', p.41.
44. Kline, *Edward VI,* pp.2–4.
45. Read, *Maids, Wives, Widows,* p.130.
46. Partridge, *Treasurie of Commodious Conceits,* ch. 67.
47. Ibid., ch. 70.

Chapter Six – To Be with Child

1. Jacques Guillimeau, *Child-birth, or The happy deliverie of women* (1612), p.2.
2. Read, *Maids, Wives, Widows,* p.131.
3. Partridge, *Treasurie of Commodious Conceits,* ch. 117.
4. Jane Sharp, *The Midwives Book: or the Whole Art of Midwifery* (1671), p.92.
5. Ibid.
6. Ibid., p.103.
7. Ibid., pp.103–4.
8. Guillimeau, *The happy deliverie of women,* p.4.
9. Ibid.
10. Ibid., p.5.
11. Anna Whitelock, *Mary Tudor: Princess, Bastard, Queen* (2009), p.280.

12. Kline, *Edward VI,* p.169.
13. Pollock, 'Embarking on a rough passage', p.44.
14. Licence, *Living Like a Tudor,* p.314.
15. Anne Clifford Herbert, *The diary of the Lady Anne Clifford* (1923), p.107.
16. Kline, *Edward VI,* p.2.
17. Pollock, 'Embarking on a rough passage', p.44.
18. Raynalde, *The Byrth of Mankynd,* fol. iii.
19. Guillimeau, op. cit., p.8. (Cited in Norton, *The Hidden Lives of Tudor Women,* p.8.)
20. Norton, *The Hidden Lives of Tudor Women,* p.8.
21. Read, *Maids, Wives, Widows,* p.133.
22. Norton, *The Hidden Lives of Tudor Women,* p.89; Carla Spivack, 'To "Bring Down the Flowers": The Cultural Context of Abortion Law in Early Modern England' in *William & Mary Journal of Race, Gender, and Social Justice* (2007), pp.120–21.
23. Spivack, 'To Bring Down the Flowers', p.121.
24. Ibid., p.113.
25. Read, *Maids, Wives, Widows,* p.135.
26. Ibid., p.134.
27. Thomas Raynalde, *The Byrth of Mankynde* (1565), fol. xlii.
28. Pollock, 'Embarking on a rough passage', p.46.
29. Ibid.
30. Read, *Maids, Wives, Widows,* p.133.
31. Ibid.
32. Ibid.
33. Pollock, 'Embarking on a rough passage', p.47; Cressy, *Birth, Marriage, and Death,* p.30.
34. Andrew Gregory, 'UK has second highest maternal death rate in eight-country European study' in *The Guardian,* 16 November 2022, https://www.theguardian.com/society/2022/nov/16/uk-has-second-highest-maternal-death-rate-in-eight-country-european-study.
35. Roger Schofield, 'Did the mothers really die?', pp.259–60. (Cited in Pollock, 'Embarking on a rough passage', p.47.)

36. Elizabeth Jocelin, *The Mothers Legacie to her unborne Childe* (1624), p.44.
37. Ibid., pp.8–9.
38. Ibid., pp.10–11.
39. Julia Martins, 'Maternal Mortality and "The Mother's Legacy to her Unborn Child"', Secrets of Women, 1 June 2023, https://juliamartins.co.uk/maternal-mortality-and-the-mothers-legacy-to-her-unborn-child.

Chapter Seven – The Expectant Tudor Mother

1. It is worth noting that the title of this painting is 'Portrait of a Woman, probably Catherine Carey, Lady Knollys', and therefore may not actually depict Catherine Carey.
2. Licence, *Living Like a Tudor,* p.35.
3. Ibid., pp.36–7.
4. Lydia Figes, 'Portraying pregnancy: from prehistoric art to Jacobean portraiture', Art UK, 29 January 2020, https://artuk.org/discover/stories/portraying-pregnancy-from-prehistoric-art-to-jacobean-portraiture.
5. Ibid.
6. Licence, *Living Like a Tudor*, p.37.
7. Figes, 'Portraying pregnancy', Art UK, 29 January 2020, https://artuk.org/discover/stories/portraying-pregnancy-from-prehistoric-art-to-jacobean-portraiture.
8. Ibid., p.35.
9. Norton, *The Hidden Lives of Tudor Women,* p.9.
10. Alden O'Brien, 'History of Maternity Dress', Love to Know, https://www.lovetoknow.com/life/style/history-maternity-dress
11. Pollock, 'Embarking on a rough passage', p.49.
12. Cressy, *Birth, Marriage, and Death,* p.47.
13. William Gouge, *Domesticall Duties,* p.506; Schnucker, 'The English Puritans', p.639. (Cited in Pollock, 'Embarking on a rough passage', p.52.)

14. ScotRO, Melville MS GD26/13/401/22 (1695). (Cited in Pollock, 'Embarking on a rough passage', p.50.)
15. Guillimeau, *The happy deliverie of women,* p.20.
16. Ibid.
17. Ibid.
18. Pollock, 'Embarking on a rough passage', pp.50–51.
19. Michael Kaye Eshleman, 'Diet in pregnancy in the sixteenth and seventeenth centuries' in *Yale Medicine Thesis Digital Library* (1974), p.38.
20. Guillimeau, *The happy deliverie of women,* p.20.
21. Pollock, 'Embarking on a rough passage', p.50.
22. Ibid.
23. Guillimeau, *The happy deliverie of women,* p.21. Hydromel is also known as 'mead' – an alcoholic beverage made by fermenting honey mixed with water, and sometimes fruits, spices, grains, or hops.
24. Guillimeau, *The happy deliverie of women,* pp.19–20.
25. BL, Add. MSS 29571, fo. 76 (*c*.1667). (Cited in Pollock, 'Embarking on a rough passage', p.51).
26. Guillimeau, *The happy deliverie of women,* p.23.
27. Ibid.
28. NRO, Isham MS IC 580 (1668). (Cited in Pollock, 'Embarking on a rough passage', p.51.)
29. Herbert, *The diary of the Lady Anne Clifford,* p.112; Pollock, 'Embarking on a rough passage', p.51.
30. NRO, Finch Hatton MS FH 4331 (*c*.1678). (Cited in Pollock, 'Embarking on a rough passage', p.51).
31. NLS, Fletcher MS 17851/132 (late seventeenth century). (Cited in Pollock, 'Embarking on a rough passage', p.51).
32. Guillimeau, *The happy deliverie of women,* pp.23–4.
33. Ibid., p.24.
34. Ibid.
35. Ibid., p.23.
36. Ibid., pp.22–3.
37. Ibid., pp.24–5.

38. Read, *Maids, Wives, Widows,* p.135.
39. Thomas Lupton, *A thousand notable things, of sundry sortes* (1589), p.83.
40. Grueninger, Natalie (Host), 'Reproduction and the Female Body with Julia Martins'.
41. Read, *Maids, Wives, Widows,* p.137.

Chapter Eight – Preparing for Delivery

1. Read, *Maids, Wives, Widows,* pp.141–2.
2. Norton, *The Hidden Lives of Tudor Women,* p.11.
3. BodL, Herrick MS C474, Vol. 1, fo. 132 (1590). (Cited in Pollock, 'Embarking on a rough passage', p.53).
4. D. Gardiner (ed.), *The Oxinden and Peyton Letters 1642–1670* (1937), p.185. (Cited in Pollock, 'Embarking on a rough passage', p.53).
5. Cressy, *Birth, Marriage, and Death,* p.57.
6. Orme, *Tudor Children,* p.1.
7. Ibid.
8. Kline, *Edward VI,* p.11.
9. Orme, *Tudor Children,* p.2.
10. Read, *Maids, Wives, Widows,* p.143.
11. Cressy, *Birth, Marriage, and Death,* p.55.
12. *Syr Bevis of Hampton* (1585). Early English Books Online Text Creation Partnership, 2011.
13. Pollock, 'Embarking on a rough passage', p.52.
14. Cressy, *Birth, Marriage, and Death,* p.30.
15. Norton, *The Hidden Lives of Tudor Women,* p.12.
16. Grueninger, Natalie (Host), 'Reproduction and the Female Body with Julia Martins'.
17. Norton, *The Hidden Lives of Tudor Women,* pp.12–13.
18. Ibid., p.13.
19. Reginald Scot, *The Discoverie of Witchcraft* (1886), p.165. (Cited in Norton, *The Hidden Lives of Tudor Women*, p.12.)

20. John Oliver, *A present for teeming women, or, Scripture-directions for women with child how to prepare for the houre of travel* (1663).
21. Mary Fissell, 'The Politics of Reproduction in the English Reformation' in *Representations,* Vol. 87, No. 1 (2004), p.44.
22. Norton, *The Hidden Lives of Tudor Women*, p.12.
23. Orme, *Tudor Children,* pp.2–3.
24. Grueninger, Natalie (Host), 'Reproduction and the Female Body with Julia Martins'; Orme, *Tudor Children,* p.3.
25. Read, *Maids, Wives, Widows,* p.145.
26. Orme, *Tudor Children,* p.3.
27. Raynalde, *The Byrth of Mankynd,* Prologue.
28. Guillimeau, *The happy deliverie of women,* p.85.
29. Norton, *The Hidden Lives of Tudor Women,* p.16.
30. Pollock, 'Embarking on a rough passage', p.48.
31. Ibid., pp.48–9.
32. Read, *Maids, Wives, Widows,* p.144.
33. Norton, *Hidden Lives of Tudor Women,* p.15.
34. Barbara Winchester, *Tudor Family Portrait,* p.101. (Cited in Pollock, 'Embarking on a rough passage', p.53); Catherine Myerick, 'Early Modern Women – Sabine Johnson (*c*.1521–1597?), Catherine Meyrick, 31 July 2020, https://catherinemeyrick.com/2020/07/31/early-modern-women-sabine-johnson-c1521–1597/.
35. Sharp, *The Midwives Book,* pp.187–88.
36. Ibid., pp.198–99.

Chapter Nine – The Tudor Birthing Chamber

1. Raynalde, *The Byrth of Mankynd,* fol. Ii–Iii.
2. *King James Bible Online,* https://www.kingjamesbibleonline.org/Genesis-Chapter-3/.
3. Cressy, *Birth, Marriage, and Death,* pp.20–21.
4. Grueninger, Natalie (Host), 'Reproduction and the Female Body with Julia Martins'.

5. Raynalde, *The Byrth of Mankynd,* fol. Iiii.
6. Ibid., fol. Iiii–Iiiii.
7. Guillimeau, *The happy deliverie of women,* p.91.
8. Raynalde, *The Byrth of Mankynd,* fol. Ivi.
9. Guillimeau, *The happy deliverie of women,* p.92; Raynalde, *The Byrth of Mankynd,* fol. Ixi.
10. Ibid.
11. Raynalde, *The Byrth of Mankynd,* fol. Iii.
12. Ibid.
13. Ibid., fol. Ixiii.
14. Ibid.
15. Cressy, *Birth, Marriage, and Death,* p.21.
16. Ibid., p.22.
17. Read, *Maids, Wives, Widows,* p.146.
18. Raynalde, *The Byrth of Mankynd,* fol. Ixi.
19. Cressy, *Birth, Marriage, and Death,* pp.51–2.
20. Ibid., p.52.
21. Raynalde, *The Byrth of Mankynd,* fol. Ixii.
22. Ibid.
23. Cash, Cassidy (Host), 'Cesarean Section Surgery in 16th Century England with Mary Fissell', That Shakespeare Life Podcast (Episode 238) 7 Nov 2022, https://www.cassidycash.com/cesarean-section-surgery-in-16th-century-england/.
24. Pottiee-Sperry F. '"L'hysterotomotokie ou enfantement caesarien" de François Rousset (Paris, 1581). Le livre d'un imposteur ou celui d'un précurseur?' ['"The hysterotomotokie or Caesarian birth" of Francois Rousset (Paris, 1581). The book of an impostor or that of a precursor?'] in *Histoire des Sciences Médicales*, 1996; 30(2): pp.259–68. French. PMID: 11624881.
25. Ibid.
26. Cash, Cassidy (Host), 'Cesarean Section Surgery in 16th Century England with Mary Fissell'.
27. Kline, *Edward VI,* p.7.
28. Cash, Cassidy (Host), 'Cesarean Section Surgery in 16th Century England with Mary Fissell'.

29. Ibid.
30. Cressy, *Birth, Marriage, and Death,* p.80; Orme, *Tudor Children,* p.4.
31. Orme, *Tudor Children,* p.4.
32. Cressy, *Birth, Marriage, and Death*, pp.80–1.
33. Grueninger, Natalie (Host), 'Reproduction and the Female Body with Julia Martins'.
34. Orme, *Tudor Children*, p.5.
35. Ibid., pp.4–5.
36. Read, *Maids, Wives, Widows,* p.147.
37. Norton, *The Hidden Lives of Tudor Women,* p.22.
38. Jacob Rueff, *The Expert Midwife* (1637), p.97. (Cited in Cressy, *Birth, Marriage, and Death,* p.81.)
39. Cressy, *Birth, Marriage, and Death,* pp.81–2.
40. Ibid., p.82.
41. Read, *Maids, Wives, Widows,* pp.147–48.
42. Ibid., p.148.
43. Cressy, *Birth, Marriage, and Death,* pp.82–3.
44. John Day, *Day's Festivals or, Twelve of His Sermons* (1615), p.236. (Cited in Cressy, *Birth, Marriage, and Death*, p.83.)
45. Sharp, *The Midwives Book,* pp.233–4.
46. Cressy, *Birth, Marriage, and Death,* p.84.
47. Ibid; Read, *Maids, Wives, Widows,* p.151.
48. Cressy, *Birth, Marriage, and Death,* pp.198–99.
49. Ibid., p.206.
50. Ibid.
51. Read, *Maids, Wives, Widows,* pp.152–53.
52. Cressy, *Birth, Marriage, and Death,* p.203.
53. Traditionally, breastfeeding women were instructed to abstain from sexual intercourse with their husbands until after their babies were weaned, though as with the Church's guidance on abstinence during her healing period, it is difficult to know how many couples adhered to this advice.
54. Norton, *The Hidden Lives of Tudor Women,* pp.40–1.
55. Orme, *Tudor Children,* p.6.

56. Ibid., p.16. In cases where the baby had died before birth and the sex could not have been determined prior to the midwife seeing it, a unisex name would have been given as part of its baptism.
57. Orme, *Tudor Children,* p.7.

Chapter Ten – Nursing and Nursemaids

1. Orme, *Tudor Children,* p.7.
2. Ibid.
3. Ibid., p.14.
4. Ibid., p.15.
5. Ibid.
6. John Sadler, *The Sicke Womans Private Looking-Glasse* (1636), p.10. (Cited in Cressy, *Birth, Marriage, and Death,* p.87.)
7. Raynalde, *The Byrth of Mankynd,* fol. C.
8. Ibid., fol. Cii–Ciii.
9. Piemontese, *The Secrets of Alexis,* p.13.
10. Read, *Maids, Wives, Widows,* p.158.
11. Cressy, *Birth, Marriage, and Death,* p.87.
12. Raynalde, *The Byrth of Mankynd,* fol. C; Cash, Cassidy (Host), 'Infant Formula in the 16th Century with Carla Cevasco', That Shakespeare Life Podcast (Episode 224) 1 Aug 2022, https://www.cassidycash.com/infant-formula-in-the-16th-century-with-carla-cevasco/.
13. Raynalde, *The Byrth of Mankynd,* fol. C.
14. Ibid.
15. Orme, *Tudor Children,* p.18.
16. Cressy, *Birth, Marriage, and Death,* p.88.
17. Read, *Maids, Wives, Widows,* p.155.
18. Elizabeth Clinton, *The Countesse of Lincolnes Nurserie* (1622), (University of Michigan). Early English Books Online Text Creation Partnership, 2011.
19. Ibid.
20. Ibid., pp.10–11.
21. Ibid., p.13.

22. Ibid., pp.13–14.
23. Ibid., p.16.
24. Ibid.
25. Orme, *Tudor Children,* p.19.
26. Sharp, *The Midwives Book,* p.353.
27. Ibid., pp.362–3.
28. Rick Bowers, *Thomas Phaer and The Boke of Chyldren, 1544* (1999), p.37.
29. Sharp, *The Midwives Book*, p.363.
30. Licence, *Living Like a Tudor,* p.77.
31. Cressy, *Birth, Marriage, and Death,* p.89.
32. Norton, *The Hidden Lives of Tudor Women,* p.28.
33. Orme, *Tudor Children,* p.20.
34. Norton, *The Hidden Lives of Tudor Women,* pp.28–9.
35. Cash, Cassidy (Host), 'Infant Formula in the 16th Century with Carla Cevasco'.
36. Orme, *Tudor Children,* p.20.
37. Francis Oscar Mann (ed.) *The Works of Thomas Deloney* (1912), p.103. (Cited in Orme, *Tudor Children*, p.21.)
38. Aradia Wyndham, 'The Boke of Children | Tudor Pediatrics', The Baby Historian, 10 May 2019, https://thebabyhistorian.com/2019/05/10/the-boke-of-chyldren-tudor-pediatrics/.
39. Cash, Cassidy (Host), 'Infant Formula in the 16th Century with Carla Cevasco'.
40. Ibid.
41. Read, *Maids, Wives, Widows,* pp.158–59.
42. Pierre Erondelle, *The French Garden* (1605), sigs G6v-7v. (Cited in Orme, *Tudor Children,* p.24).
43. Norton, *The Hidden Lives of Tudor Women,* p.29.
44. Paul Hair, *Before the Bawdy court: selections from church court and other records* (1972), p.103. (Cited in Orme, *Tudor Children,* p.25.)
45. Orme, *Tudor Children,* p.25.
46. Ibid., p.27.
47. Norton, *The Hidden Lives of Tudor Women,* pp.48–9.
48. Ibid., p.33.
49. Ibid.

Chapter Eleven – 'Infancy' and Young Childhood

1. Norton, *The Hidden Lives of Tudor Women,* p.2.
2. Shakespeare, *As You Like It,* Act II, Scene VII, Line 143, Shakespeare Online, https://www.shakespeare-online.com/plays/asu_2_7.html.
3. Kline, *Edward VI,* p.14.
4. Sharp, *The Midwives Book*, p.367.
5. Orme, *Tudor Children,* p.20.
6. Read, *Maids, Wives, Widows*, p.60.
7. Kline, *Edward VI,* p.14.
8. Raynalde, *The Byrth of Mankynde,* fol. LX.
9. Alexander Barclay, *The Eclogues of Alexander Barclay,* Beatrice White (ed.) (1928), eclogue 5, lines 280–5. (Cited in Orme, *Tudor Children,* p.36.)
10. Orme, *Tudor Children,* p.191.
11. Aradia Wyndham, 'Leading Strings', *YouTube,* uploaded by The Baby Historian, 8 October 2022, https://www.youtube.com/shorts/GFbLNV91Z2Y.
12. Juan Luis Vives, *Instruction,* Bk. II, sig. K4. (Cited in Betty S. Travitsky, '"A Pittilesse Mother"?: Reports of A Seventeenth-Century English Filicide' in *Mosaic: An Interdisciplinary Critical Journal* (1994), p.65.
13. William Gouge, *Of Domesticall Duties, Eight Treatises* (1622), pp.554–55. (Cited in Travitsky, 'A Pittilesse Mother', p.65.)
14. Hugh Rhodes, *The Boke of Nurture, for Men, Servauntes, and Chyldren* (1867), p.5.
15. Ibid.
16. Ibid., p.14.
17. Orme, *Tudor Children,* p.53.
18. Ibid.
19. Ibid., p.98.
20. Ibid., pp.99–105.
21. Ibid., p.105.
22. Ibid., p.107.
23. Norton, *The Hidden Lives of Tudor Women,* p.23; Orme, *Tudor Children,* p.42.

24. Orme, *Tudor Children,* p.25.
25. Barbara Winchester, *Tudor Family Portrait* (1955), p.224. (Cited in Sim, *The Tudor Housewife,* p.xxiii.)
26. Orme, *Tudor Children,* pp.55–6.
27. Bowers, *The Boke of Chyldren,* p.31.
28. Ibid., pp.52–4; pp.49–50; pp.56–61.
29. Ibid., pp.34–5.
30. Ibid., p.40.
31. Ibid., pp.39–40.
32. Ibid., pp.64–5.

Chapter Twelve – Daily Life: Discipline and Play

1. Rhodes, *The Boke of Nurture,* pp.14–5.
2. Ibid., p.15; Orme, *Tudor Children,* p.51.
3. Rhodes, *The Boke of Nurture,* p.15.
4. Anthony Fitzherbert, *The Boke of Husbandry* (1534), p.95.
5. William Harrison, *The Description of England* (1577), p.140.
6. Goodman, *How to Be a Tudor,* p.87.
7. Orme, *Tudor Children,* p.46.
8. Goodman, *How to Be a Tudor*, pp.87–8. An Act in 1495 dictated that 5.00 a.m. be the start of the working day.
9. Ibid., p.90.
10. Ibid., pp.89–90.
11. Ibid., p.94.
12. Sim, *The Tudor Housewife*, p.xxiii.
13. Orme, *Tudor Children*, p.49. The definitions for Erasmus' terms are: 'Churl' – a mean-spirited person; 'Carter' – a man who drives a cart; and 'Ploughman' – a man whose job it is to direct a plough by leading a horse or other animal.
14. Harrison, *The Description of England*, pp.449–50.
15. Sir Thomas Elyot, *The Book named The Governor* (1531), p.16.
16. William Nelson (ed.), *A Fifteenth Century School Book* (1956), p.13.
17. William Caxton (trans.), 'A Yonge thief and of his moder' in *The fables of Aesop* (1889), pp.210–11.

18. Orme, *Tudor Children*, p.48.
19. John Dee, *The Private Diary of Dr. John Dee* (1842), pp.30–1.
20. Travitsky, 'A Pittilesse Mother', pp.58–9.
21. '1616: Margaret Vincent, "Pittilesse Mother"', *Executed Today,* 18 May 2015, https://www.executedtoday.com/2015/05/18/1616-margaret-vincent-pitilesse-mother/.
22. Neonaticide is defined as the murder of a newborn infant within twenty-four hours of birth.
23. Travitsky, 'A Pittilesse Mother', p.57.
24. Nelson, *A Fifteenth Century School Book*, p.14, p.xxii.
25. Sir Thomas More, 'Pageant Verses' in *Luminarium Editions* (2007).
26. Orme, *Tudor Children,* p.64.
27. Norton, *The Hidden Lives of Tudor Women,* pp.35–6.
28. Dee, *The Private Diary of Dr. John Dee,* p.14.
29. Norton, *The Hidden Lives of Tudor Women*, p.36.
30. Ibid., pp.36–7.
31. Thomas Ravenscroft, *Deuteromelia* (1609), p.13.
32. William Wager, *The Longer Though Livest the More Fool Thou Art* (1565), sig. A3r. (Cited in Orme, *Tudor Children,* p.164.)
33. 'Margery Paston to John Paston, 21 January 1486' *Paston Footprints,* https://thisispaston.co.uk/index.php.
34. Goodman, *How to Be a Tudor,* p.121, p.142.
35. 'Ember days' – days of fasting and prayer – took place on the Wednesday, Friday, and Saturday during the weeks following four significant religious days in the Catholic Church's liturgical calendar: St Lucy's Day, the first Sunday in Lent, Pentecost, and Holy Cross Day.
36. Orme, *Tudor Children,* p.45.
37. Goodman, *How to Be a Tudor*, p.230–33.
38. Orme, *Tudor Children,* p.171.
39. King Henry VII naming his firstborn son and heir 'Arthur' insinuates a belief in the legendary King Arthur, and a desire to strap his own son's legacy and reputation to him.
40. Orme, *Tudor Children,* pp.172–73.
41. Ibid., p.172.

42. William Shakespeare, *The Merry Wives of Windsor,* Act IV, Scene IV, Lines 29–36. Folger Shakespeare Library, https://www.folger.edu/explore/shakespeares-works/the-merry-wives-of-windsor/read/4/4/.
43. Orme, *Tudor Children,* p.42.

Chapter Thirteen – Educating Sons and Daughters

1. Norton, *The Hidden Lives of Tudor Women,* p.53. Formal education would not become a legal requirement in England until the 1870s.
2. Shakespeare, *As You Like It,* Act II, Scene VII, Lines 144–6, Shakespeare Online, https://www.shakespeare-online.com/plays/asu_2_7.html.
3. Orme, *Tudor Children,* p.130.
4. Ibid., p.123.
5. Ibid., p.125.
6. Ibid.
7. Norton, *The Hidden Lives of Tudor Women,* p.54.
8. Edward Herbert, *The Autobiography of Edward, Lord Herbert of Cherbury* (1886), p.36.
9. Ibid.
10. David Cressy, *Literacy and the Social Order: Reading and Writing in Tudor and Stuart England* (1980), p.22.
11. Orme, *Tudor Children,* p.128.
12. Kline, *Edward VI,* p.20.
13. Ibid., p.31.
14. Foster Watson, *Vives and the Renascence Education of Women* (1912), pp.162–3. (Cited in David Cressy, *Education in Tudor and Stuart England* (1975), p.107.)
15. Thomas Becon, *The Catechism of Thomas Becon* (1844), p.376.
16. Ibid.
17. Ibid., p.377.
18. Ibid.
19. Norton, *The Hidden Lives of Tudor Women,* p.55.
20. Orme, *Tudor Children,* p.130.

21. Ibid., p.129.
22. Norton, *The Hidden Lives of Tudor Women,* p.55.
23. James Daybell, *Women Letter-Writers in Tudor England* (2018), p.12. (Cited in Norton, *The Hidden Lives of Tudor Women,* p.55.)
24. D. Hickman, 'From Catholic to Protestant: The Changing Meaning of Testamentary Religious Provisions in Elizabethan London' in Tyacke, N. (ed.), *England's Long Reformation 1500–1800* (1998), p.97. (Cited in Norton, *The Hidden Lives of Tudor Women,* p.56.)
25. Norton, *The Hidden Lives of Tudor Women,* p.56.
26. Ibid., p.68.
27. Ibid.
28. Nicholas Orme, *Medieval Schools* (2006), pp.143–4. (Cited in Orme, *Tudor Children,* p.132.)
29. Orme, *Tudor Children,* p.132.
30. Ibid., p.133.
31. Thomas Tusser, *Five hundred pointes of good husbandrie* (1878), p.207.
32. Shakespeare, *As You Like It,* Act II, Scene VII, Lines 144–6, Shakespeare Online, https://www.shakespeare-online.com/plays/asu_2_7.html; Francis Segar, *The Schoole of Vertue* (1557), sigs A7v–8r. (Cited in Orme, *Tudor Children,* p.135.)

Chapter Fourteen – Parenting the Adolescent

1. Lipscomb, 'Suzannah Lipscomb: Women, Sex and Power in the Sixteenth Century', YouTube, 28 June 2020, https://www.youtube.com/watch?v=TY5mrshQT3o&t=342s.
2. Anne Kussmaul, *Servants in Husbandry in Early Modern England* (1981), p.144. (Cited in Orme, *Tudor Children*, p.199.)
3. Norton, *The Hidden Lives of Tudor Women,* p.73.
4. Ibid., p.106.
5. M. Davies, 'Thomasyne Percyvale, "The Maid of Week" (d. 1512)' in Barron, C.M., 'Introduction: The Widows' World in Later Medieval London' in Barron, C.M. and Sutton, A.F. (eds.), *Medieval*

London Widows 1300–1500 (1994), pp.185–208. (Cited in Norton, *The Hidden Lives of Tudor Women,* p.106.)

6. P. Humfrey, *The Experience of Domestic Services for Women in Early Modern London* (2011), p.7. (Cited in Norton, *The Hidden Lives of Tudor Women,* p.73.)
7. Orme, *Tudor Children,* p.198.
8. Ibid.
9. Muriel St. Clare Byrne, *The Lisle letters: an abridgement* (1983), pp.330–31.
10. Muriel St. Clare Byrne, *The Lisle letters,* vol. VI (1981), p.2.
11. Ibid., p.276.
12. Orme, *Tudor Children*, pp.200–1.
13. Ibid., p.202.
14. William Kremer, 'What medieval Europe did with its teenagers', BBC News, 23 March 2014, https://www.bbc.com/news/magazine-26289459.
15. Charlotte Augusta Sneyd, *A Relation, Or Rather A True Account, of the Island of England* (1847), pp.24–5.
16. Ibid., pp.25–6.
17. Kremer, 'What medieval Europe did with its teenagers', BBC News, 23 March 2014, https://www.bbc.com/news/magazine-26289459.
18. Orme, *Tudor Children,* p.198.
19. Ibid., p.199.
20. Norton, *The Hidden Lives of Tudor Women,* p.110.
21. Orme, *Tudor Children,* p.199.
22. Norton, *The Hidden Lives of Tudor Women,* p.73.
23. Ibid., p.74.
24. Orme, *Tudor Children*, p.199, 204.
25. Norton, *The Hidden Lives of Tudor Women,* pp.78–9.
26. Linda Pollock, *With Faith and Physic: the life of a Tudor gentlewoman, Lady Grace Mildmay 1552–1620* (1993), p.28. (Cited in Orme, *Tudor Children,* p.217.)
27. Orme, *Tudor Children*, pp.205–6.
28. Elizabeth Norton, 'Tudor women: what was life like?' in *History Extra,* 11 March 2019, https://www.historyextra.com/period/tudor/tudor-women-what-was-life-like/.

29. Norton, *The Hidden Lives of Tudor Women,* pp.104–5.
30. Orme, *Tudor Children,* pp.205–6.
31. Kremer, 'What medieval Europe did with its teenagers', BBC News, 23 March 2014, https://www.bbc.com/news/magazine-26289459.
32. Ibid.
33. 'Lady Katherine Paston to William Paston, 11th June 1624', *Paston Footprints,* https://thisispaston.co.uk/pastonletters2.html.
34. Byrne, *The Lisle Letters.*

Chapter Fifteen – The Ageing Mother and Her Adult Children

1. Godfrey, *Attitudes Toward Post-Menopausal Women,* p.10.
2. Norton, *The Hidden Lives of Tudor Women,* p.272.
3. John Freind and Thomas Dale (trans.), *Emmenologia* (1729), p.1.
4. Sara Read, *Menstruation and the Female Body in Early Modern England* (2013), p.171.
5. James Drake, *Anthropologia nova, or, a new system of anatomy* (1750), pp.189–90.
6. William Shakespeare, *Macbeth,* Act I, Scene V, Lines 48–53, *Folger Shakespeare Library, https://www.folger.edu/explore/shakespeares-works/macbeth/read/1/5/.*
7. Jointures were financial protections for wives in the case of widowhood, established and agreed upon by both families prior to the marriage.
8. Wall, 'For Love, Money, or Politics?', p.515.
9. McNabb, 'She is but a girl', pp.77–8.
10. Anne O'Brien, 'The delicate matter of mustard and candles: a Paston family scandal' in *Historia,* 16 January 2023, https://www.historiamag.com/the-delicate-matter-of-mustard-and-candles-a-paston-family-scandal/.
11. Wall, 'For Love, Money, or Politics?', p.514.
12. Ibid.
13. Ibid., p.516.
14. Ibid.

15. James Daybell, *Women Letter-Writers in Tudor England,* (2006), p.111.
16. Wall, 'For Love, Money, or Politics?', p.520.
17. 'Bess of Hardwick to Gilbert Talbot, Master Clarke, and William Cavendish, earl of Devonshire, 31 January 1580/1', *Bess of Hardwick's Letters: The Complete Correspondence c.1550–1608,* https://www.bessofhardwick.org.
18. 'Bess of Hardwick to Robert Dudley, Earl of Leicester, 18 May 1577' *Bess of Hardwick's Letters: The Complete Correspondence c.1550–1608,* https://www.bessofhardwick.org.
19. Houlbrooke, 'Love and marriage in Tudor England'.
20. 'Spain: May 1502', in *Calendar of State Papers, Spain*, Volume 1, 1485–1509 (1862), pp.267–9. British History Online, https://www.british-history.ac.uk.
21. 'Spain: August 1502', in *Calendar of State Papers, Spain*, Volume 1, 1485–1509 (1862), pp.276–86. British History Online, https://www.british-history.ac.uk.
22. Joel Thomas Rosenthal, *Old Age in Late Medieval England* (1996), p.57.
23. Barbara J. Harris, *English Aristocratic Women, 1450–1550* (2002), p.56. Alison Wall points to contemporary evidence that between 1480 and 1679, grooms in the peerage averaged the age of 24 at the time of marriage, with brides averaging 19 ('For Love, Money, or Politics?', p.514).
24. Rosenthal, *Old Age in Late Medieval England,* p.57.
25. Johnson, *So Great a Prince,* p.91.
26. Ibid., p.123.
27. Godfrey, *Attitudes Toward Post-Menopausal Women*, p.30.
28. Norton, *The Hidden Lives of Tudor Women,* p.291.
29. Ibid., p.293.
30. Rosenthal, *Old Age in Late Medieval England,* pp.59–60.
31. Ibid., pp.78–9.
32. Andreas Capellanus, *The Art of Courtly Love,* John Jay Parry (trans.) (1960), p.17. (Cited in Godfrey, *Attitudes Toward Post-Menopausal Women,* p.29.)
33. As is the case in the modern period, life expectancy for a Tudor woman was greater than that of a man.

Conclusion – A Mother's Legacy

1. Licence, *Living Like a Tudor,* pp.78–9.
2. Ibid., pp.77–8.
3. Ibid., p.77.
4. Oxfordshire wills: will.oxfordshirefhs.org.uk. (Cited in Licence, *Living Like a Tudor,* pp.115–6.)
5. According to legend, the Chequers Ring was removed from Elizabeth's finger upon her death by Robert Carey, who rode with it to the Scottish border in order to bring the news of the queen's death to her heir, the future King James I of England. (Maev Kennedy, 'Ring that could hold clue to Elizabeth I' in *The Guardian,* 26 July 2002, https://www.theguardian.com/uk/2002/jul/26/humanities.monarchy.)
6. Ibid.
7. This theory is a curious one, because although Elizabeth and Katherine were very close for a time, Elizabeth's later scandal with Katherine's fourth husband, Thomas Seymour, caused a rift between the two women that would have made it unlikely for Elizabeth to wear a ring with Katherine's image in it until her own death.
8. 'William Brooke Baron Cobham and his family, dated 1567', Wikimedia Commons, https://commons.wikimedia.org.
9. 'Edward 3rd Lord Windsor and his family', Wikimedia Commons, https://commons.wikimedia.org.
10. Licence, *Living Like a Tudor,* p.34.
11. Alison Weir, *Elizabeth of York: A Tudor Queen and Her World* (2013), p.453.
12. 'Henry VII in Mourning', Wikimedia Commons, https://commons.wikimedia.org.
13. Weir, *Elizabeth of York*, p.450.

Bibliography

Primary Sources

Adams, Francis (ed.), *Aretaeus of Cappadocia, De causis et signis acutorum morborum* (lib. 1), (Tufts University; http://www.perseus.tufts.edu)

Archer-Hind, R.D., M.A. (ed.), *Plato, The Timaeus of Plato,* (New York, 1888).

Barrough, Philip, *The Method of Physick, contaning the causes, signes, and cures of inward diseases in mans body, from the head to the foote*, (London, 1624).

Becon, Thomas, *The Catechism of Thomas Becon*, (London, 1844).

Boorde, Andrew and Furnivall, F.J. (ed.), *Andrew Boorde's Introduction and Dyetary with Barnes in the Defence of the Berde*, (London, 1870).

Bowers, Rick, *Thomas Phaer and The Boke of Chyldren, 1544*, (Tempe, 1999).

British Medical Association – *British Medical Journal*, (London, 1857).

Byrne, Muriel St Clare, *The Lisle letters: an abridgment*, (Chicago, 1983).

Byrne, Muriel St Clare, *The Lisle letters, Vol. VI*, (Chicago, 1981).

Calendar of State Papers, Spain, Volume 1, 1485–1509, (London, 1862). British History Online, https://www.british-history.ac.uk/cal-state-papers/spain/vol1.

Caxton, William (trans.), *The Fables of Aesop (1484)*, (London, 1889).

Certain sermons or homilies appointed to be read in churches in the time of Queen Elizabeth of famous memory and now reprinted for the use of private families, in two parts, (London, 1562). Early English Books Online Text Creation Partnership, 2011; https://quod.lib.umich.edu)

Clinton, Elizabeth, *The Countesse of Lincolnes Nurserie*, (London, 1622). Early English Books Online Text Creation Partnership, 2011; https://quod.lib.umich.edu)

Culpeper, Nicholas, *The Complete Herbal*, (London, 1850).

Dee, Dr John, *The Private Diary of Dr. John Dee: and the catalogue of his library of manuscripts, from the original manuscripts in the Ashmolean museum at Oxford, and Trinity college library, Cambridge*, (New York, 1842).

Drake, James, *Anthropologia nova, or, a new system of anatomy*, (London, 1750).

Elyot, Sir Thomas, *The Book Named The Governor*, (London, 1531).

Elyot, Sir Thomas, *The Castel of Helth*, (London, 1541).

Fitzherbert, Anthony, *The Boke of Husbandry*, (London, 1534).

Freind, John and Dale, Thomas (trans.), *Emmenologia*, (London, 1729).

Guillimeau, James, *Child-birth or, The Happy Deliverie of Women*, (London, 1612). Early English Books Online Text Creation Partnership, 2011; https://quod.lib.umich.edu)

Harrison, William, *The Description of England*, (Ithaca, 1968). Herbert, Anne Clifford, *The Diary of the Lady Anne Clifford with an Introductory Note by V. Sackville-West*, (London, 1923).

Herbert, Lord Edward, *The Autobiography of Edward, Lord Herbert of Cherbury*, (London, 1886).

Jocelin, Elizabeth, *The Mothers Legacie to her unborne Childe*, (London, 1624). Early English Books Online Text Creation Partnership, 2011; https://quod.lib.umich.edu)

Jonas, Richard, *The Byrth of Mankynde*, (London, 1540).

Jorden, Edward, *A briefe discourse of a disease called the suffocation of the mother*, (London, 1603). Early English Books Online Text Creation Partnership, 2011; https://quod.lib.umich.edu)

Lupton, Thomas, *A thousand notable things, of sundry sortes Wherof some are wonderfull, some straunge, some pleasant, divers necessary, a great sort profitable and many very precious…*, (London, 1589). Early English Books Online Text Creation Partnership, 2011; https://quod.lib.umich.edu)

More, Sir Thomas, *Pageant Verses*, (Luminarium Editions, 2007). https://www.luminarium.org/editions/morepageant.htm.

Nelson, William (ed.), *A Fifteen Century School Book from a Manuscript in the British Museum*, (Oxford, 1956).

Oliver, John, *A present for teeming women, or, Scripture-directions for women with child how to prepare for the houre of travel*, (London, 1663). Early English Books Online Text Creation Partnership, 2011; https://quod.lib.umich.edu)

Paré, Ambroise and Johnson, T.H. (trans.), *The Workes of that famous Chirurgion Ambrose Parey*, (London, 1678).

Partridge, John, *The Treasurie of Commodious Conceits,* (London, 1573). Transcription by Johnna Holloway (2010); http://www.medievalcookery.com/notes/treasurie.pdf.

Piemontese, Alessio, *The Secrets of Alexis: containing many excellent remedies against divers diseases, wounds, and other accidents*, (London, 1615).

Ravenscroft, Thomas, *Deuteromelia*, (London, 1609).

Raynald, Thomas, *The Byrth of Mankynde: otherwise named the womans booke*, (London, 1565).

Rhodes, Hugh, *et al.*, *The Boke of Nurture, for Men, Servauntes, and Chyldren*, (Suffolk, 1867).

Rivière, Lazare; Cole, Nicholas; Culpeper, Nicholas; and Rowland, William (trans.), *The Fifteenth Book of the Practice of Physick: Of Womens Diseases*, (London, 1655).

Shakespeare, William, *As You Like It*, (London, 1623).

Shakespeare, William, *Macbeth*, (London, 1606).

Shakespeare, William, *The Merry Wives of Windsor*, (London, 1602).

Sharp, Jane, *The Midwives Book: or the Whole Art of Midwifery*, (London, 1671).

Sneyd, Charlotte August, *A Relation, Or Rather A True Account, of the Island of England: with sundry particulars of the customs of these people, and of the royal revenues under King Henry the Seventh, about the year 1500*, (London, 1847).

Stockwood, John, *A Bartholomew Fairing for Parents*, (London, 1586).

Stow, John and Kingsford, C.L. (ed.), *A Survey of London*, 2 vols., (Oxford, 1908).

Syr Bevis of Hampton, (London, 1585). Early English Books Online Text Creation Partnership, 2011; https://quod.lib.umich.edu)

Tilney, Edmund, *A briefe and pleasant discourse of duties in marriage, called the flower of friendshippe*, (London, 1568). Early English Books Online Text Creation Partnership, 2011; https://quod.lib.umich.edu)

Tusser, Thomas, *Five hundred pointes of good husbandrie*, (London, 1878).

Vives, Juan Luis, *A Very Fruitful and Pleasant Book Called the Instruction of a Christian Woman*, (London, 1529).

Secondary Sources

Bonnard, Jean-Baptiste, 'Male and female bodies according to Ancient Greek physicians' in *When Medicine Meets Gender*, edited by Nicole Edelman and Florence Rochefort (2013).

Cash, Cassidy (Host) 'Cesarean Section Surgery in 16th Century England with Mary Fissell', That Shakespeare Life Podcast (Episode 238; 7 November 2022). https://www.cassidycash.com/cesarean-section-surgery-in-16th-century-england/.

Coch, Christine, '"Mother of my Contreye": Elizabeth I and Tudor Constructions of Motherhood' in *English Literary Renaissance*, Vol. 26, No. 3 (Chicago, 1996).

Cressy, David, Birth, *Marriage, and Death: Ritual, Religion, and the Life-Cycle in Tudor and Stuart England*, (Oxford, 1997).

Cressy, David, *Education in Tudor and Stuart England*, (London, 1975).

Cressy, David, *Literacy and the Social Order: Reading and Writing in Tudor and Stuart England*, (Cambridge, 1980).

Daybell, James, *Women Letter-Writers in Tudor England*, (Oxford, 2006).

Emtiazy M *et al.*, 'Relation between Body Humors and Hypercholesterolemia: An Iranian Traditional Medicine Perspective Based on the Teaching of Avicenna' in *Iran Red Crescent Medical Journal*, (1 March 2012). https://www.ncbi.nlm.nih.gov.

Eshleman, Michael Kaye, 'Diet in pregnancy in the sixteenth and seventeenth centuries' in *Yale Medicine Thesis Digital Library*, (New Haven, 1974).

Faraone, Christopher A., 'Magical and Medical Approaches to the Wandering Womb in the Ancient Greek World' in *Classical Antiquity*, Vol. 30, No. 1 (Berkeley, 2011).

Figes, Lydia, 'Portraying pregnancy: from prehistoric art to Jacobean portraiture', Art UK, 29 January 2020. https://artuk.org/discover/stories/portraying-pregnancy-from-prehistoric-art-to-jacobean-portraiture.

Fissell, Mary, 'The Politics of Reproduction in the English Reformation' in *Representations*, Vol. 87, No. 1 (Oakland, 2004).

French, Katherine L.; Smith, Katheryn A.; and Stanbury, Sarah, 'An Honest Bed: The Scene of Life and Death in Late Medieval England' in *Fragments: Interdisciplinary Approaches to the Study of Ancient and Medieval Pasts*, Vol. 5 (Ann Arbor, 2016).

Gilman, Sander L.; Helen King; Roy Porter; G. S. Rousseau; and Elaine Showalter, *Hysteria Beyond Freud*, (Berkeley, 1993).

Godfrey, Jessica, *Attitudes Toward Post-Menopausal Women in the High and Late Middle Ages, 1100–1400*, (Middletown, 2011).

Goodman, Ruth, *How to Be a Tudor*, (New York, 2015).

Green, Monica, 'Flowers, Poisons, and Men: Menstruation in Medieval Western Europe' in *Menstruation: A Cultural History*, (London, 2005).

Green, Monica, 'From "Diseases of Women" to "Secrets of Women": The Transformation of Gynecological Literature in the Later Middle Ages' in *Journal of Medieval and Early Modern Studies*, 30, (Durham, 2000).

Grueninger, Natalie (Host), 'Reproduction and the Female Body with Julia Martins', Talking Tudors Podcast (Episode 161; 19 June 2022). https://onthetudortrail.com/Blog/2022/06/20/episode-161-reproduction-the-female-body-with-julia-martins/.

Hales, Sally, 'We explore the lives of Tudor women' in *BRITAIN* Magazine, (21 October 2016). https://www.britain-magazine.com/carousel/lives-of-tudor-women/.

Harris, Barbara, 'A New Look at the Reformation: Aristocratic Women and Nunneries, 1450–1540' in *Journal of British Studies*, Vol. 32, No. 2 (Cambridge, 1993).

Harris, Barbara, *English Aristocratic Women, 1450–1550*, (New York, 2002).

Howlett, Libby, 'A Long Winter's Nap', Agecroft Hall & Gardens Blog, (31 January 2023). https://www.agecrofthall.org/single-post/a-long-winters-nap.

Jouanna, Jacques, 'The Legacy of the Hippocratic Treatise The Nature of Man: The Theory of the Four Humours' in *Greek Medicine from Hippocrates to Galen: Selected Papers*, Philip van der Eijk (ed.), (Leiden, 2012).

Kenny, Amy, 'Returning the Wandering Womb with "Fetid and Rank Smells"', The Recipes Project, (7 October 2018). https://recipes.hypotheses.org.

Kline, Stephanie, *Edward VI: Henry VIII's Overshadowed Son*, (Yorkshire, 2023).

Kremer, William, 'What medieval Europe did with its teenagers', BBC News, (23 March 2014). https://www.bbc.com/news/magazine.

Licence, Amy, *Living Like a Tudor – Woodsmoke & Sage: A Sensory Journey Through Tudor England*, (New York, 2021).

Lipscomb, Suzannah, 'Suzannah Lipscomb: Women, Sex and Power in the Sixteenth Century', YouTube, uploaded by Oxford Festival of the Arts, (28 June 2020).

Martins, Julia, 'Flowers', CEMS KCL Blog, King's College London, (25 June 2021). https://kingsearlymodern.co.uk/keywords/flowers.

Martins, Julia, 'Maternal Mortality and "The Mother's Legacie to her Unborn Child"', Secrets of Women, (1 June 2023). https://juliamartins.co.uk/maternal-mortality-and-the-mothers-legacy-to-her-unborn-child.

Martins, Julia, 'What are the "Non-Naturals"?', Secrets of Women, (1 August 2022), https://juliamartins.co.uk/what-are-the-non-naturals.

Martins, Julia, 'What is the "Wandering Womb"?', Secrets of Women, (16 January 2023), https://juliamartins.co.uk/what-is-the-wandering-womb.

Norton, Elizabeth, *The Hidden Lives of Tudor Women*, (New York, 2017).

Orme, Nicholas, *Tudor Children*, (London, 2023).

Pollock, Linda, 'Embarking on a rough passage: the experience of pregnancy in early-modern society' in *Women as Mothers in Pre-Industrial England: Essays in Memory of Dorothy McLaren*, (London, 1990).

Read, Sara, *Menstruation and the Female Body in Early Modern England*, (London, 2013).

Read, Sara, '"Thy Righteousness is but a menstrual clout": Sanitary Practices and Prejudice in Early Modern England' in *Early Modern Women: An Interdisciplinary Journal*, Vol. 3 (Chicago, 2008).

Read, Sara, *Maids, Wives, Widows: Exploring Early Modern Women's Lives, 1540–1740,* (Yorkshire, 2015). Kindle.

Rosenthal, Joel Thomas, *Old Age in Late Medieval England*, (Philadelphia, 1996).

Sim, Alison, *The Tudor Housewife*, (Phoenix Mill, 1996).

Spivack, Carla, 'To "Bring Down the Flowers": The Cultural Context of Abortion Law in Early Modern England' in *William & Mary Journal of Race, Gender, and Social Justice*, Vol. 14, Issue 1, (William & Mary Journal of Women and the Law, Williamsburg, 2007).

Traister, Barbara, '"Matrix and the pain thereof": a sixteenth-century gynaecological essay' in *Medical History 35*, (Cambridge, 1991).

Travitsky, Betty S., '"A Pittilesse Mother"?: Reports of A Seventeenth-Century English Filicide' in *Mosaic: An Interdisciplinary Critical Journal*, Vol. 27, No. 4 (Manitoba, 1994).

van de Walle, Etienne, 'Flowers and Fruits: Two Thousand Years of Menstrual Regulation' in *The Journal of Interdisciplinary History*, Vol. 28, No. 2 (Cambridge, 1997).

Wall, Alison, 'For Love, Money, or Politics? A Clandestine Marriage and the Elizabeth Court of Arches' in *The Historical Journal*, Vol. 38, No. 3 (Cambridge, 1995).

Weir, Alison, *Elizabeth of York: A Tudor Queen and Her World*, (New York, 2013).

Whitelock, Anna, *Mary Tudor: Princess, Bastard, Queen*, (London, 2009).

Wyndham, Aradia, 'The Boke of Chyldren | Tudor Pediatrics', The Baby Historian, (10 May 2019). https://thebabyhistorian.com/2019/05/10/the-boke-of-chyldren-tudor-pediatrics/.

Wyndham, Aradia, 'The Byrth of Mankynde, 1540 | Book History', The Baby Historian, (7 February 2020). https://thebabyhistorian.com/2020/02/07/the-byrth-of-mankynde-1540/.

Index